Who Shall Enter Paradise?

NEW AFRICAN HISTORIES SERIES

SERIES EDITORS: JEAN ALLMAN AND ALLEN ISAACMAN

Books in this series are published with support from the Ohio University National Resource Center for African Studies.

David William Cohen and E. S. Atieno Odhiambo, *The Risks of Knowledge: Investigations into the Death of the Hon. Minister John Robert Ouko in Kenya, 1990*

Belinda Bozzoli, *Theatres of Struggle and the End of Apartheid*

Gary Kynoch, *We Are Fighting the World: A History of the Marashea Gangs in South Africa, 1947–1999*

Stephanie Newell, *The Forger's Tale: The Search for Odeziaku*

Jacob A. Tropp, *Natures of Colonial Change: Environmental Relations in the Making of the Transkei*

Jan Bender Shetler, *Imagining Serengeti: A History of Landscape Memory in Tanzania from Earliest Times to the Present*

Cheikh Anta Babou, *Fighting the Greater Jihad: Amadu Bamba and the Founding of the Muridiyya in Senegal, 1853–1913*

Marc Epprecht, *Heterosexual Africa? The History of an Idea from the Age of Exploration to the Age of AIDS*

Marissa J. Moorman, *Intonations: A Social History of Music and Nation in Luanda, Angola, from 1945 to Recent Times*

Karen E. Flint, *Healing Traditions: African Medicine, Cultural Exchange, and Competition in South Africa, 1820–1948*

Derek R. Peterson and Giacomo Macola, editors, *Recasting the Past: History Writing and Political Work in Modern Africa*

Moses E. Ochonu, *Colonial Meltdown: Northern Nigeria in the Great Depression*

Emily S. Burrill, Richard L. Roberts, and Elizabeth Thornberry, editors, *Domestic Violence and the Law in Colonial and Postcolonial Africa*

Daniel R. Magaziner, *The Law and the Prophets: Black Consciousness in South Africa, 1968–1977*

Emily Lynn Osborn, *Our New Husbands Are Here: Households, Gender, and Politics in a West African State from the Slave Trade to Colonial Rule*

Robert Trent Vinson, *The Americans Are Coming! Dreams of African American Liberation in Segregationist South Africa*

James R. Brennan, *Taifa: Making Nation and Race in Urban Tanzania*

Benjamin N. Lawrance and Richard L. Roberts, editors, *Trafficking in Slavery's Wake: Law and the Experience of Women and Children*

David M. Gordon, *Invisible Agents: Spirits in a Central African History*

Allen F. Isaacman and Barbara S. Isaacman, *Dams, Displacement, and the Delusion of Development: Cahora Bassa and Its Legacies in Mozambique, 1965–2007*

Stephanie Newell, *The Power to Name: A History of Anonymity in Colonial West Africa*

Gibril R. Cole, *The Krio of West Africa: Islam, Culture, Creolization, and Colonialism in the Nineteenth Century*

Matthew M. Heaton, *Black Skin, White Coats: Nigerian Psychiatrists, Decolonization, and the Globalization of Psychiatry*

Meredith Terretta, *Nation of Outlaws, State of Violence: Nationalism, Grassfields Tradition, and State Building in Cameroon*

Paolo Israel, *In Step with the Times: Mapiko Masquerades of Mozambique*

Michelle R. Moyd, *Violent Intermediaries: African Soldiers, Conquest, and Everyday Colonialism in German East Africa*

Abosede A. George, *Making Modern Girls: A History of Girlhood, Labor, and Social Development in Colonial Lagos*

Alicia C. Decker, *In Idi Amin's Shadow: Women, Gender, and Militarism in Uganda*

Rachel Jean-Baptiste, *Conjugal Rights: Marriage, Sexuality, and Urban Life in Colonial Libreville, Gabon*

Shobana Shankar, *Who Shall Enter Paradise? Christian Origins in Muslim Northern Nigeria, ca. 1890–1975*

Who Shall Enter Paradise?

Christian Origins in
Muslim Northern Nigeria, ca. 1890–1975

Shobana Shankar

OHIO UNIVERSITY PRESS ∽ ATHENS

Ohio University Press, Athens, Ohio 45701
ohioswallow.com
© 2014 by Ohio University Press
All rights reserved

To obtain permission to quote, reprint, or otherwise reproduce or
distribute material from
Ohio University Press publications, please contact our rights and permissions
department at (740) 593-1154 or (740) 593-4536 (fax).

Cover photo: Discharge ceremony at the Sudan Interior Mission Leprosarium,
Kano, ca. 1940. (Collection of SIM International Archives.)

Printed in the United States of America
Ohio University Press books are printed on acid-free paper.∞ ™

20 19 18 17 16 15 14   5 4 3 2 1

Library of Congress Cataloging-in-Publication Data

Shankar, Shobana.
 Who shall enter paradise? : Christian origins in Muslim northern Nigeria, ca. 1890–1975 / Shobana Shankar.
   pages cm. — (New African histories)
 Includes bibliographical references and index.
 ISBN 978-0-8214-2123-9 (hc : alk. paper) — ISBN 978-0-8214-2124-6 (pb : alk. paper) — ISBN 978-0-8214-4505-1 (pdf)
 1. Christianity—Nigeria, Northern. 2. Missions—Nigeria, Northern. 3. Religion and politics—Nigeria, Northern. 4. Nigeria, Northern—Religion—19th century. 5. Nigeria, Northern—Religion—20th century. 6. Nigeria, Northern—Ethnic relations. I. Title. II. Series: New African histories series.
 BR1463.N5S33 2014
 276.69'08--dc23
                                                                    2014031510

For my grandmother,
who told me that maybe all doors are meant to be opened.

Contents

List of Illustrations	ix
Acknowledgments	xi
Introduction	xiii
Note on Language and Acronyms	xxix

PART ONE   THE WORD TRAVELS

Chapter 1	"A Place to Lay Our Head" *A Sect of Strangers, 1890–1918*	3
Chapter 2	A New "Middle" Class in the Muslim City, 1918–1925	25
Chapter 3	A Christian Feminist Freelance *Policing Propaganda and Piety, 1920–1935*	47

PART TWO   FOLLOWERS OF THE WORD

Chapter 4	Christian Medical Missions as Muslim Charity *Paternalist Alliances, Maternal Alienation, 1928–1942*	71
Chapter 5	Joining in the Melee *Soldiers, Youth, and Rural Revivalism, 1945–1950*	94
Chapter 6	Security and Secrecy in the Era of Independence, 1950–1975	116

Conclusion	136
Notes	145
Bibliography	181
Index	199

Illustrations

PHOTOS

Cover:	Discharge ceremony, Sudan Interior Mission Kano Leprosarium, ca. 1940	
1.1	Biamuradi and Inusa, evangelists at Wushishi, ca. 1930	22
2.1	*Teaching Soldiers to Read Numbers*, Geidam Barracks, Borno, Northern Provinces, ca. 1913	39
2.2	James Cotton and schoolboys in Kano, ca. 1927	41
3.1	Maikwando, evangelist's daughter, and babies at Wushishi orphanage	51
5.1	Opening of the Kano SIM Eye Hospital, 1947	99
5.2	Waifs from Kano City bound for SIM Boys' Home, ca. 1946	103
5.3	Boys' Brigade, SIM Company 2, Kano, July 1947	109
5.4	Christian villagers at Tasa, Kano, led by lay evangelist Malam Idi, ca. 1947	109

MAPS

1.1	A Christian missionary view of the Sudan, 1906	4
1.2	Inusa's journey, 1916	20
4.1	Places of origin of leprosy sufferers at Kano SIM Settlement, and sites of itinerant evangelism by African Christians, 1937–1939	84

Acknowledgments

A great many people made this book possible. I must first thank Ladi Wayi, Halima, Baba, Aisha, and Ibrahim for their generosity, hospitality, and warmth. In Sabuwar 'Kofa, Alhaji Aminu Shariff Bappa and his family, Alhaji Ujdud Shariff Bappa, Hajiya Saliha and their children, and Bello and Ummi Mai Wada were constant sources of companionship. Dr. Bassey and Nseobong Nkanga always made a place for me at their home.

At Bayero University Kano, Professor M. S. Abdulkadir and Professor M. D. Suleiman graciously welcomed me as a visiting researcher. The late Professor Philip Shea was a friend and critic who is sorely missed.

Professor Hamidu Boboyi and Dr. Hajiya Aisha Shehu facilitated greatly my research at the Arewa House Archives and Kano History and Culture Bureau, respectively. Staff at those institutions and at the National Archives in Kaduna were helpful and patient. Bob Arnold was my first guide to the voluminous archives of the SIM, and his successor, Tim Geysbeek, has become a good friend and collaborator on various projects.

Archival and field research was conducted with support from the Fulbright Institute of International Education; the Wenner-Gren Foundation for Anthropological Research (Grant 6482); the American Historical Association Bernadotte E. Schmitt Grant; a Mellon postdoctoral fellowship from Barnard College–Columbia University; and the Georgetown University Graduate School of Arts and Sciences.

The invitation to present this research at various institutions has helped the manuscript become stronger, though any errors it contains are entirely my own. I thank Brian Larkin at Barnard College–Columbia University, Cati Coe at Rutgers University–Camden, and Beth Whitaker at the University of North Carolina at Charlotte. Michael Gomez and Edmund Abaka helped immeasurably in making possible my affiliation at their institutions. At Georgetown, I had the fortune to have a fine group of scholars offer constructive criticism: Thanks in particular to Adam Rothman, Bryan McCann, Meredith McKittrick, John McNeill, Aviel Roshwald, Carol

Benedict, Scott Taylor, and John Tutino. Conversations with and questions from several members of the Stony Brook history department helped me in the final preparation of the book; I am grateful to be part of such a collegial group. Murray Last, Lahra Smith, and John Voll also read and commented on whole or parts of drafts. Jean Allman, Allen Isaacman, and Gillian Berchowitz were superbly encouraging and helpful. I am grateful to Annie Schwendinger and Gerry Krieg for helping me create maps from raw data.

Ned Alpers, Richard Elphick, Ray Kea, and Chris Ehret have been wonderful mentors. The lessons LaRay Denzer, Alhaji Maina Gimba, Russell Schuh, Brenda Stevenson, Karen Leonard, Sondra Hale, and Vinay Lal taught me have stayed with me. For their camaraderie, I thank Ralph Austen, Paul Barclay, Judi Byfield, Bill Bissell, Brandi Brimmer, Carolyn Brown, Conerly Casey, Barbara Cooper, Roquinaldo Ferreira, Karen Flint, Cymone Fourshey, Lloys Frates, Alan Frishman, Rudi Gaudio, Ibrahim Hamza, Nara Milanich, Moses Ochonu, Akin Ogundiran, Toja Okoh, Ben Soares, Samuel Roberts, Heather Sharkey, Judy Stevenson, Aparna Vaidik, and Liz VanderVen.

My family has been supportive in so many ways, especially my mother, Avayam; my father, Mani; my sister, Kalpana; and my in-laws, Nancy and Charlie Green. Sachin, who is the real historian in this family, inspired me to write better with his persuasive essay on why one should play soccer. Kavya made me think harder when she put the bathtub plug on her head and asked, "Professor, what is the meaning of life?" Marcus has given me the answer through his unwavering commitment to our partnership.

Introduction

John Mamman Garba saw history as a special problem for Christians in the predominantly Muslim North of Nigeria. Among the Hausa, the largest ethnic group in the region, "Christianity is just some eighty years old while Islam has been with us since . . . about the fourteenth [century]." He continued, "It could be said that Christianity with us is but skin-deep."[1] Garba's autobiography is a memorial of sorts to Christians who converted from Islam as he did, but were lost: "Not a few Hausa Christians have (unobtrusively and unnoticed) disappeared into the big jostling Islamic society in which they live, never to be heard of again as Christians, just as a small pebble thrown into a big pond does not rise any more! The Parable of the Sower readily comes to mind."[2]

The Central Sudanic region we now call Northern Nigeria was not inhospitable to Christianity. Written and oral histories mention place-names and ethnonyms suggestive of ancient Middle Eastern and Abrahamic sects within the region's dominant Muslim religious culture,[3] and *Injil* (the New Testament) was a sought-after book.[4] Yet Christianity as such did not have followers until the colonial era, when European and North American missionaries established schools, hospitals, and churches. Christians like Garba belonged to the time of foreign rule, not to the vague and venerable Islamic past.

Garba spoke of the "communicativeness" of Christians to Muslims, reflected in indigenous names for the new believers. Christians were *'yan mission*, meaning "people of the mission," but also *Masihiyawa*, or followers of the "messiah," from the Arabic word. Today, some Hausa-speaking Christians prefer to be known as *masu bi*, which in Hausa means "those who follow," and echoes the notion of submission in Islam. These Christians identify themselves with Hausa and Arabic languages and even Islamic influences, and emphasize their piety as part of a conscious effort to dispel their colonial association in the minds of many Muslims.

This book traces the origins of this new religious community in the north-central emirates of Nigeria and the development of a new competitive religious politics from roughly 1890 to 1975, focusing on indigenous Hausa-speaking Christian communities and their relationships with their Muslim neighbors. The Christians in this book explain their origins in relation to Northern Nigerian Muslim society as much as to foreign-built Christian mission institutions. This book tells the history of these Northern Nigerian Christians, belonging to a community distinct from that of the more visible Southern Nigerian Christian settlers bearing more obvious ethnolinguistic differences and ties back home.

The story of Northern Nigerian Christians, whose fluid identities Garba describes, reveals the dynamic construction of religious difference marked by the politics of history and of forgetting. Garba writes of a kind of pluralism in Muslim Northern Nigeria that is all but forgotten today. To illustrate, the history lesson with which novelist Chimamanda Adichie begins her review of Chinua Achebe's memoir of the Biafran War is all too familiar to Nigerian schoolchildren (and to academic historians): Nigeria was forged in 1914 by the force of Frederick Lugard because "the British colonial government needed to subsidise the poorer North with income from the resource-rich South. With its feudal system of emirs, beautiful walled cities, and centralised power systems, the North was familiar to Lugard—not unlike the Sudan." Adichie continues: "Missionaries and their Western education were discouraged, to prevent what Lugard called their 'corrupting influence' on Islamic schools. Western education thrived in the South."[5] In this narrative, the stagnation of the North, owing to British colonial and Muslim rejection of outside intervention, is the root of Nigeria's failure as a modern nation. This facile version has no place for the complicating factor of Northern Nigerian Christianity.

Today, history is now being forcibly rewritten by the Islamist group Boko Haram, whose name is often translated as "Western education is prohibited," a conscious attack on modern innovations, some inspired by Christian mission translation and writing, of Hausa Muslim literary culture.[6] Boko Haram has killed thousands of people, destroyed property, and forced both Muslims and Christians to flee their homes.[7] The group has also committed violence against Hausa language and culture, erasing the richness of meanings boko once had and further exploiting myths of the unchanging Muslim character of Northern Nigeria.[8] Excavating boko from under the weight of the present shows that, although it conveyed different ideas—inauthenticity, literacy in the Roman script, academic subjects of non-Arabic and non-Islamic origin—boko was almost always a competitive enterprise, assiduously sought after by Christian and Muslim Northern Nigerians.

The history of Northern Nigerian Christianity, and especially the notion that Christians can genuinely be Hausa, Fulani, or Kanuri (predominantly Muslim ethnic groups), does not readily fit the usual political narratives, whether British colonial, Islamist, secular, or even those that dwell on Christian victimization. Conventional histories often repeat the self-serving claims of British colonial sources that attest to the unchanging character of the Muslim Northern Nigerian aristocracy—in many cases proud descendants of nomadic Fulani jihadists who conquered the Hausa city-states in the early nineteenth century and created the Sokoto Caliphate—as the archetypal Native Authority and indirect rulers. Indeed, the pioneering scholarship of the 1960s that celebrated the Fulani Empire, its clerical families and its literature, has been used by partisans as evidence that Northern Nigerian Muslim society is somehow impervious to non-Islamic influences.[9]

Yet Muslim Northern Nigerians did not keep Christians outside their walled cities and villages, even in the instances when they may have wanted to do so. Christians—both foreign missionaries and indigenous evangelists—were not contained by the official colonial policies designed to prevent them from moving and finding opportunities among Muslims, especially opportunities to speak and preach about their faith. In Northern Nigeria, more than the "social gospel" of education and medical work, Christian evangelism deeply influenced Muslim society well beyond the relatively small number of converts.

Today, despite international and local fears about the consequences of the implementation of shari'a law for non-Muslims, not all Christians share the apprehension.[10] A powerful Christian leader—an ordained minister who converted from Islam as a young man—referred to the Qur'an in response to a question about the future of Christian-Muslim relations in Nigeria: "In Sura 23, 'Al-Muminun,' it is said, 'In the Name of Allah, Most Gracious, Most Merciful, Successful are the Believers,—Those who humble themselves in their prayers, Who avoid vain talk. . . . Those who faithfully observe their trusts and their covenants, And who (strictly) guard their prayers, These will be the heirs Who will inherit Paradise; they will dwell therein (for ever).' Only God knows. We do not worry."[11] Many Christians claim they are reformers who hold truer to the words of the Qur'an than those they see as lapsed Muslims around them. Northern Christians defend their indigeneity,[12] and they feel emboldened to proselytize in spite of escalating violence. Muslims, for their part, feel that Christians have overstepped their place.[13]

Colonial narratives of Muslim stagnation, variously repackaged, ignore transformations in Islamic culture that have occurred in Northern Nigeria over the last century. Moreover, the sometimes celebratory notion that Christian missions in colonial Africa translated into lasting Christian communities and postcolonial social, political, and economic "development" may equally require revision.[14] Christianity and Islam were co-created in Northern Nigeria in unexpected and unpredictable ways.

This book does not claim that the history of Christian missions among Muslims explains the origins of contemporary religious animus. Nor does it seek to diminish the victimization that Christians have experienced. Instead, it marshals powerful new evidence of the historical, indigenous, and local development of religious interactions and differences that is simply incompatible with conventional narratives that overcredit colonial policies. It demonstrates the agency of both nonelites and elites, both Muslim and Christian, in shaping religious politics. Muslim-Christian competition in Northern Nigeria, however much outsiders have intervened, is an intimate affair.

Analyzing the origins of the Rwandan genocide, scholars of the African Great Lakes region have noted the processes by which Hutu-Tutsi ethnic differences, rooted in precolonial political economy, significantly hardened and became racialized under German and Belgian colonialism and postcolonial autocracy.[15] History-writing was crucial, particularly in the schools of Catholic and Protestant missions, which did not purely "invent ethnicity" but played a complex and catalyzing role in fostering Rwandans' revisionist histories of precolonial politics.[16] Though religious difference in Africa is rarely historicized in the same ways as ethnicity,[17] the burgeoning scholarship on Christian-Muslim interactions throughout Africa—including Sudan, Niger, Eritrea, Ethiopia, Benin, Ghana, and in the southern region of Nigeria—reveals the rich and dynamic constructions of religious differences in many spheres of activity, from literary culture to public health.[18] Muslim-Christian differences have been shaped within ethnic, gender, occupational, generational, and class dynamics; missions to Muslims were the scenes of many kinds of struggles.

Writing the past in Northern Nigeria, as elsewhere, has been "a powerful vehicle of political argument because it is addressed to a collective 'we,' not the individual 'I.'"[19] As Murray Last keenly observes, there is an "economy of panic" surrounding Muslim-Christian relations in Nigeria.[20] History is the hard currency in that economy. Christians and Muslims alike have imagined and passionately adopted histories that readily support separatist agendas of all kinds. But Northern Nigeria's history requires a sober revision that locates the disappeared witnesses of whom Garba wrote and reveals the conditions of their origins, movements, and disappearance in the very politics of history-making.

MISSIONS TO MUSLIMS: A NEW EVANGELICAL CULTURE, MAKING WEALTH IN PEOPLE

The Central Sudan was a prized foreign mission field for Christians in the late 1800s at the time of British and French conquest, in some sense, because it was a political minefield. Anglo–North American Christian activists developed a "special burden for the Sudan" and a distinct historiography of the region in which the nomadic Fulani jihadists who founded the Sokoto Caliphate, one of the largest precolonial states in Africa, were seen to have brought "Wahabi propaganda."[21]

Driven to counter this movement and convert the Hausa, whom the missionaries then believed to be a conquered people recently converted to Islam by force, missionaries tried to enter the Hausa city-states from the West African coast. They failed. Some subsequently traveled to Mediterranean North Africa to study Hausa language with slaves and pilgrims who had stopped on their way to Arabia. The Anglican Church Missionary Society (CMS) managed to open a station in 1900 in Girku, in Zaria Emirate, and then a station within the walls of Zaria City itself in 1904. The North American Sudan Interior Mission (SIM) opened stations on the Niger River in 1902 and 1903 and at Wushishi in 1904, all in towns that were ruled by Muslim chiefs and populated by Hausa and Yoruba traders and Nupe and Fulani scholars. Neither mission could establish a foothold in Kano. Frederick Lugard, the first High Commissioner of Northern Nigeria after Britain's formal occupation in 1900, restricted the placement of Christian missions to outside *dar-al-Islam* (the abode of Islam), on the southern marches of the newly conquered caliphate.

In imagining the Sudan as the battlefield between Christianity and Islam, Christian missions also refigured the spaces of Northern Nigeria itself. The region's geography was not simply divided between *dar-al-Islam* and *dar-al-harb* (the abode of war). Murray Last describes a frontier zone between these two spheres that was heavily militarized to enable Muslim powers to extract taxes from non-Muslims and raid for slaves.[22] The British invaded these frontier zones from the south, and Christian missionary work in or near them added a new dimension to the colonial remaking of the region, particularly in relation to the British efforts to abolish slavery. The colonial government turned over its freed slave home to the Sudan United Mission (SUM) in 1908, taking in mostly young girls and women who were freed during British raids or who were runaways.[23] Former slaves—girls and boys—became Christians and were among the first Northern Nigerians to possess many cultural and economic goods and skills not available in Muslim areas: literacy in Roman script (*boko*), books and paper, farming techniques, maps, medicines, and more. These early Christians also became migrant workers for whom official boundaries often held little importance. Furthermore, mission stations located in these interstitial zones became havens for Muslim dissenters; historians have underestimated how incomplete the jihad was in Northern Nigeria before 1900.[24]

Scholarship on Christianity in Muslim Northern Nigeria often overemphasizes the *sabon gari*, or new town enclave, which the British and Muslim Native Administrations created to segregate non-Muslim settlers from Southern Nigeria on the outskirts of Muslim towns.[25] Muslims were a majority in these enclaves for many years. Zaria's Sabon Gari was the first, founded in 1911, one year before the railway from Lagos to Kano was completed. Enclaves were not entirely new, though. Before the colonial era, itinerant Tuareg traders and their Buzu slaves occupied designated sections of Kano. The sabon gari did eventually add new religious and regional difference to residential segregation, thereby "dramatically altering host-stranger relations," a transformation that was not unique to British Northern Nigeria but also obtained in French West Africa and elsewhere.[26] White Christian missionaries were often made to reside and operate institutions in or near sabon gari, but Northern Nigerian Christians, for their part, treated the place as a transit zone.

After the British Colonial Office began to invest more resources in welfare for Africans in the late 1920s, missions were allowed to play a greater role in education in many parts of Northern Nigeria.[27] In the emirates, missions moved from urban Kano into suburban areas of Kano and other Muslim cities such as Sokoto and Katsina, where they founded leprosariums and clinics from the late 1930s.[28] Into the 1940s and 1950s, African Christian patients, workers, and freelance sellers of medicines and tracts penetrated rural Muslim areas that had never been exposed to the Christian gospel.

In the expansion of mission institutions from freed slave homes to leprosariums, the colonial authorities and, to a lesser extent, the Muslim governments, used different types of segregationist rationales: the state's moral arguments concerning the problem of slave girls and the medicalization of an ancient disease that Islamic charity had previously addressed.

Christians used these sites for interaction and exchange with Muslims. They moved from such locations and created autonomous spaces, usually against the wishes and without the knowledge of colonial and missionary authorities. Christians, though often regarded as strangers who were former slaves, migrants, and guest workers, used the goods, texts, and preaching of Christianity to establish their authority in new areas. Mission commodities, furthermore, traveled without the presence of Christians. Vigorous yet highly controlled trades in books and traditional medicines over networks that predated Christian missions' arrival in Hausaland stretched much further than evangelists themselves.[29]

Christians' mobility in the region has always been political, beginning with the earliest grassroots evangelism in Muslim areas in 1913. Itinerant evangelists flouted established political authorities and required the charisma to attract listeners and the cunning to convince them to purchase tracts or to barter for food and lodging. Evangelists were entrepreneurs whose literacy, wages garnered in the whites' employ, clothes, and medicines gave them prestige among Africans outside institutional spheres. Most importantly, evangelists assembled people around them. Whereas Muslims referred to spiritual grace, *baraka*, of the especially elect in their community,[30] noted Christians gathered *masu bi*, "those who follow." An entire spectrum of Christian authorities existed under the label of "lay evangelist." Evangelists who knew both the Qur'an and the Bible, and boko and Arabic, held a higher status over other evangelists. Itinerant evangelists in African history cannot be understood apart from the complex story of migrant labor in colonial Africa.[31]

The mobility of women, too, shaped evangelical culture. The first freed slave girls at mission stations in the early 1900s were migrants who seemed ripe for conversion out of their presumed desperation, but Christian missionaries and colonial officials wanted them married off. The missionaries even suspected that Islam was more appealing for them than Christianity, as polygyny offered co-wives with whom to share domestic duties, and the possibility of seclusion offered an escape from agricultural labor. Indeed, many African women did not see monogamy as a benefit, and missionaries' insistence on monogamy and opposition to divorce (more readily available in Muslim marriages) placed Christianity at a competitive disadvantage in terms of reproduction vis-à-vis Islamic marriage patterns. In this context, women who remained faithful Christians claimed a special piety for favoring gifts of the Spirit over worldly possessions. The freed slave girls and women who knew nothing of their own ethnic backgrounds were among the first to prioritize religious over ethnic identities and the idea of conversion as thoroughgoing rebirth, later to become the hallmarks that separated the new religion from the old.

The gendered patterns and problems of Christian social reproduction in a Muslim land worried Christians like John Garba. He remarked on the sexual and social loneliness of Christian men and women converts, suggesting that many cases of infertility and barrenness had hurt the growth of Christian Hausa communities.[32] Northern Nigeria was not unique for Christians' perceived demographic insecurity,[33] but the forms of evangelical networks that were created in response were innovative, perhaps exceptional. Medical evangelism in particular became the means by which new migrants such as demobilized soldiers could tap networks of alms-seekers, youth, and seekers of mobile health care to garner more clients. The search for healing has inspired grassroots systems of care in many African contexts, and Christian medical missions had an unintended effect more important than creating distinctions between traditional and modern medicine: It invigorated novel forms of lay African authority, not foreign missionary or Muslim governmental control.[34]

It was the productive capacity of Christianity that began to reshape Muslim-Christian relations in the 1940s and 1950s. Sensing that converts were becoming more valuable than mere clients, Alhaji Ahmadu Bello, who held both the traditional title of Sardauna and the constitutional title of Premier of Northern Nigeria in the 1950s, set out to convert to Islam entire Christian communities en masse,[35] many including just recently converted "pagans," who, before the colonial period, lived beyond the limits of dar-al-Islam. This mode of conversion to Islam was a distinct departure from precolonial precedent and a direct result of Christians' increasingly evangelical mobility and its particular forms. Christian missionary and indigenous evangelism altered the course of and gave shape to modern Muslim politics in Northern Nigeria.

Religious difference was not created by colonial policies of segregation or by elites holding sway over faithful and passive followers. It emerged out of interaction, just as "pagans" and Muslims were identified by reference to one another in precolonial Hausaland.[36] Comparing African conversion to Islam and Christianity decades ago, Robin Horton observed that Islam was content with its role as a catalyst, allowing for a continuum of converts to remain within the fold. In contrast, missionary Christianity drew its boundaries rigidly and drove off "a great many adherents . . . [who joined] the proliferation of breakaway sects.[37] In their interaction, however, conversion became profoundly unstable.

While Muslims and Christians fundamentally disagree about the nature of God pertaining to the status of Isa (Jesus), they have a shared cosmology in which to debate. On one hand, Horton's contention—that without "radical change in cosmology," the propriety of the term "conversion" is doubtful—has some utility in the context of the early mission period in Northern Nigeria from a theological perspective.[38] Distinguishing between Muslims and Christians was often impossible (as in the leprosariums, as the cover photograph shows), and Christian religious identities emerged over several years. On the other hand, "conversion," whether or not deemed somehow authentic, became more immediate. Some pagans were converts twice over, between Islam and Christianity, while recantation of Christianity was usually undertaken expeditiously among the men who took positions in Muslim government in the 1950s. Conversion was impermanent and notably difficult to manage by political authorities and within courts. Without an effective overarching or parallel legal system, British officials recognized that Christians were dependent on the benevolence of Muslim authorities, a condition that persists as evidenced by the shar'ia conflicts that have occurred in more recent decades.

That the modes of conversion multiplied in the Muslim-Christian encounter reflects the growing importance of evangelism to both religions. While scholars have tended to focus on conversion, its historicity and changing definition within broader processes of evangelism have received less attention. "Evangelism" is a term not ordinarily associated with Islam. The ways in which modes of aggregating clients and converting people were borrowed and exchanged may better be expressed not in the language of Christian missions, but as part of a dynamic and widening "prayer economy," a concept that scholars of Islam have usefully employed.[39] In Islamic Africa, Nehemia Levtzion notes, the prayer economy involved "the learned urban 'ulama'" and the "rural rustic divines," who met with mystics of other religions to engage principally in two kinds of religious experiences: a search for the divine and "the recruitment of supernatural aid."[40] Christians and crypto-Christians in Northern Nigeria at times participated in this economy by trading in texts and "bible touches," and selling medicines along roadways. However, these networks remained the province of Muslims, who themselves were subject to a distinct occupational hierarchy. Christian evangelists, while still trying to sell goods, some that did not effect cures, began to compete more to accumulate people, a crucial concept for understanding sub-Saharan Africa, where wealth in land was rare, but clients, dependents, slaves, wives, and children constituted wealth and created influence. Christian evangelists of widely disparate origins created a new panethnic Hausa-speaking *jamaa*, or community, as they migrated among Muslims conducting colportage and medical work.[41]

The autonomy of itinerant evangelists and their "wealth" enabled a profoundly new appetite among ethnic and religious minorities for political independence from Muslim officials in the 1940s and 1950s.[42] Moses Ochonu rightly notes that Christian Northern Nigerians prioritized anti-Fulani politics, in contrast to Southerners' anti-British rhetoric.[43] Yet another difference is perhaps more striking: Northern Nigerian Christians' claims of moral and religious superiority over Muslims' corrupt politicking. Christianity inserted new divisions into the historically pronounced Hausa system of stratification, the most obvious distinctions being between *masu sarauta* (rulers) and *talakawa* (nonrulers), Muslims and pagans (*arna*). In Kano, Hausa and Fulani Muslims claim that the nineteenth-century jihad disciplined and schooled them in their own religion but left many in other ethnic groups as "pagans without clothes." Christianity a century later "suited" these lower social orders. Many, including former "pagans" themselves, speak quite literally of missions' "clothing pagans." In the town of Dass, Christians spoke of their transformation from a state of witless savagery and nudity, using the phrase of a child's coming of age (*ba mu da wayo*) to describe their Christian awakening and their authority to evangelize the Hausa, the very group that had held political and cultural sway over them for centuries.[44] This shared language of conversion among Christians and Muslims, referring to pagans, clothing and civilizing influence, is local, historical, and rehearsed. It has become increasingly competitive in the service of modern religious nationalism.[45]

DEBATING TEXTS AND TRUTH

In 2001, Justice Haruna 'dan Daura spoke on the Nigerian Television Authority program *A Chance to Meet*. An eminent Anglican Hausa Christian who was by then quite elderly, and has since died, he told his story of conversion to bolster his credentials for delivering a public address in the wake of violence that broke out over the declaration of shari'a. In the late 1910s, 'dan Daura's uncle Istifanus returned to Nigeria from serving with the British troops in World War I. Accused of engaging in sorcery by his family, Istifanus was outcast and joined the CMS. Soon after, he and his wife learned they were infertile and adopted Istifanus's dying brother's children, Haruna and Ramilat. Haruna was eight years old at the time and sent to a secret Christian missionary school operating within Kano Township. He eventually became a policeman and, in 1958, was appointed by the British and Muslim authorities to oversee the Mixed Court in Kano's Sabon Gari. On *A Chance to Meet*, Haruna 'dan Daura discussed at length his learning of Christ, or Isa, through Qur'anic passages.

The letters he received after the program aired were not responses to his discussion of political affairs but instead preoccupied with his personal history.[46] One response attacked the validity of 'dan Daura's conversion as a child, arguing that he did not choose his religion, his uncle did: "You were eight years and you were praying with the man and his family in [a] Christian way. . . . You must know the actions of your uncle [were] 'unethical.'" The writer denounced 'dan Daura's "murmuring" of Al-Fatiha, the Muslim creed in the first Sura, implying that 'dan Daura, as a Christian, had no right to recite from the Muslim scripture. In another letter, titled "YOU ARE VERY WRONG," a man from Sokoto denounced 'dan Daura for wanting "us to beli[e]ve that Christians are those with faith (in Jesus), Muslims in particular do not have faith, and they are the ones who rejected Jesus; therefore, you believe they will be [the] ones who will be punished. Your assertions are deceptive, wicked and wrong." He went on to quote at length from Qur'anic passages to support his view. A Christian writer questioned 'dan Daura on his self-deprecating statement on the program that he had not accomplished anything in his life: "Don't you reckon your decision at less than 10 years of age to pick Christianity as a way of life is an achievement?" 'Dan Daura answered the letters carefully and in great length. He also wrote directly to then President Olusegun Obasanjo, expressing his worry over the new and more expansive shar'ia courts. He cited Nigerian constitutional history, explaining how Muslim jurists deciding on independent Nigeria's penal code in 1959 carefully considered but decided not to establish shari'a and customary courts for criminal matters because different standards would be set for different citizens.

Texts have been at the center of many controversies between Muslims and Christians in Nigeria.[47] Over the objections of most Muslims, Christians contend they can read and imbibe the teachings of the Qur'an. Older Christians used the English translations produced by Indians like Muhammad Ali, while today, cheap Hausa and English pamphlets with Qur'anic passages are common in marketplaces. The Qur'an incorporates Injil, the New Testament, and contains stories of Isa, Christians argue, so why can't Christians read Muslim scripture? Throughout much of the twentieth century, disputes over apostasy, interreligious adoptions, land rights, and inheritance in the context of conversions and recantations were settled outside the courts in private informal negotiations. On the eve of Nigerian independence, foretelling the future conflict over the imposition of shari'a, the British worried about their failure to adequately provide institutionally for the resolution of disputes involving non-Muslim populations living under Muslim authority. The TV series *A Chance to Meet* was an attempt at public dialogue, but the letters 'dan Daura received, aside from engaging in the usual theological debates, reflected the fixation with questions about the authenticity of 'dan Daura's personal religious identity, either celebrating his courage or disparaging his uncle's decisions.

Although many of the sources collected for this book are new and offer exciting interpretive possibilities, they were created under conditions of intense scrutiny and overt competition for moral legitimacy. I collected original sets of handwritten diaries by three young men of Muslim Hausa and Zarma (another largely Muslim ethnic group) ethnicity, all of whom entered Christian mission networks before 1930. Many colonial-era Christians, in their written narratives (ordinarily in the mode of diary or memoir), self-consciously claim Muslim and ethnic ancestry out of the desire for a place among Muslims. As Karin Barber has pointed out in her introduction to the unique collection of essays *Africa's Hidden Histories*, African literacy "embodied aspiration and aspiration was founded upon lack—a sense of personal inadequacy associated with an education perceived as incomplete."[48] Northern Nigerian Christian literacy was the product of "unremitting effort," often undertaken in isolation from others, and thus self-conscious, particularly about origins and family history. The unpublished writings of Northern Nigerians I collected reveal anxiety over isolation and a search for belonging, often told as a spiritual journey.[49] A diary written by a man named Inusa starting in 1916, given to me by his daughter (then an elderly woman living in Jos), supported her claim that her father was one of the first Muslim converts to Christianity. But a second memoir attributed to her father, located in the SIM International Archives in Fort Mill, South Carolina, also disclosed Inusa's prior involvement in a millennial Islamic uprising against colonial and Muslim authorities and his flight as a refugee. Painful dislocation, dissent, and moral righteousness are themes further reflected in two new sources: sets of diaries written by the Anglican converts John Mamman Garba and Joseph Mohammed Sani.

The more conventional sources are of course not free of divergences in public and private versions. Sources from the British National Archives in Kew, England; Rhodes House Library, Oxford University; the Nigerian

National Archives in Kaduna; Arewa House in Kaduna; and the Kano History and Culture Bureau demonstrate an abiding skepticism on the part of British officials toward Christian missionaries, indigenous Christians, and Muslim "indirect rulers," though they often assumed politeness in public notices about these figures. At the CMS archives in Birmingham, England, among the well-used papers of Dr. Walter Miller, the head Anglican missionary in Zaria and a colorful figure who remained in Nigeria for decades, I found unpublished portions of the memoir of his sister Ethel Miller, a missionary who left the CMS and went "freelance," settling near Kano City on her own in the 1910s. This longer and unvarnished version reveals the frustrations of a feminist fundamentalist missionary who felt she shared more with pious Muslims than with lapsed Christians. Other white missionaries and colonial officials disdained Ethel Miller, who wished to die in Nigeria but instead was forced by the authorities to spend her final days in a Brighton nursing home.

Multiple texts by and about these individuals reveal the constructedness of religious discourses by the very actors historians presume to study. Archival sources, primarily from the SIM archives and the CMS archives, as well as published pamphlets and autobiographies, show how religious narratives were heavily scripted for communal, social, and political use. Each text had many existences, deployed variously as oral testimony at church, reprinted in missionary newspapers, and cited in the occasional legal case.

Oral sources show the same kinds of contested "writing" of religious history. I visited rural locations of former SIM and CMS stations, covering hundreds of miles between Bauchi, Kano, Kaduna, and Katsina States. Many rural folk had moved to the cities of Jos and Kaduna, where I met women and men who had lived in mission stations, either as pupils or workers for the missionaries. Out of roughly 100 conversations and interviews, I was permitted to make audio recordings of approximately 70. The interviews are of Christians and Muslims, many of whom were referred to me by others who had firsthand knowledge of and experiences with missions before 1975. The continuing ties between people across wide distances helped me to better understand how the social world of the Christian community was created and grew through informal networks. In the communal memory, well-known Christians were remembered by their nicknames or unique preaching styles. Often entire life histories recounting how a particular person ended up within the mission fold are well known throughout the wider regional Christian community. So, too, are there whispered histories of suspect conversions, backslidings, and recantations.

The circumstances of many Christian women's life histories, without the benefit of information about their origins, were particularly amenable to the theological notion of being born again. Similarly, the idea of "secret belief," following the New Testament's story of Nicodemus, is a thread that grows increasingly common in oral testimonies concerning suspected but unconfirmed Christian conversions of Muslim Hausa and Fulani.[50]

There are relatively few written sources compared to the much more voluminous oral narratives by African Christians. The written conversion testimonies echo what Derek Peterson observed in East Africa, where revivalists aimed to "plot a passage to new life" and position themselves in relation to political structures through their writings.[51] They also show that access to literacy remained highly specialized and restricted in the early years of Christian-Muslim encounter in Northern Nigeria. Further, the types of sources reflect the changing repertoire of indigenous evangelism over time. Mass public conversions became important spectacles at Christian leprosariums, in deep rural Hausaland, and during the campaigns of the Sardauna, Ahmadu Bello. As evangelism gained steam, and with the urgency of the imminent End that has been a strong belief running through various religious communities in Northern Nigeria,[52] the conditions prevailed for oral exhortation in favor of private scribbling in diaries. This is not to suggest that orality replaced written religious cultural production altogether, only that social circumstances and religious timekeeping informed the nature and prevalence of particular modes of communication: ritual, written, spoken, and conveyed by dress or bodily adornment, constituting an increasing and more religiously defined sense of difference.

STRUCTURE AND OVERVIEW OF THE BOOK

The book is divided into two parts, which break roughly around 1930, when Muslim-Christian encounters shifted from the grassroots and the pace of mission medical institutionalization prompted new competitive evangelism and, as a consequence, more attention to religious affiliation in the era of nationalist politics.

In part 1, the first chapter treats the earliest British, Canadian, and German missionary efforts in Muslim Northern Nigeria. While missionaries were generally Islamophobic, they also believed in the racial and religious superiority of Muslim Central Sudanese in relation to other sub-Saharan Africans. Christian evangelical culture in Northern Nigeria was shaped as much by Muslim reformism as by any Christian tradition. Within it, African women and men created and adopted new religious identities as stranger-migrants. Chapter 2 describes the urban politics of religious segregation and subversion in Kano following World War I. Transient families became crypto-Christians who settled in Zaria and Kano, the larger cities in Northern Nigeria, where they became a class of consumers of mission books and sent their children to secret schools. The Emir of Kano at once sought to incorporate crypto-Christians into his administration as workers, but he altered course after he saw that Christian teachers were attracting many clients. While Christian evangelism had given earlier Christians mobility, mission education was beginning to limit it. Chapter 3 shows how the possibilities for urban religious integration were diminished when, in the 1920s, Ethel Miller, a woman missionary freelancer who left the Anglican CMS, began a consciously feminist Christian anti-Muslim propaganda campaign, propagated through British women's networks from South Africa to India. She provoked the ire of the British colonial officers and male missionaries alike, who at every opportunity distanced themselves from her in their efforts to negotiate formal agreements to work in Muslim areas. The era of grassroots evangelism was effectively forestalled as official mission-Muslim cooperation progressed. While Ethel Miller's activism created a silence around the "woman question" in colonial Muslim Northern Nigeria at a time when gender reform was increasing elsewhere in the colonies, her status rose among indigenous Christians, particularly girls and women, who sought to prioritize religious work over the white missionaries' medical schemes.

Part 2 follows the rise of Christian medical work, informal schools, and formal orphanages that grew in Muslim areas, mostly through the work of the SIM because American Christian economic investment proved more robust than the European commitments after the Depression. Chapter 4 describes leprosy segregation facilities and rural dispensaries. They were successful in terms of medical outreach and cooperation, but also fostered religious offshoots and created social fractures. After women patients deserted the leprosariums, young males and older men became the majority of patients, leading to tensions between missions and Muslim authorities. The Emirs were also uncomfortable with the growing power of African Christians as medical and educational authorities, and debates about the ethics of converting youth arose. While the mission medical work was intended to curb and contain freelance evangelism, it instead expanded it.

Chapter 5 shows how this evangelical zeal and activism spread beyond the leprosariums to rural areas, as medical mission sites in Muslim Northern Nigeria became the "underground" where anticolonial and nationalist tendencies were percolating to counter both native and foreign authority. The postwar era brought into Northern Nigeria demobilized soldiers from French West Africa, who entered Christian medical institutions to seek care and economic opportunities, as well as to create new identities for themselves, many becoming "indigenous" evangelists in the process. These stranger-settlers developed radical new forms of evangelical culture in Muslim and "pagan" villages, creating spheres of local autonomy over which mission, colonial, and native authorities had little knowledge or supervision. The final chapter explores how Northern Nigerian Christians, whose presence had grown within both urban and rural Hausaland, became outsiders in the politics of the late colonial period. They represented an educated class ready to take government posts in a Nigerianized civil service, but their interests did not match up with either Christian Southerners or Muslim Northerners. Muslims engaged in overtly political evangelical campaigns. After the Nigerian government's takeover of most mission sites and growing regional divides between the North and South, Northern Nigerian Christian networks became largely invisible. While many histories attribute the rise of charismatic and Pentecostal Christianity in Nigeria to changing economic fortunes and the influence of Southern Nigerian Christians, the competition between Muslims and Christians in the North surely played a part in shaping new revivalist movements, occuring secretly amid growing insecurity and violence.

Note on Language and Acronyms

The names of ethnic groups appear generally according to Hausa convention: one Hausa person is *Bahaushe* (male) or *Bahaushiya* (female), while the plural is *Hausawa*. *Zabarmawa* or *Zarmawa* is another example (*Zarma* or *Zabarma* is singular).

The following glossary lists common words that appear throughout the text. The spellings may be slightly different in quoted material from missionary, colonial governmental, or other English transliteration. Following Hausa orthography, I have used an apostrophe before letters that are pronounced with ejective or implosive sounds (the most common example is 'dan). Unfortunately, the original Hausa writings in Roman script do not contain these important marks, and I have translated oral interviews into English in most cases.

GLOSSARY

alhaji — one who has completed the Muslim pilgrimage (*hajiya* is feminine)
alkali — judge in Islamic court (also appears as *qadi* or *kadi*)
arna — pagan (Hausa term)
balaga — puberty
baraka — spiritual grace
birni — walled city
boko — mostly used to mean Roman script writing or non-Islamic academic subjects
'*bori* — spirit possession
Emir — Muslim high official
galadima — important titled office in the Native Administration
Ha'be — prejihad (before 1807) Hausa states
hajj — Muslim pilgrimage to holy sites in Arabia
hijra — flight
Injil — New Testament
Isa — Jesus
Isawa — followers of Jesus

magani—medicine

Mahdi—rightly guided one

malam (pl. *malamai*)—teacher, respected person (feminine is *malama*; colonial sources often spelled it as mallam)

masu sarauta—titled officeholders

Native Administration—indigenous political authorities serving as part of the British colonial government, also referred to as Native Authority

pagan—non-Muslim; practitioner of indigenous religion. Commonly used over the 20th century in pejorative and non-pejorative senses.

Resident—British official living and serving in a colonial territory, mainly as part of the indirect rule system that included Native Administrations

sabon gari—literally "new town," enclave created for immigrant Africans in some Muslim cities (I have not capitalized the phrase unless referring to a specific city's enclaves)

sarki—chief, king, titleholder (pl. *sarakuna*; *sarauta* refers to the title system)

shar'ia—Islamic religious law

Shehu—refers to Usman 'dan Fodio, nineteenth-century jihad leader, from Arabic *sheikh*

talakawa—commoners

ulema—scholars, also spelled as *ulama*

yin wa'azi—exhort or preach

COMMON ACRONYMS USED IN THE TEXT

AMS—African Missionary Society
AMTL—American Mission to Lepers
BELRA—British Empire Leprosy Relief Association
BFBS—British Foreign Bible Service
CCN—Christian Council of Nigeria
CMS—Church Missionary Society
ECWA—Evangelical Churches of West Africa
NA—Native Authority or Native Administration (refers to indigenous rulers—Emirs, Islamic judges, etc.)
NCNC—National Council of Nigeria and the Cameroons
NEPU—Northern Elements Progressive Union
NPC—Northern People's Congress
SIM—Sudan Interior Mission
SMA—Society of Missions in Africa
SUM—Sudan United Mission

PART I

The Word Travels

1 ↬ "A Place to Lay Our Head"
A Sect of Strangers, 1890–1918

IN 1889, the Irish Protestant evangelist and activist Henry Grattan Guinness wrote an essay introducing European and American readers to the "Soudan" of Central Africa, a region greater in size and population but less well known than Congo, he claimed. This vast land was split, "half monotheist, half heathen." The name "is a witness to this mixture," Guinness wrote, where "the Semite and the Hamite dwell together in its sunny plain."[1] His preaching tour in America that same year garnered so much interest that the Soudan Pioneer Mission was formed in Minneapolis, Minnesota. A newspaper, the *Soudan and the Regions Beyond*, was established to raise awareness about this great prospect for Christian proselytizers.[2]

Over the next decade, many European and North American Christian missions with a "burden for the Sudan" were founded. Though many of the first missionaries traveling to West Africa died, physical challenges did not stop new recruits.[3] Inspired by the evangelical movement, these Christians were bent on bringing the gospel to the unreached peoples of the interior (see map 1.1).[4] Not only had the region of Sudan captivated their interest as a battleground to stop the advance of Islam, they also denounced the white "goldseeking" agents of the Royal Niger Company traders.[5] "Coastal Africans," many of whom had been evangelized in earlier decades, were dismissed as drunkards and members of unintelligent races.[6] Missionaries to Sudanic Africa believed strongly in European racial science of the time,

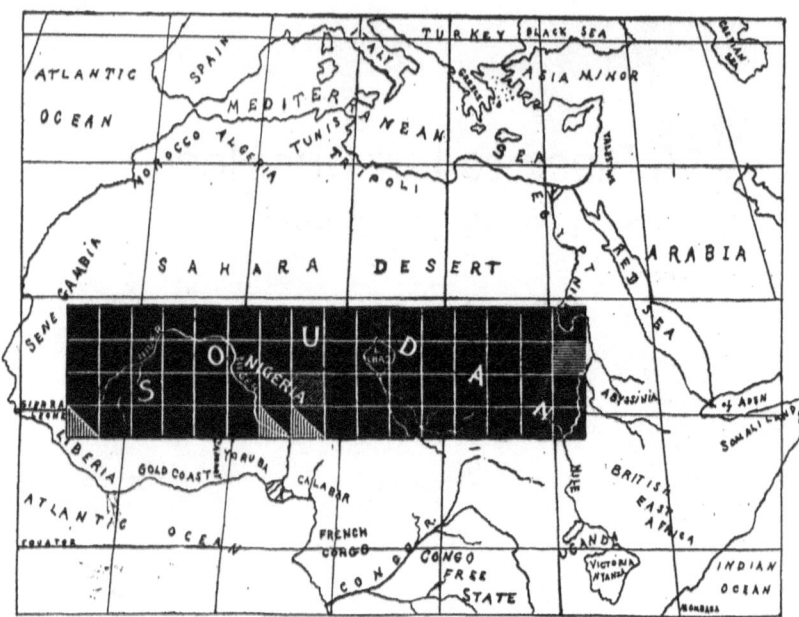

Map 1.1. A North American Christian magazine sought to interest missionaries for the Sudan, represented by black squares, where the "Gospel had never reached." (*Missionary Witness*, 25 September 1906.)

which posited the predominantly Muslim ethnic groups of the interior, such as the Fulani and the Hausa, as superior to and more civilized than other Africans. Over the years, the idea that Islam was the "archenemy of Christianity" gradually came to dominate missionary thinking in relation to Sudanic Africa.[7]

Even as Christians vilified Islam in different ways, some missionaries in the late nineteenth and early twentieth centuries admitted a grudging admiration for the means by which Muslims spread their religion in Sudanic Africa. Some missionaries insisted that Muslims had conquered with violence in West Africa, but a growing number claimed that Muslims had a kind of religious sociability that Christian missionaries should perhaps emulate. Muslims preached publicly yet were "tolerant" toward "pagan" practices of magic and superstition that allowed a less abrupt break between African indigenous traditions and Islam than Christian missions allowed.[8] This tolerance was not for lack of theological understanding, for Christian missionaries credited Muslims with a knack for sophisticated debate about eschatological and other matters. Rather, critics gently chastised Europeans and Americans for their disinterest in missions to Muslims because of their desire for quick results. "Missionary work must be honest service of friendship and love, not propaganda, which, at bottom always contains a grain of self-seeking," wrote one missionary.[9]

This chapter explores the diverse and divided currents of civilizational reform within Christian missionary movements in the North of Nigeria. Although the Sudan Interior Mission (SIM) considered its theological position to be antimodern (thus, more resistant to innovations to the Bible), Donald Donham points out that in political and social practice, the mission's evangelism had more complex effects. Noting the intriguing relationship formed between American missionaries and Haile Selassie, Donham writes, "the dialectic between anti-modernism and its shadow, modernism, was always more than a simple opposition. These two stances depended upon one another and at times feed into one another."[10] In the interreligious realm, a similar creative tension existed between Christian and Muslim evangelism developing in the 1890s and early 1900s. Both Christian missions and devout Muslims were fixated on prophecy and the imminent end of the world; for both, this fixation intensified with European conquest. Christian-Muslim encounter produced a unique revivalism; reformism became an expression of personal and political emancipation and the basis of authority for the first Christian Northern Nigerian lay leaders. Refugees, freed slaves, and other marginalized people sought to use religious renewal as the impetus for their newfound mobility amid the political, economic, and social transformations occurring after the colonial takeover of the caliphate and the abolition of slavery.

SEEKERS AFTER THE TRUTH: CHRISTIAN PROSPECTS IN THE HAUSA WORLD, 1890–1905

The spark Guinness gave to American evangelicals bent on reaching the Sudan was burning in England as well, where independent and institutionally sponsored missionaries undertook journeys to the Nigerian hinterland. Freelance English missionary Graham Wilmot Brooke tried to reach Kano first from the Mediterranean, then from the Congo, before he died in 1890. That same year, the Anglican Church Missionary Society (CMS) sponsored the trip of John Robinson and Thomas Harford Battersby. From the coast, the two reached as far as Lokoja, at the confluence of the Niger and Benue Rivers, and studied Hausa for one year until Robinson died. In Robinson's memory, the chairman of the Royal Niger Company, Sir George Goldie, founded the Hausa Association in 1891 "to promote the study of Hausa language and people."[11] John's brother, Reverend Charles

Robinson, later Canon of Ripon, led three expeditions to Hausaland in 1893, 1894, and 1895 on behalf of the association.

A distinct creation of the late nineteenth century, the association included members who were Christian but ecumenical in their outlook and their interest in Hausaland. In addition to the Archbishops of Canterbury, York, and Dublin, the eminent anthropologist and statistician Sir Francis Galton, Sir Leonard Darwin (a cousin of Charles Darwin), and the Orientalists F. Max Mueller and David S. Margoliouth, famous for their studies of comparative religions, all sat on the General Committee. Several of these men believed in Islam's positive influence on the world, especially for Africans. Sir Francis Galton grew up in a Quaker family of physicians and inventors but, after living in Syria, traveling in Africa, and reading Charles Darwin's work on evolution, experienced a "freedom of thought, a positive faith" that confirmed a personal drift away from Christian orthodoxy and toward a relativity of religion.[12] Goldie, an atheist, had lived for a few years with an Arab mistress in the Anglo-Egyptian Sudan, a place he described as "the Garden of Allah," where he met Hausa-speaking pilgrims and traders who sparked his interest in opening the Niger River hinterland to British commerce.[13] The missionaries affiliated with the Hausa Association, and the Anglicans generally, shared interests in Hausa language and history with philologists, racial scientists, and traders. Their religious relativism was a source of conflict with American evangelicals as early as 1895, when the association medical secretary, Dr. T. J. Tonkin, met the SIM's Walter Gowans not far from Zaria. The doctor had urged the missionary to get to the coast for treatment, but Gowans refused and died of dysentery in Girku. Tonkin's story of the meeting was meant, in part, to distinguish between scientifically oriented European interventions and evangelical Christian agendas in Africa.[14]

Charles Robinson of the Hausa Association took a clinical approach in his assessments of Hausa civilization. He presented relatively specific population estimates of between 10,000 and 30,000 inhabitants every 50 miles. He highlighted the thriving economic success in the commercial capital of Kano, with its market that drew an average of 25,000 to 30,000 visitors daily, and the effective political control of the Fulani-held capital of Sokoto. The main problem he saw in an otherwise-flourishing region was slave-raiding and trafficking, the "great overshadowing evil."[15] Most of the slaves, which he estimated at nearly one-third of Hausaland's fifteen million total population, "are obtained not from foreign or outside sources, but from villages or towns, the inhabitants of which are of the same tribe and race as their captors. The practical result of this is that the country is subject to nearly all the evils of a perpetual civil war. . . . There is no real security for life or property anywhere."[16] Robinson proposed two remedies: the introduction of a modern currency system and the introduction of the railway and other modern transportation, since captives were used as currency and as porters.

More evangelical Christians viewed their task in the Central Sudan as not to bring free commerce but to contain Islam as a threat to "pagan" Africans and Westerners. An anonymous writer in the *Faithful Witness* magazine, published by SIM founder Rowland Bingham, warned of the grip of "the hoary religions of the East and the new falsehoods of the West, and the Mohammedanism that holds the centre," raising fears that the British "sapping" of Muslim power in Egypt would "revive a proselytizing [Muslim] force." Yet the British were not entirely in control, for, the author noted, "there is not the slightest doubt that many European thinkers have been powerfully influenced by Mohammedanism."[17] The author cited rumors of Muslim missionaries in Paris and London. From the time of Britain's takeover of Northern Nigeria in 1900, and well after the final subjugation of Sokoto in 1903, Christian evangelicals worried about British colonial policies of noninterference with Muslims.[18] "It may be necessary that a new leader shall be raised up who shall recall the British people to the standards which have been the means of raising her to the forefront of nations," wrote the editor of the *Missionary Witness* in 1905.[19]

While missionaries disagreed among themselves about who was more fit for evangelism in Northern Nigeria, their work in Hausa translation and with Muslim inquirers began to reveal the vibrant and vigorous religious debates that contradicted earlier stereotypes of forced conversions and passive acquiescence of African Muslims. Before 1899, when the CMS was able to secure a site in Zaria, missionaries went to North Africa to study Hausa language with slaves, servants, and pilgrims on their way to Arabia. Hermann Harris, a missionary of the Central Soudan Mission in Cairo,[20] translated Hausa oral stories told by Muslims of different ethnicity—including Nupe and Hausa, showing a circulation of life histories of important Muslim figures, like Muhammad Ahmad, the Mahdi (rightly guided one) of the Eastern Sudan who was famed for his militant resistance to colonization by the Egyptians and the British.[21] A recurring theme in the stories was initial disbelief and growing conviction of the truth of the identity of righteous religious figures.

Dr. Walter Miller, who had also studied the Hausa language in North Africa before establishing the CMS Zaria mission in 1899, adopted a Hausa boy named Audu, one of Harris's young servants.[22] One of the earliest known Hausa converts to Christianity, Audu came into the ambit of missions in North Africa after his father died while the pair were traveling to Arabia for the hajj around 1897. Some Hausa travelers found Audu in Aghat in southwest Libya and took him with them to Tripoli. It is not clear if Audu was enslaved when he met an Anglican missionary, Lieutenant Nott, in the Tripoli bread market, but the boy eventually came into the care of Walter Miller, who arranged for the British consul at Benghazi to guarantee the boy's safe passage to Alexandria, where Audu worked as a servant for Hermann Harris. Audu left to complete the pilgrimage and reappeared in Egypt in 1901. From there he went to England, most likely through missionary sponsorship, and reunited with Dr. Miller in Zaria. Audu lived with Miller as his own son.[23] Audu's conversion took some time, but, even before his baptism, he "witnessed" about the pilgrimage. Miller recounted Audu's saying before a group of Muslim men, including an Arab, that "if there is anything in Islam of truth, the most Truth and holiness ought to be found in Mecca, our holy City, but it is the wickedest, most depraved City in the world."[24]

Miller's version of the "witness" concerning Islam served his purpose to illustrate the challenges of conversion for Audu, who stood to hold great esteem as an *alhaji*, one who had completed the pilgrimage, particularly at such a young age.[25] Other white observers, including the Hausa Association's Dr. Tonkin, who had little sympathy for Christian efforts to civilize people he considered already quite evolved, confirmed the power of the pilgrimage narrative, without making reference to its actual content: "As the old warrior fights his battles o'er again, so the returned Hadji day by day and week by week re-performs his pilgrimage for the benefit of listening and admiring friends and acquaintances. Whom the king conquers he converts!"[26]

Audu had no doubt sought to advance himself socially through his pilgrimage experience and, perhaps, his association with the white missionaries. In 1902, the Emir of Zaria, who had been friendly to Miller and the CMS, refused any further contact, and Miller remarked on Audu's growing despondency.[27] "All this has brought about a complete estrangement between him and his people," wrote Miller about Audu. "The first person he has yet met from his own country Katsina, a boy who was at school with him, met him here, seemed delighted beyond measure, and then after two days' intercourse stole from my poor laddie the most valuable things in his possession. . . . His people don't trust him because his affection for us is so genuine and he has even to give up seeing his own mother because his meeting her might lead to her being killed afterwards as accomplice of the white man!"[28]

British officials often accused Miller of overstating physical threats to Christian converts,[29] but Audu's crisis in the midst of increasing political opposition to Christian missions was less the result of any specific threat than a realization that the pathways between missions and his Muslim community were closing. He would have to choose. Audu received baptism in 1904, and Miller, commenting on Audu's piety, praised the young man's deceased father as "a negro Muslim, who seems to have been a very unusually good and genuine seeker after the truth."[30]

Audu's conversion was the result of distance from his family and friends, a distance Miller cultivated. Yet it was precisely this kind of distance that also made him more ascetic and reformist in his religious outlook, if we are to believe Miller's recollection of how Audu spoke about the hajj. Stripping away the self-serving element of missionary accounts of African Muslims' critiques of Islam, many sources make clear that long-distance journeys were a common beginning for dissenters who became Christian inquirers and converts.

The SIM, which had established stations at Pategi in 1902 and Bida in 1903 on the Niger River, and then Wushishi in Kontagora in 1904, told the story of another Muslim convert, Halilu, from Katagum Emirate in Bauchi Province. He spoke of specific teachers in his area, Malam Sumbo and his son Malam Suli, who was known as a great traveler who brought "back a book" and began to contradict his father about Isa's death.[31] The SIM, whatever their problems with the more moderate missions, could not deny their claims of the importance of language and stories to the Hausa, whom missionaries considered special Africans for their love of books.[32] Writing about Halilu's visits as a child to hear Malam Suli's "stories of travel in a strange land," an SIM missionary wrote, "Sometimes he would ask to see the wonderful book. Imagination readily reconstructs the scene—the Mallam taking with reverent hands the worn volume from its leather case, and the little boy . . . gazing with curious, awestruck eyes on the pages that held for both of them the possibilities of the infinite."[33]

Missionaries of both evangelical and more modern views saw the Hausa as largely devoid of Islamic evangelical zeal and advised Christian countrymen to learn from Muslims in the marketplace and use their methods of "passive" evangelism through communal prayer.[34] Yet the missionaries underestimated the reformist zeal that was simmering throughout the region, particularly as the interethnic and interreligious relations—between Muslims and non-Muslims—were radically altered with the ongoing and messy process of European colonization of the Central Sudan. British authorities and Muslim rulers who survived or were put in place after the conquest drew ever closer together, enraging some Christian missionaries while bringing others firmly under government control. Rebels and refugees were driven in larger numbers into the missions' ambit. Migration and flight within this context took new directions and new meaning in ways that few authorities—white missionaries, British officials, or Muslim rulers—could hardly appreciate, much less predict or control.

PROTEST MOVEMENTS AND FLIGHT, 1906–1910

In November 1898, Lieutenant Laussu arrived in Dosso, less than three hundred kilometers west of Sokoto, with forty *tirailleurs* (soldiers), but the *zarmakoy*, the chief, refused to submit.[35] Instead, Auta, the son of a former zarmakoy, began helping the French troops. This mutually beneficial relationship gave the French local levies and allowed Auta to build an empire by conquering towns neighboring Dosso. Auta styled himself as a traditional chief to the French but took unprecedented powers in overriding the relatively democratic appointment of zarmakoy. He was much hated by his countrymen and tried to break them through punitive raids. He did not have slaves before his relationship with the French, but, defying their stated goal to abolish slave-raiding, he took scores of captives between 1899 and 1905. The last raid occurred in Kobkitanda.

Kobkitanda was not a "traditional" village but, instead, a haven for resisters. Yarima Inusa, who was about fifteen years old, lived in a nearby village. Many years later, after he had fled the area and worked for the SIM, Inusa called Kobkitanda a place that had "sprung up in the bush because many people had settled to farm."[36] Kobkitanda's main leader was Shaibu, a blind cleric, whom Inusa described as "a tall, dark thin man" who claimed to be the Mahdi, one called to lead Muslims in the End Time. Mahdism existed in many parts of the Muslim world, and, in the early colonial context of social and political disorder, it flourished.[37] Inusa said that Shaibu's claims of invincibility, supported by rumors that he possessed medicine to render white men's guns powerless, spread quickly throughout the area. The authorities at Dosso sent three soldiers to investigate the rumors in late 1905. When they arrived in Kobkitanda, Inusa recalled that Shaibu rallied his followers, stating, "What are we waiting for? Let us kill the infidels." The response was swift. Two soldiers were killed, "thrown into the bush for wild animals to devour, their guns buried, but the horses were retained because they were quite valuable." The third soldier escaped and raised the call for reinforcements.

The revolt in Dosso led to reprisal attacks, then revolts down along the Niger River, and the flight of Shaibu across the border to Satiru, a village near Sokoto that was similar to Kobkitanda in its anticolonial and anti-"collaborator" orientation.[38] In Satiru, the Mahdists joined with fleeing slaves. The British had issued a proclamation freeing from slavery all children born after March 1901 and outlawing slave-raiding, but they had wanted to prevent a mass exodus of slaves from destabilizing native rule and the fragile peace only recently established. The Satiru uprising, however, swelled into a protracted rebellion, leading the British and the pro-British Sokoto forces to kill an estimated 2,000 rebels and drive 3,000 women and children seeking protection into Sokoto, where "many [were taken] into servitude."[39]

The postmortem on the revolt showed clearly an antiaristocratic and antislavery vein running through various Muslim communities. Ethnic tensions were simmering, for not even a single Fulani body could be identified among the dead. Oral accounts mentioned many Hausa subgroups among the participants but no Fulani or even non-Hausa. The Zabarma cleric Shaibu, who survived the bloodshed but was imprisoned and later executed, and any fellow countrymen who had made it to Satiru from Dosso, were "Hausaized" in the analysis of the conflict on the Northern Nigerian side of the border. The British authorities minimized the role of slave deserters in the destruction to avoid alarming the aristocracy who had supported them to put down the Satirawa.[40] It was politically expedient to downplay ethnic tensions as well, since only non-Fulani were slaves.

Inusa survived the ravages of the French and Dosso armies as they razed town after town. "They set fire to our houses, even though we had no part in the uprising," he recalled. "No matter, they killed and plundered, for they were athirst for revenge. It was at this time my father was killed, together with my uncle and maternal grandfather."[41] His mother had died two years earlier. As the eldest, he took his younger brothers and went to live with his paternal uncle, a Qur'anic teacher. Inusa did not do well in school, however, and left in 1909 to wander, heading first for Jebba, south on the Niger River in Nigeria.

The post-Satiru exodus of dissidents and runaway slaves, groups now fairly mixed together, flooded the western corridor of Northern Nigeria. While the Dosso-Satiru uprising had a profound impact on solidifying political power and the alliance of Europeans and their indigenous allies, it also reshaped the demography and economy by dispersing many refugees into jobs as porters, laborers, and other menials in the colonial service.[42] Uprooted people fled down the Niger, toward the confluence with the

Benue, to Lokoja and Zungeru, the centers of colonial trade and administration and presumably to other parts of the colony. "Pagan" slaves emancipated during the unrest sought to return to their natal lands, perhaps as far east as Lake Chad and Adamawa, from which many slaves had come into Hausaland. East and south of the "core" Muslim areas, dispersed slaves and dissenters encountered Christian missionaries. Whereas the missionaries had been unable to reach these populations, the dislocation following Satiru brought the refugees to them. The SIM stations on the Niger and the SUM stations at Ibi on the Benue received many runaways.

Frederick Lugard, the high commissioner, worried for the missionaries' safety at the hands of Muslim resisters but relied on them to assist the government's abolitionist work.[43] The colonial authorities knew runaways and other freed slaves worked for the CMS and SIM.[44] It is no coincidence that the formal negotiations regarding the Christian mission takeover of the government freed slave homes began in late 1906 and early 1907, immediately following Satiru.

Dr. Karl Kumm, the son-in-law of the Irish preacher Grattan Guinness and founder of the Sudan United Mission (SUM), approached the British authorities in November 1906 to ask for one hundred acres of land to establish a freed slave colony.[45] Unlike other missionaries in Northern Nigeria, he wanted to locate his missions among non-Muslims, especially on slave routes. Kumm hoped to cultivate militant Christianity, in contrast to the gradual and Muslim-focused strategy of Miller in Zaria. The British colonial administration was, in his estimation, not a friend of Christianity but a supporter of Islamic domination. He wrote sarcastically: "We have brought the Pagan tribes in Central Africa into subjection; we have established peace; we have built roads, and we protect the Moslem trader, the Moslem pilgrim and the Moslem teacher. Yea! And we go so far as to send Moslem administrators to the Pagans."[46] He claimed that the people of the Sudan should be seen as the guardians of Christendom, akin to the Swiss peasants who drove back the dukes of Austria. "Theirs was the first Republic of modern days, and what the Swiss accomplished in Europe, the Ethiopians, including the Christian Abyssinians and the warlike mountain Pagans, succeeded in doing in Africa," he wrote. This was political Christianity to rival what Kumm called 'dan Fodio's "Wahabi desire for reform and conquest."[47]

A modern Christian colony within the larger Islamic Northern Nigeria was the best means of abolition, he wrote, and contrasted the American situation: "How very much more satisfactory the results would have been, and all the race hatred, the lynching, and sacrificing of coloured criminals avoided, had the trade and traffic in slaves been abolished, and domestic slavery gradually come to an end, through the compulsory education of the free children of domestic slaves, or the establishment of one or two free negro states under the control of wise, white administrators."[48]

The British accepted his proposal for a freed slave colony in 1907 and, in 1908, decided to hand over to the SUM the freed slave home founded by the government at Zungeru. William Wallace, acting High Commissioner of Northern Nigeria, visited the home and advised the Colonial Office that it was "a philanthropic institution, not a suitable Government Department."[49] A major problem at the home was the government's inability to dispose of the girls and women. Males could be conscripted as soldiers or manual laborers, but, as J. C. Sciortino, Resident of Nassarawa Province, explained, the authorities had to prevent the formation of an "undesirable class of unattached females."[50]

According to freed slave registers of 1906–1907, out of 627 freed slaves, 403 were females. Girls of the prime age of marriage by local standards constituted more than 53 percent of the female freed slaves, and, among them, older girls between the ages of sixteen and twenty accounted for nearly one-quarter of all freed slaves. Some of these older girls had their own children, the mission records show. Females were preferred in the trans-Saharan trade, unlike in the Atlantic, where males were in far greater demand.[51] Islamic law allowed four wives and as many concubines as a master could afford. The British, often by inaction, allowed girls who remained in slavery to be "absorbed" into Muslim households, and the authorities used the terms "master" and "husband" interchangeably. Freed girls, on the other hand, were conspicuously alienated, but not free.

These girls joined males like Inusa at the mission stations. Both kinds of refugees became laborers—colonial conscripts and domestic workers at Christian stations who would produce children in the first Christian Northern Nigerian households. Thus, Satiru was a turning point not just for the political order but also for the religious and social reordering of Northern Nigeria.

Not all missions wanted or could handle the freedpeople. The CMS station in the Muslim city of Zaria was not a ready-made haven for runaways or rebels. Dr. Walter Miller, the head missionary, had a complicated relationship with the Emir of Zaria and the British Residents. Miller was quite vocal in his criticism of Fulani rulers in general and the British administration after Satiru. As early as 1904, he recorded Fulani rulers' abuses, as reported by "trustworthy Hausas and some royal Fillanis," and informed Frederick Lugard of them.[52] In 1907, he sent to Lugard a letter detailing atrocities committed by troops under British command against Satiru rebels. Lugard replied that Sokoto Native Authority police had committed these acts.⁵³ Yet Lugard's brother, Edward, had information corroborating Miller's story. A British Resident told him about the license given to African troops by Major Alder Burdon, in charge at Sokoto during the rebellion: "It is well not to spoil a Club carpet by vomiting on it, but he dropped out such items as the spitting of their mallam on a stake, the cutting off the breasts of women!!—imagination can supply the rest."⁵⁴ Yet Edward insisted that if any action were to be taken against Burdon, it should be attributable only to Miller's reporting. In the end, Burdon was not officially reprimanded. Miller, perhaps as an appeasement, was permitted to remain within the walls of Zaria City, the only Christian site in a Hausa emirate before the 1920s.⁵⁵ Miller was considered to be too involved with politics and was never again trusted fully by the colonial officers. He could no longer count on them for support, nor did British officers place as many freed slaves with him as with the SIM and SUM.

These other missions worked closely with the British government in antislavery work, accepting funds for upkeep of their wards. In this regard, they became effectively a government department. They viewed Miller with suspicion, and, because he was in charge of the Hausa translation work upon which all of the Christian societies depended, the self-avowedly fundamentalist SIM feared his theological "modernism" would creep into the Hausa Bible and, through it, indigenous Christian culture.⁵⁶ Miller, in turn, viewed the SIM as unequipped intellectually for work among Muslim Hausa.⁵⁷ These missionary interests and their positions relative to the political authorities, now wary of religious revolts, shaped the kinds of identities and the attendant opportunities for mobility that converts could find in Christianity.

CAPTURING THE FLOW OF MANY STREAMS

Construction on the railway connecting Lagos to Kano began in 1907, and Inusa, with another Zabarma man, Audu, consulted a diviner before heading down the Niger to Jebba.⁵⁸ It is very likely that they joined many streams of other Zabarmawa who migrated to Gold Coast and the Southern Nigerian Provinces and then returned home after earning wages as porters, ditchdiggers, timber sellers, and other menials. The rail had not yet been built as far as Jebba, and Inusa and Audu meandered south down the Niger. When they stopped to rest in the market at Pategi, a man rounding up carriers for a white traveler approached them. Inusa refused to carry the man's loads, but Audu went and, after the trip, stayed on as horseboy for the traveler, who was SIM missionary E. F. Lang. Inusa, meanwhile, worked as a servant to a Nupe *malam* (teacher) who had a Qur'anic school. The teacher agreed that if Inusa worked for him as a manservant, he would teach Inusa the Qur'an from the fourth chapter, where he had left off in Dosso.[59]

Inusa made a point of refusing to carry loads, at least in the retelling, because it was a job associated with slaves. He also resisted Audu's invitations to hear the white people's preaching because he was sure that whites did not believe in God.[60] When Inusa eventually did visit the SIM missionary at Pategi, he could understand very little, for the missionary in charge spoke only Nupe. Inusa then met Paul, a Laka man from Adamawa, far to the east, who spoke Hausa and showed Inusa a map. "He pointed out to me the name of many towns in my own country. I was amazed and asked him whether he had been to my country, but he answered no. I said, how can you know all these places, even Dosso, without ever going to my country," Inusa wrote.[61] Though neither Audu nor Inusa understood the missionary's Nupe preaching, they were both captivated. It took a Hausa-speaking Christian, a foreigner like Inusa himself, likely of slave descent, to induce Inusa to leave his Muslim teacher.

In Zaria at around the same time, Dr. Miller called together about ten converts, not yet baptized, and told them about a sect founded in the 1850s or 1860s after a pilgrim named Ibrahim, a member of the retinue of Kano's Emir-apparent Abdullahi, returned from Mecca and preached that Muhammad was not the true prophet of Allah.[62] When Ibrahim refused to repent, Abdullahi ordered him to be impaled in the Kano market. His followers fled to the border between Kano and Bauchi, where they settled and built alliances with "pagan hordes" to fight the Fulani.[63] Evangelizing the Isawa, as Miller called the sect on account of its Isa- or Jesus-centered reading of the Qur'an, was "the privilege and duty" of Africans, not foreign missionaries.[64] Afterward, one young illiterate man reportedly brought out twelve coppers and, saying that he could not travel out to the villages because of his cattle, offered to help someone else go. Several volunteers went each week to the Isawa outposts thereafter.

It is doubtful that uncommitted Christians actually evangelized the Isawa, but men who had had more exposure to white men and their books than others could indeed attempt to present themselves as "teachers." However, whereas a malam possessed authority and students, or clients, these men had little standing as Christians, and their status as Muslims decreased with each day spent at the mission. They were not even valued as teachers to white missionaries, who studied Nupe and Hausa in Arabic script with advanced Muslim scholars.⁶⁵ Itinerant preaching, therefore, was not simply religious exhortation so much as a method of social networking that preceded any contemplated Christian conversion.

Knowledge and learning were as a general matter competitively taught and sought in Muslim West Africa,⁶⁶ and learning about the whites became a new curiosity among competing and even isolated sects. Paul Krusius, a German missionary in Zaria, met a young pagan Hausa at the Zaria market in 1914 and accompanied him to his remote village, where he was met with wonder.⁶⁷ The villagers believed that whites came to earth fully grown from the water or the sky. When Krusius explained that whites were as human as they, the Maguzawa (non-Muslim Hausa) blamed Kano men for spreading misinformation.⁶⁸ The Muslim Hausa and Maguzawa often blamed one another for misinformation and misdeeds, such as tempting good Muslims to drink beer.⁶⁹ They also relied on each other for certain services. Maguzawa purchased Imams' performances of certain rites like baby-naming, while Muslims sometimes traveled to rural Hausaland to seek Maguzawa treatment for spirit-caused illnesses, like madness.⁷⁰ Over the twentieth century, Christian evangelists reached the Maguzawa who lived in deep rural Kano, Katsina, Bauchi, and Zaria Emirates.⁷¹ Isawa and Maguzawa, whose paths reportedly crossed, tended to be reclusive.

Finding them was a path for upward mobility for men like Inusa. Christian teachers like Paul were usually raised from youth within the missions. Men like Inusa, and the unbaptized seekers in Zaria, on the other hand, had to work as cooks, stewards, and carriers to trekking missionaries.⁷² For example, one of the Zaria men, Malam Fati, had a better job purchasing cotton for the British Cotton Growing Association in Katsina in 1916. He was, however, imprisoned for extortion, and the Emir of Katsina threatened to kill him. According to Miller's account in a letter to the British Resident in Kano, H. R. Palmer, Miller (unsurprisingly) believed the Emir threatened to kill Fati because of his religion.⁷³ However, the Emir of Katsina apparently had even earlier deemed Fati to be a worthless opportunist.⁷⁴ To be sure, the Emirs were interested in limiting the mobility of the missionaries' migrants and trekkers, but not necessarily out of dislike of Christianity. And the migrants who tested these boundaries, as Fati and Inusa did, showed mettle that missionaries themselves did not have.

Missionaries, for their part, policed such men, owing both to doubts of their fidelity and to fear of losing their investment. Walter Miller of the CMS, who saw the precariousness of Audu's conversion, kept him close with the promise of marriage to a girl of his same social standing. Eight years after Audu's baptism, when he was in his twenties, Audu was betrothed to a twenty-year-old Christian Fulani girl named Hawa'u.[75] The couple waited nearly three more years to wed. Inusa, on the other hand, was of uncertain background. He did not tell the SIM missionaries that he was a Zabarma and folded himself with their Hausa-speaking seekers. Working as a steward, cook, and washman, he studied Hausa writing and reading until 1913, when he began evangelizing in rural areas around Wushishi. The same year, the SIM engaged him to a young freed slave named Rifkatu at Wushishi. Inusa returned to Dosso after this, taking with him tracts to sell, but his people teased him that he would have been better off making the pilgrimage to Mecca. They tried to marry him to a local girl, and, when Inusa told them he was already betrothed, they insisted he take two wives. Instead, Inusa returned to Nigeria to receive baptism and his new name, Samuila (Samuel), in 1914 and to marry Rifkatu the following year.

In Zaria, Miller lengthened the process of betrothal and marriage to manage gender disparities and make ethnic matches. He commented on the lack of Hausa Christian girls and noted that for the five boys that his assistant W. A. Thompson had recently brought to the CMS, his sister, CMS missionary Ethel Miller, had baptized just two girls.[76] Walter Miller told three Hausa boys vying for the same fifteen-year-old girl that they had to wait for at least two years to begin courting her.

The situation at the missions that took in freed slave girls and refugee men like Inusa was completely the reverse. The numbers of girls overwhelmed the missionaries, most of them being men. According to costs for food, medicine, and clothes provided by the government in 1908, total annual expenditure for 220 residents was anticipated to be about thirteen hundred pounds.[77] This was a large amount for a single mission, and slave children continued to be parceled out to various missions. The missionaries wanted to marry these girls off to relieve themselves of the burden of their care and to keep men Christian.

The problem was also to keep the girls Christian. J. Lowry Maxwell of the SUM, who led the freed slave work from 1909, had little hope about the prospects for Christianity among freed slave girls, who numbered well over half of the SUM freed slave home residents. He believed that they did not work hard enough and were easily seduced by town life.[78] He refuted the claim of his mission's founder, Karl Kumm, and others that Islam endangered African women, citing their recourse to justice in shari'a courts and the Islamic prohibition on drinking, which kept Muslim men in check while "pagan" men were drunkards. Maxwell implied that Islam in

Northern Nigeria was a better option than "paganism" or even Christianity. Maxwell also understood that running away from slavery did not mean that girls did not want to marry Muslim men.

Maxwell's view of Islam, ironically, was shaped by watching not young mobile men but the majority female population of the freed slave home. The home colored his view even of Christianity's potential for non-Muslim males: "Islam is the system of the country. Pagans hate it first but grow to appreciate the order, trade goods. And so the pagan is patient with the stranger and his pack, and the first missionary to many a pagan community may have taken the impersonal form of a sack of salt."[79] He did not believe that Christianity should bring any "democratic spirit" to Africa, complaining in 1911 that his male wards "do not realize that they are not by their accepting Christ emancipated from their position as inferiors, boys, ex-slaves. They must be taught firmly (and forcibly, if necessary) that they must accord proper respect and proper courtesy to native elders and *dattibai* [gentlemen]."[80] He worried about making unions between these useless young men and uncontrollable girls. "The girls can't marry trees, rocks, equally they can't marry the Basa heathen or the Igbirra or Hausa Muslim; whom shall they meet at Umaisha [the location of the home]?"[81] Missionaries like Maxwell sought to insert Christians into the existing social hierarchy, not upend it.

Throughout Africa, Christian missions expected African girls to bear the norms of respectability of the new religion,[82] and girls at the freed slave home and other missions in Northern Nigeria also were trained for the domestic realm. The missions did not differ from the Muslim household in this regard, yet Christian missions had a harder time in assimilating these girls than the Muslim household would have. Had these girls remained as slaves with Muslim masters, they would have belonged as wealth to the household. In the missions, the girls were clearly marked as a financial burden and a challenge to marry, without having ethnic or familial origins to speak of. The marriage registers of SIM's Minna station reported on occupations and origins of brides and grooms, and, more often than not, the brides' descriptions were "widow," with no family known or ethnicity; the only specific details were their jobs, such as domestic, maid, or washer.[83] At the same time, their husbands' fathers' occupations and their ethnic origins were mostly known, though very few men continued to farm as their fathers had, but were instead laborers and evangelists.

The story of Benani, an older freedwoman, reveals the challenge of rewriting an erased identity.[84] Yangola, later renamed Benani, arrived at the government freed slave home after trying to flee raiders with five of her children. She was freed by British troops and remained with the SUM after the turnover of the home. She later went to the SIM station in Wushishi. Though she was older by the time she met the missionaries, her oldest child being sixteen years old and a mother herself, Benani told missionaries she did not know her ethnicity. Her lips were pierced and she practiced *'bori*, the Hausa spirit possession cult. The confusion in her story was perhaps intentional but also in stark contrast to the much clearer markers Christianizing men used—Laka, Zabarma, Hausa, Fulani. Why men had ethnicity and women did not is not entirely clear, but it seems that men's greater ability to return to their original places endowed them with some sense of place, or at least a reason to create or maintain that aspect of their identities.

Working at the mission station in Zaria, Ethel Miller appreciated that monogamy could actually alienate women from Christianity. She told the story of an African Christian convert who struggled to choose one of his two wives but could satisfy no one. The abandoned wife became a divorcée, and the wife he chose to keep was "very spiteful because she knows he is half a Christian and won't divorce her or get another."[85] No longer a full Muslim herself, she had no one to share the work of managing a household, raising children, and keeping a husband happy. She refused to shake Ethel Miller's hand out of anger. To make Christian marriage more valuable, the missionaries collectively agreed to retain the practice of dowry, the money with which a bride went to her groom, despite disapproving of the practice. But instead, the plan mostly had the opposite effect. The missionaries set a payment of one pound to go eventually toward the "common benefit of husband and wife,"[86] a sum that made Christian girls feel cheap and of little interest within their new community.[87]

LIVING BETWEEN

In March 1916, in the middle of the dry season, Inusa set off for Dosso from Idda, a journey of more than 250 miles. He stopped in Sokoto before crossing the border into French territory to sell Hausa Christian tracts printed in *boko*, Roman characters. The Imam at a village mosque seemed friendly at first, but after asking about Inusa's origins, ordered him to leave immediately. "There is a natural dislike between the Filani [sic] and Zabarmawa," Inusa wrote.[88] "They would not even give us a drink of water or a place to lay our head. They always remember the trouble our people caused them.

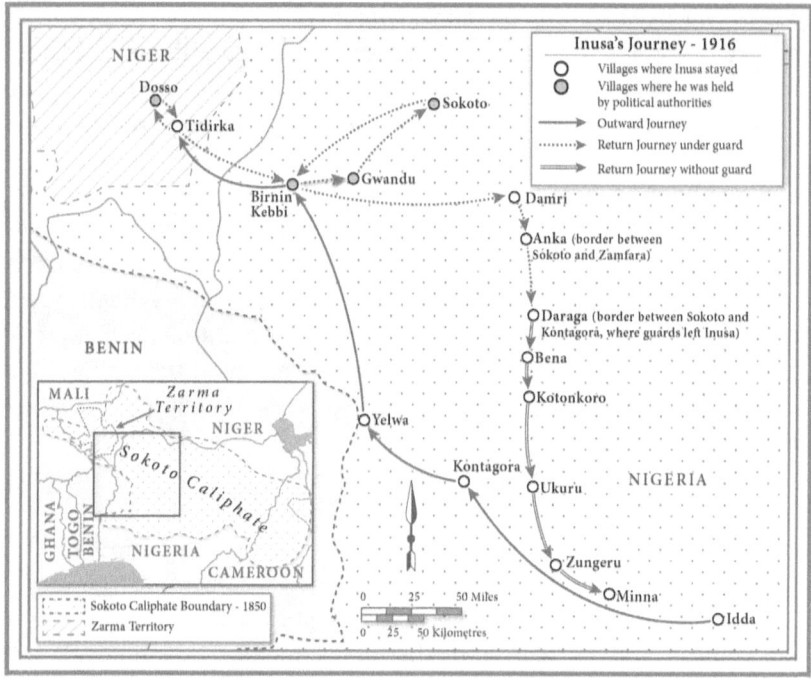

Map 1.2. The route of an African Christian evangelist crossing the borders of the former Sokoto Caliphate and the Anglo-French colonial boundary, 1916. (Drawn by Gerry Krieg; developed from information in Inusa's diaries.)

That is why we were called infidels and driven away, because our people refused to follow Shehu. It was not because I was a follower of Jesus but because we as a people were hated by the Filani."

The cleric dismissed the Zabarmawa by invoking their disloyalty to Usman 'dan Fodio, the leader of the jihad in 1807. Inusa had no claim to sell texts. His people, to the elite of the Sokoto area, were known as "hewers of wood and drawers of water in the dry season."[89] Dosso people were truly on the fringes of the Fulani world, and now also enemies of the British allies of the Sokoto aristocracy (see map 1.2).

Inusa wrote that "when the imam called me an infidel and told me to get out of the mosque for were it not for the rule of the white man they would kill me, it was necessary then to continue our journey."[90] Both the Imam and Inusa wanted to avoid the British authorities and decided on a pragmatic approach. Yet, once in Dosso, Inusa's preaching attracted the attention of the French commandant, who ordered him to leave immediately. Inusa and his brother and nephew crossed back into Nigeria and stopped for the night in Birnin Kebbi. The native police posted a guard at their door and, the following morning, sent an escort to take Inusa and his companions to the British district officer. Inusa wrote, "He insulted me and [asked], 'Who gave you the power to come through here to preach and sell books about Jesus in Muslim territory?'" Taking one of the books out of Inusa's bags, he demanded that Inusa read aloud: "The officer listened to what I read, and two clerks who were with him said they would buy books, which I sold for three shillings." Whereupon he was marched to the district officer's superior, the Resident at Sokoto, E. J. Arnett, held in jail, and then taken under guard to the provincial border.

Inusa, by this time, had improved his literacy in boko. Though less a mark of distinction than the hajj or literacy in Arabic, the language of God's revelation, literacy in a few boko characters was enough for the house servant of Major Arthur Tremearne, a Hausa folklorist, "to shave his head and wear a turban like a malam or learned man."[91] It is not possible to know exactly how the clerks or other Africans in the offices of political officials saw Inusa, but the colonial authorities feared his entry into Sokoto for many reasons. First, the amalgamation of Northern and Southern Nigeria in 1914 made British officers serving in the North worry about a rapid influx of immigrants. Second, the religious revivalism at Dosso and Satiru ten years earlier was not forgotten, and some British officers felt that the French were not doing enough to police their side of the border.[92] Third, the British colonial administration was anxious to prevent Muslim agitation in relation to the situation in Turkey after World War I began.[93]

The colonial authorities treated Inusa just roughly enough to convey a threat. At Sokoto, the Resident told Inusa that he could spend the night only in the "dark house" (*'dakin dufu*), the jail. He was put into the hands of a native guard, who marched him to the border. Verbally assaulted and denied food, Inusa nonetheless escaped imprisonment. The white missionaries were unsympathetic, and he made a special note in his diary of the failure of missionaries to support him while Africans gave him money to pay the porters who carried his loads. An official letter went to the British Resident of Niger Province, "telling him that he had a troublemaker and rebel in his district."[94] SIM missionary Reverend John Hay, who was having tea with the Resident when the letter arrived, burst out laughing at the idea that Inusa, their evangelist, was seen as a threat.

SIM was not willing to make a complaint about the native or British authorities for Inusa, in contrast to Walter Miller of the CMS, who was quick to lodge such complaints, but was eventually not taken seriously. Yet, by their inattention, white missionaries and colonial officials enabled

Photo 1.1. Biamuradi and Inusa, evangelists at Wushishi, ca. 1930. (Collection of SIM International Archives.)

fluid encounters between Christians and Muslims to continue. Inusa had crossed farther north into Muslim spheres by 1916 than any white missionary. His respectability among Africans, for carrying Christian tracts while also holding on to the religion of his birth, enabled him to evangelize so widely. He kept both the Qur'an and the Bible and grew a long beard in the manner of a malam. He wore the long white robe, *babbar riga*, much as the Isawa and strict Muslims were known to do.[95] He and his second wife, Biamuradi, evangelized often in rural and urban areas near Wushishi (see photo 1.1). He was not ordained a pastor until 1955, despite his long service in the SIM, but he clearly built his identity from other credentials with significance among Africans.

After Inusa was forced out of Dosso, he preached to non-Muslim Mawri, neighbors of the Zabarmawa, to their "great happiness," he wrote. Though the Mawri were completely resistant to Islam, Inusa seems to have achieved among them a status as a malam.[96] After 1917, Inusa directed his evangelical efforts to the Gbagyi people in Abuja, trekking often to Dagbada, the village where Yepwi, a young man converted to Christianity under Inusa's influence, resided. One day, after Yepwi backslid, Inusa restored Yepwi's faith and won the entire village to Christianity by spending hours "destroying idols of all descriptions from stones and pots to altars." Inusa recalled, "From morning, right on to evening, we destroyed the devil's work." A white missionary came to investigate. "Of course, it was found to be absolutely true. However, one blind man had thrown out his idols, but his children replaced them."[97]

Inusa's trek to Dosso was, as far as available sources suggest, exceptional. However, the ambiguous and autonomous religious life of men like Inusa is reflected again in the establishment of an Isawa village in Zaria, itself another exception. Like Inusa's life between religions, the missionaries (in this case Dr. Miller) fostered an independent existence for the Isawa and secured from Frederick Lugard a remote piece of land at Gimi, in Zaria Emirate, for a settlement, on the condition that the Isawa pay taxes to the Emir of Zaria. After this, an Isawa malam and W. A. Thompson, a black West Indian missionary, took over. Thompson helped bring a sugar-crushing machine to Gimi and set up a sugar production business.[98] Gimi was for a time a self-supporting Christian village and a major sugar supplier in Northern Nigeria. Thus, a sect of dissenters was moved from militant outposts, which the missionaries called "freebooter's country," onto a model colonial plantation.[99] These figures between religions shared commonalities— most importantly a dissenting past, and the missions and colonial administration worked together to segregate them. Placing dissidents on the fringes but under the watchful gaze of white authority was a useful strategy of containment.

But the Gimi experiment was short-lived. In 1919, during the rainy season, sleeping sickness decimated the village's population, and the survivors "stole away from the death-smitten area, tormented by reproaches of those who attributed all this misfortune to apostasy from Islam."[100] The women married Muslims and "disappeared." Only the children who had been taken to the main CMS school in Zaria survived and were raised by missionaries and African converts.[101] Disconnected from their histories and their origins, these children and women were much easier to convert both to Islam and to Christianity. Thus, Muslim heads of households, perhaps slave masters, and Christian missionaries alike, valued bringing them into their fold.

CONCLUSION: SETTLERS AS STRANGERS

Looking back, Walter Miller remarked that before 1914, the year of the amalgamation of the territories of Southern and Northern Nigeria, mission work "was all about saving souls," but thereafter, it became a veritable "government department."[102] However, this turning point came earlier, from the vantage point of Muslims and women, in 1906, when Satiru, through direct and indirect effects, sent alienated people into the missions. Christianity worked to erase and remake dissidents and slaves into stranger communities.

In this process, migrant males and females shaped distinct ethnic and religious identities. Men's ability to remain connected to their pre-Christian identities, to be itinerant evangelists but also to retreat from evangelism when the need arose, was valuable both for themselves and for the missions. Female mobility, however, was a threat to social stability and moral order. In the end, men married into their rootless wives' patrimony but used their ethnic and religious origins strategically beyond the mission sphere. It is significant that Inusa did not tell the missionaries about his connection to the Dosso revolt until the 1950s. Thus, he was able to live as an iterant evangelist for many years.

The native evangelist became the most effective means by which Christianity penetrated the large urban centers of Hausaland, where survival as a dissenter could be more difficult, as the Isawa origin story showed. Walter Miller had a base in Zaria City, but the railway and the amalgamation of Southern and Northern Nigeria were new openings in Zaria and Kano. How Christians entered Kano and changed it from inside the city's walls is the subject of the next chapter.

2 ∽ A New "Middle" Class in the Muslim City, 1918–1925

IN 1911, JOURNALIST EDMUND DENE MOREL, who had helped expose Belgian atrocities in Congo, published a series about Nigeria in the *Times* of London. The first part covered the Southern Provinces, and the second was titled "Northern Nigeria and Its Problems." He apprised his readers: "Nigeria is not merely by far the most considerable of our West African possessions, but the only British Dependency in any part of the world which approaches the Indian Empire in magnitude and variety. Our administrators there, in most inadequate numbers and under very difficult conditions, but with our Indian experiences to help them, are confronting problems as large and delicate as those which first inspired the administrative genius of Great Britain in the East." He listed several reasons for Nigeria's importance to the empire: its size, wealth, and Muslim population, already in the millions and increasing "rapidly." He wrote, "Until a few years ago the work of Great Britain in West Africa, apart from a few trifling exceptions, was confined to the administration of the Pagan negro. The position is very different now." The British had governed in Southern and Northern Nigeria in very different ways and mostly as regions independent of each other, but amalgamation into a single colony was imminent. Morel wanted his readers to understand how diverse Nigeria's peoples were and what might be the challenges for a single Nigerian colony, starting with the railway connecting Lagos to Kano that was completed in 1911.[1]

For the emirates, Morel focused on Kano, its history, and commerce, and described his interview with the Emir Abbas. Morel asked Abbas pointedly about his views on the prospects for Christian missionaries in Kano. Could these workers serve strictly as teachers and not as proselytizers? Abbas reportedly answered, "What is the use of the Christian missionary if there are no converts?" The Emir made clear his reservations about having whites settle in close proximity to Africans, believing that his subjects would become "troubled in their minds." He warned: "The lion and lamb cannot lie down together."[2]

Abbas's words have often been cited as evidence of Muslim rulers' opposition to Christian missionaries in Muslim population centers, which was purportedly a key factor in British policies restricting Christian proselytism. However, a closer reading of the full interview as Morel published it suggests that Abbas had a more studied view of missionaries than the excerpted portions suggest. At Morel's request, Abbas confirmed his position in a written letter, which was reproduced in translation in the *Times*. The Emir reiterated his apprehension about the preaching of Christianity but seemed to agree with Morel about the "practical work" of missionaries: "On the other hand, as regards secular matters and the affairs of this world, we can do anything—however great a change it might be—since our people are accustomed to law and to obey orders of their rulers as their fathers and grandfathers before them." He addressed the issue of whites living in Kano City as a separate matter, using the metaphor of the lion and lamb, but clarifying that the power of whites was so great that blacks could not live with them. Every white man, he wrote, "is in our eyes a great man and powerful." His distinctions implied that religious differences could be settled and subject to law, but race and racial inequality, more specifically, necessitated physical separation. He recommended a separate town for whites wishing to settle in Kano.[3]

The exceptional Church Missionary Society (CMS) station in Zaria aside, the struggle for missions to secure a site in Kano became connected to wider debates about racial segregation and colonial urban politics. Ethnic and racial enclaves predated the colonial era in Kano. For example, the Fagge neighborhood, adjacent to the wall of Kano City, was the place where the Buzu slaves of the Tuareg were known to live and trade. Arabs settled within the city walls in a ward called "Unguwan Turawa" (neighborhood of the whites). As Alhaji Muhammadu 'Ko'ki, a Kano teacher, put it, "The Arabs and the Tuareg were the only pale-skinned people we knew before you Europeans came. And after them, the Fulani. All the rest of the people were black."[4] Within this socially variegated landscape, the plan of

Emir Abbas for a white European enclave in Kano was implemented, and a neighborhood for African settlers from outside Kano was also established, called Sabon Gari (new town). Such enclaves, established in other Muslim cities as well, came to be known as the Christian part of town and, by that association, the space of new markets, goods, and workers who came after the British, the railway, and new commerce.

The exchange between Abbas and Morel and the beginnings of Muslim policies toward Christians represent an important milestone in the longer process of placing Christian missions in Muslim spheres of Northern Nigeria and, in relation to them, defining the powers of the Muslim Native Administration. Abbas acknowledged that Christian conversions occurred where missionaries preached and suggested further that Christian missionaries, though threatening like other whites as powerful people, had specific functions in "things of this world." In previous centuries, foreign settlers, including the Wangarawa or Jula of the Senegambia and North African Arabs, settled in Kano as traders and as religious scholars and jurists. Urban quarters were named "the place of" the Arabs, the Turks, and the like.[5] The Emir recommended that Christians focus on worldly work, which need not have meant nonreligious activities but, instead, healing or trade that required trust and belief but also perhaps superior skills.[6] How Christianity's material associations shaped Muslim views of newly converted Africans who were freed slaves and others of clearly lower socioeconomic status is a crucial question. Religious identity became inseparably intertwined with class and occupation as Christian colonial missions entered urban Muslim areas of Northern Nigeria. Christian status became a spatial and professional identification in Muslim cities like Kano. These new settlers, though not large in number, became the focus of new strategies to manage religious, ethnic, and class differences.

ASSIMILATING CHRISTIAN MISSIONS IN KANO

In December 1911, Abbas sent three of his subjects—a farmer and two boys—to travel about three hundred miles south to the Catholic mission station at Shendam, below the Jos Plateau.[7] The French Society of Missions in Africa (SMA) had established an agricultural station at Shendam, and the British Resident of Muri, the province where the mission was located, invited the Emir to witness the introduction of an oxen-drawn plow. The pupils returned to Kano during the dry season, and the Emir planned to send the three men with additional recruits to learn more techniques before the next rainy season.

The Emirs and other royal Muslims commonly passed off slaves or sons of slaves as their own in British schools; perhaps these students of the Catholic missionaries also were slaves. Clearly they were nonroyal dependents, and Abbas's use of such intermediaries to take advantage of the Resident's invitation to the Catholic experimental farm was similar to practices among Emirs and other Muslim elites seeking to capitalize on colonial-era changes. Abbas was especially interested in the experimental farm because of the potential for maximizing his farms' production of groundnuts for export.[8] Abbas's farm estates increased output during the "peanut boom" that followed the opening of the railway in 1911.

Slavery, continuing because of the halfheartedness of British abolition, was crucial to agricultural expansion on the farms of wealthy landholders. Kano had no freed slaves home or other mechanism for self-emancipation. Abbas actually increased the number of slaves on one of his better-studied royal plantations, Fanisau. The slaves belonging to small private holders, who had fewer slaves and tended to extract more from them with less prestige, ran away most often and fled to royal estates.[9] Royal slaves also hired free peasants. Hausa merchants in Kano, who had earlier been kola traders traveling as far as Gold Coast, invested in slave trafficking up to the 1930s. They set themselves up in non-Muslim areas specifically to fill the strong demand for slaves that abolition and export crop production drove. Christian missions' association as places for teaching freed slaves how to farm, like the Catholic Shendam outpost, provided Muslim elites a place to acquire a different kind of wealth—technical knowledge and manual training for their laborers. This tutorship of the Emir's wards continued, though the sources contain few details. The Catholic mission secured a place in Kano's Sabon Gari a few years later, seemingly with little conflict. Abbas and the Catholic mission at Shendam brokered this informal relationship through the exchange of people.[10]

The British authorities, on the other hand, were locked in battle with Christian missions over formal negotiations for a plot of land in Kano city. The Anglican CMS secretary, Thomas Alvarez, negotiated in 1910 with the Governor of Nigeria, Hesketh Bell, for a permanent Christian mission station to be built in Kano when the rail was completed. Governor Bell made several stipulations, including the requirement that the CMS locate their future station in Kano Sabon Gari and that unmarried women missionaries be barred from serving in Muslim areas for fear of offense to native sensibilities.[11] The CMS, however, built huts outside the 'dan Agundi wall gate on the south side of the city at a place called Gandun Albasa (the onion farm); this was the only site the mission would accept because enough land was available for an experimental farm. The Residents in Kano and Zaria, however, prevented missionaries from lodging there. They wanted to send the missionaries to the whites' residential neighborhood established in Bompai, an area farther from the Old City and on a slightly higher elevation, a key consideration from the view of colonial sanitation concerns. The British authorities destroyed the huts, the CMS rebuilt them, and then finally, around 1918, the government took the huts for good and compensated the CMS.

No Muslim Kano authority had been consulted. In all the negotiations, the acting Resident at Kano only guessed that the Emir might be suspicious about the purpose of the huts.[12] Tensions had already arisen in Northern Nigeria over the 1910 Land and Native Rights Act, which vested land in communal African ownership instead of individual property rights based on European tenure.[13] The act was irritating to some elite African landowners because, as one experienced British legal adviser noted, some of them did own land privately.[14] The Emir was one such private holder. No British officer wanted yet to broach the subject of renting land to white missionaries for fear of creating further resentment, though Abbas may not have minded, given his interest in agricultural development.

During this row over the huts, the 'dan Agundi gate became the area associated with a small group of Hausa Christians or crypto-Christians.[15] Local Kano people acknowledged the presence of these Christians as men who worked for the missionaries and for the British officials. It is quite likely, then, that the Emir knew of these Africans' presence, even as the British authorities attempted to push the missionaries out.

White missionaries were asked to live either with other whites in Bompai or in the African aliens' areas (*sabon gari*) of Muslim towns from 1914 forward. Some British officers, including the Resident of Zaria, W. F. Gowers, believed it "most undesirable that missionaries should live [in the European section of town], as it would identify them, in the eyes of the natives, with the Government."[16] Acting governor C. L. Temple argued, on the other hand, that missionaries improved political officers' moral authority:

> In my opinion the prestige of the Government would gain rather than lose by our having Ministers of our official religion living amongst us. In fact, the absence of such ministers is, I believe, freely commented on by the better class Moslems, especially those who have visited Tripoli and Egypt and have become accustomed to assume that the European nations are not without a religion which they respect. An even more important point is, I think, that the presence of Ministers has undoubtedly an excellent effect on the Christian employees of the Government. In fact, in my

opinion, it is clearly the duty of the Government to afford them opportunities for worship.[17]

He recommended that the CMS be allowed to establish a station in Kano, provided the mission agreed not to preach outside of the government areas and the "township." In other words, they were prohibited from preaching inside the Old City.

British officials implied that they could not protect the safety of missionaries, but the only evidence of violence appears to have been directed at African government workers, who experienced a great deal of hardship in Kano in the early years of Emir Abbas's reign. Courtiers physically attacked them. Eventually, ostracism, material incentives, and threats of demotion were used as disincentives for working with the Europeans, and were used to ensure loyalty to the Native Authority.[18] Christian missionaries claimed that Muslim clerics added religious pressure by threatening excommunication. Andrew Stirrett of the Sudan Interior Mission (SIM), after working at stations on the Niger River, observed about the "vernacular speaking blacks, employed by Government as labourers, carriers, policeman, soldiers, cooks, domestics, interpreters, train hands, messengers, etc.": "Many of these were disowned by their own religionists, the Mohammedans, because they are working for a kafir or heathen government (British). One dear fellow, well up in the military circles, questioned me quite seriously as to whether there was any hope at all of salvation for such as he had been informed by his own priests that he could not be saved on account of his occupation. The Mohammedan priests are constantly taunting the British soldiers (native) in this way."[19] The idea that proximity to whites was polluting was, for the Christian missionaries, partly self-serving since it justified their "necessity" as moral guardians of African government workers. The British officer Temple promoted the use of missionaries in an attempt to increase the cultural authority of whites and blacks who worked for the colonial government.

Morel observed that indirect rule through Muslim rulers impeded the development of the modern "secretarial, judicial, police and military" classes, echoing Stirrett's observation.[20] He cited as an example a comparison of the effectiveness of the British government native police in Kano versus the emirate police. While just ninety emirate guards could reportedly police the large population (rural and urban) of the entire emirate effectively, native police from other parts of Nigeria instead actually "raised crime." Morel believed that Islamic law was an effective deterrent on its own, for in Northern Nigeria, Muslim judges maintained jurisdiction over criminal matters, possessing powers well beyond that of the Egyptian *qadi* (judge who administers

Islamic law). Morel suggested that the Native Authority effectively used social pressure and threats of violence that worked less well with "foreign populations," whose numbers were, of course, to increase with amalgamation. He believed that the Native Administration would be slow to encourage literacy in Roman script or the bearing of arms among its employees, for these "skills" would be taken as signs of waning Muslim power.

While Morel perceived growing conflicts over the changes brought by colonial rule in urban Kano, Muslim elites adopted certain novel practices of incorporating new people and practices. Abbas's relations with Christian agricultural workers were a means to retain male slave or servile labor, even if they were intermediaries to Christian missions. Marriage was a means of incorporating non-Muslim slave women, practiced through Abbas's reign. Malam 'Ko'ki, a Kano judge and interpreter, recalled that the slave trade in Kano continued. Male slaves were sent to the government's craft school to learn "carpentry and smithing and leatherwork, while women slaves were, along older models, sent to different homes in the town."[21] "The pretence of free marriage" absorbed many girls and women into households. Malam 'Ko'ki's family took in two girls, an older one who had already been married and a second girl of eleven or twelve. 'Ko'ki recalled that the customary way for a male slave to seek manumission was to ask his master for the cost of his freedom and pay in increments, all the while demonstrating his loyalty. He did not distinguish if the same held true for female slaves, but the "pretence of free marriage" suggests that freed slave women had to become more Muslim in their identities, as compared to earlier times, when women slaves had reputations as adherents of non-Muslim religious or crypto-Muslim practices. Through conscription into government service and marriage, former slavers had increasingly to "profess" their religious loyalties. While men could find other employment, women had to seek a divorce.

The gradual and intimate process of traditional modes of manumission conflicted with the British raids on slave caravans and universal emancipation by proclamation. In Kano, where the British avoided methods of immediate emancipation, the news of abolition spread by rumor that slaves could petition for freedom.[22] Yet the Muslim authorities did not take kindly to such petitions. In one legal case, Abbas refused to rule on the fate of a freed slave woman wishing to return to her master, stating that her situation came under British, not Islamic, law. Her emancipation did not conform to the traditional mode. Inclusion and exclusion were highly subjective and mediated through structures of authority, like the Emir's palace.

Servile men who worked for the colonial administration or Christian missions were useful to Muslim elites. The case of the freedwoman shows that women were more vulnerable after leaving the Muslim domestic sphere. Her case and the informal Shendam Christian mission–Muslim connection suggest that the Kano Emir did not have a categorical position on Christians or others deemed "outside" Islam. Instead, his position was fluid and opportunistic.

"HUNGER FOR BOOKS": THE MAKING OF PROPAGANDA

On May 14, 1915, the Resident of Kano reported that a "Native Christian Missionary" arrived in Kano, apparently on "a begging pilgrimage." The itinerant apparently visited the Arab quarter with an "archaic" and unsigned letter stating that the Governor-General of Nigeria approved his visit. He "deftly" collected 4 pounds, 6 shillings, and, before leaving on May 16, "romanced" about garnering a number of Muslim converts to Christianity.[23]

That Kano authorities were interested at all in such "native preachers" reflects the political climate of World War I and the anxiety over the amalgamation of the Northern and Southern Provinces of Nigeria. The British worried that the war against the Ottoman Empire would inflame animosity among Muslim subjects of the empire. Islamic anti-British propaganda in the North of Nigeria was cited in official correspondence as a specific concern in 1914, but, by the end of the war, the authorities concluded that the Emirs had remained largely loyal to Britain, demonstrating their steadfastness through money, supplies, and relief for Nigerian war veterans.[24] Germans tried but failed to infiltrate Muri Province, in the east on the border with German Kamerun. However, the British noted, their "efforts to stir up Mohammedan feeling by proclamations, letters and leaflets were carried out in a bungling way and proved fruitless."[25]

While fearing Muslim agitation, the British authorities also worried that the growing Christian presence, including white and "native" missionaries, in Kano and other emirates would threaten Muslim and British authority. White or foreign Christian missionaries in Muslim areas were increasingly seen by the British authorities as expedient allies to keep African Christians in check. The British authorities understood that they could not themselves effectively police indigenous religious agents, Christian or Muslim.

In 1919, the Governor-General of Nigeria, Sir Hugh Clifford, argued that the North should be opened to missionaries. He expressed concern that economic stagnation resulted from the segregation of Europeans from Africans, promoted through colonial medical and sanitary regulations like the "440 yards rule," which required this minimum distance between African areas and European residential and commercial areas. These restrictions applied across Nigeria, from Kano in the North to Calabar in the Southeast.[26] In the Northern Provinces, Clifford claimed that local British Residents' uses of the "segregation principle" had brought Christian missionaries "to the brink of despair."[27] Thereafter, the numbers of foreign missions, including Christians and Muslims, in Kano increased.

The CMS rented a small building in the Fagge area around 1920 to open a bookshop. In 1922, Indian missionaries of the Ahmadiyya, a sect begun by a Muslim in India, were granted a plot in the Kano Sabon Gari.[28] Significantly, while this sect was a problem in India, in Nigeria and other parts of West Africa, the British authorities seemed quite sympathetic to them. When the Secretary of State for the Colonies questioned the sect's intent, believing that "Mohammedans did not have organised missionaries," an officer responded that the "Ahmadiyya is a 'modernist' movement, which endeavours to impart a more spiritual meaning to the more grossly materialistic tenets of Islam." The converts, he wrote, were "mostly of feeble intellect," and their missionaries "mostly mild brown old gentlemen with white beards and green turbans, wandering about."[29]

Among British officers, a feeling grew that missionaries could provide a positive influence amid the many changes converging upon Africans. The CMS bookshop at Minna, opened around 1914 by Reverend James Cotton, sold "Scriptures and Bible Stories in Hausa, Yoruba, Nupe, Arabic, and English, besides a lot of educational supplies."[30] Cotton commented that the thronging crowds at the new rail station were ready customers for "a bright picture for their eye, a warm message for their ears, a helpful tract for their intellect." "There is such a hunger for books that it is sometimes pathetic," Cotton noted.[31] Meanwhile, the British worried that "traditional" authorities were completely preoccupied in their own affairs and disinterested in the welfare of commoners. Alcohol sales and consumption, though officially outlawed in Muslim areas, were vigorous in Kano. "It seems strange," the Resident wrote, "that there are not found in all the City men of sufficiently strong religious views and moral courage to make a stand on behalf of prohibition but their neglect to do so is, I fear, merely a sign of the times."[32] In such a vacuum of political authority, religious revivalism, as the Resident saw it, was on the rise among poorer folk. The cerebrospinal meningitis epidemic in 1924 was a crucial factor in the revivalism, and the Sufi *turuq* (paths), Qadiriyya and Tijaniyya, not to mention the millennial Mahdists, all competed with one another on this fertile ground. The British authorities closely watched the activities of religious and worldly "enterprises" through the 1920s.[33]

The Christian bookshop was a unique meeting place for menials employed by Europeans who taught them to read and for literate Kano

Muslims, mostly elites educated in the Native Administration schools. Both groups sought new reading materials, paper, and perhaps literacy classes. Christian missionaries' reputation as literally "people of the book" grew in the 1920s, when Governor Hugh Clifford directed the former CMS missionary Reverend G. P. Bargery to compile a new Hausa dictionary. In 1923, the Kano Emir chose Alhaji Mahmudu 'Ko'ki, then a Kano surveyor and later a judge, to work with Bargery on this project. According to Malam 'Ko'ki, he and Bargery met with Dr. Walter Miller of the CMS, though it had been several years since Bargery left the mission. "We used to collect words that were giving us trouble," Malam 'Ko'ki recalled, "to get [Miller's] ruling on them; and when we got that, we would follow it." 'Ko'ki did not specifically mention the bookshop but discussed the fact that religion had little to do with his conversations about Hausa language with Bargery. "I know he was a Christian but in all the years that we were together, we never discussed religion for he wasn't interested in interfering with Islam; and he never criticised it or tried to convert me to an interest in Christianity."[34]

Over decades, Malam 'Ko'ki came to know Dr. Miller; his sister Ethel Miller, the freelance missionary; and Cyril Sanderson, head of the team translating the Hausa Bible in the 1930s. Malam 'Ko'ki and his father were both proud of the intellectual work done together with the white missionaries. The Christian bookshop raised the esteem of the missionaries in Muslims' eyes and garnered them bigger audiences and greater interest from more well-to-do people than the British authorities anticipated.

In 1926, the Lieutenant Governor of Nigeria asked the Resident of Kano about rumors that Christian missionaries preached "regularly in the Market place of Kano City."[35] Reverend Cotton, the bookshop manager, reportedly admitted these activities to Dr. Raymond Leslie Buell, a Harvard University scholar who traveled to Nigeria and other African colonies in 1926 to conduct research for his book, *The Native Problem in Africa*. After Buell's revelation, the Kano Resident scrambled to investigate missionaries' activities around the province, only to find that, in addition to Christians' public preaching, mission tracts had reached rural areas of Kano. A teacher at the Native Administration crafts school apparently converted from Islam to Christianity as a result of reading such tracts. He was not alone, according to an article titled "Baptisms at Kano" that appeared in *West Africa* magazine, a publication with a wide audience. Eight Hausas had been baptized near the 'Kofar Mata gate to the Old City in February 1926, a few months prior to Buell's remark to the secretary.[36]

The District Officer of Kano Township believed that CMS employees and other whites flagrantly carried on "missionary enterprise," flouting

British authority and using the bookshop as a first step to get a religious site in a Muslim center, in spite of the simple business terms laid out in the certificate of occupancy.[37] The investigations further showed that Reverend Cotton's wife and Ethel Miller, the sister of Dr. Walter Miller of the CMS, and several other whites had openly spoken about Christianity to Kano city and country dwellers. Ethel Miller and Dugald Campbell, a "missionary explorer,"[38] were not affiliated with any mission. The political authorities implied that the bookshop had outgrown its CMS affiliation and was used almost like a church by any Christian with the motive of religious activism. "Do the Cottons and Miss Miller think that we are unaware of their activities," wrote Carrow, the Resident of Kano, "[or] alternatively do they think that we do know and are afraid to say anything?"[39]

The British authorities were surprised that the Emir did not share their sense of outrage against the missionaries. The apparent "apathy" of the Emir of Kano and of many of his subjects alarmed the Resident. When villagers from Ungogo, a district southwest of the city, arrived with three Bibles, the Emir allowed them to do as they liked with them.[40] The freelance missionary Ethel Miller penned a tract titled the *Truth about Mohammed*, which explicitly insulted the Prophet of Islam, but the Kano Muslim authorities were singularly uninterested in her propaganda (discussed in greater length in chapter 3). Further reports that Christian Africans had bought houses within the Old City of Kano under the previous Emir (Usman, who ruled from 1919 until his death just before the bookshop opened) did not upset his successor, Abdullahi.

Through these investigations, it came to light that Malam Ari Biu, a teacher of *boko*, in the government crafts school, converted from Islam to Christianity. Fred Beminster, the superintendent of the school, fired him and sent him to the Emir. The emirate council interviewed Ari following Beminster's action and confirmed that the story of conversion was true. The council did not, however, label him an apostate or seek any formal legal action such as imprisonment or death, which might have been allowed under certain interpretations of the shari'a or hadith.[41] The Emir chose to strip Ari of authority as a teacher and offered him a position instead in the Public Works Department. The Emir concluded that the school was a Muslim sphere because the Native Administration paid for it and for teachers' salaries. The Emir believed that Ari should still be allowed to earn a Native Administration salary, but he could not order, control, or hinder anyone, as the Emir put it in a letter on the matter (domin chewa shi a chikin wannan aikin ba zai umarchi wani ba, ba zai hana ba). Ari declined the Emir's offer because he would have been required to work and travel on Sundays.[42]

Ari was a convert twice over. He was born of nonroyal "pagan" parentage, according to Superintendent Beminster, and, "on his father's death, the Emir of Biu [in Borno Province] had the boy looked after out of compassion because his mother was the daughter of Mai Ari Pasku [a chief in Biu]. The Emir of course was never married to her."[43] Ari was quite young when the Emir of Biu sent him to the Kano school for chiefs' sons, which was established to train children to serve in the Native Administration. After finishing school, Ari received the post of teacher in the Crafts School, and, to Beminster's knowledge, became a Muslim, "attending the big Mosque very regularly and at one time having three and even four wives in a harem. In company with the rest of the staff he saluted the Emir every Friday and went to the mosque."[44]

With conversion to Christianity, Ari lost a privileged place, presumably several wives (the missionary sources mention just one wife and a servant who converted with him), and the patronage of Muslim royalty. At the same time, Beminster's version of Ari's story makes clear that Ari had no "real" claims as the Biu Emir's heir. The Emirs, in British view, provided charity to the poor boy. Yet both the Emir of Biu and the Emir of Kano clearly felt some greater responsibility toward the young man in trying to bring him into the fold of Islam and perhaps to each other.

Ari's path from paganism through Islam to Christianity shows both the possibilities and the limits of mobility. The paths to Islam and to Christianity clashed. While modern institutions like the colonial education system facilitated the conversion of pagans to Islam, Christian conversion curtailed social and economic opportunities within the Native Administration, showing how urban religious politics operated in a manner that African Christians in Northern Nigeria had not yet experienced in the towns and villages. The Emir of Kano felt that Ari tried to rise above his station through knowledge of *boko*, Roman literacy. The Emir's response, removing Ari from a position of authority, was to diminish the value of boko. Ari's case no doubt made Muslim elites more attentive to increasing opportunities for and disloyalty of "pagans."

Ari, his wife, and servant went to live at the CMS bookshop. His primary role was to collect and teach children. He recruited about seven boys whose parents either assented to Christian education or were absent. Another bookshop figure, a Zaria man known as Mijinyawa, managed to rent or buy a house within the Old City walls, to the consternation of the colonial authorities.[45] White missionaries and African Christians visited the house and the bookshop often, which the Native Administration appeared to ignore. The Emir, in fact, saw people like Ari as simpletons and victims of a particular kind, suggesting once again that Christian missionaries had unfairly swayed "the natives [who] have no power of knowing whether it is the intention of (His Excellency) the Governor to upset our religion or not. . . . How could native peasants refuse when they assume that the White missionaries are carrying on this work under the authority of the Government."[46] The Emir did not force Ari to return to Islam. He implied rather that it was the British who were improperly using religion as a political tool if they allowed Christian missionaries to convert Africans in positions of any kind of authority.

Kano Emir Abdullahi complained about native missionaries carrying Christian propaganda throughout the province and about white women missionaries, but he and his council placed responsibility for enforcing any limits squarely on the British authorities. For their part, the colonial authorities investigated possible legal means to forcibly repatriate Christian missionaries holding British citizenship but concluded that this action would be unpopular at home because it conflicted with the exercise of "religious freedom." The British Resident at Kano suggested that the Emir be responsible for dealing with African Christians and the British be responsible for limiting white missionaries in Muslim spheres by judging their educational qualifications and their previous experience in Nigeria, rather than trying to remove them altogether.[47] Governing Christian converts became a particular problem.

In 1927, the Emir issued an unprecedented proclamation that prohibited preaching of any kind in any walled or unwalled towns, villages, neighborhoods, or on roads.[48] Preaching was allowed only within mosques or a room (*d'aki*). The proclamation was silent as to preaching in churches or other places of worship, but its wording seemed to address public Christian and alternative Muslim evangelism for which no spaces existed without political authorities' approval. It covered indigenous and foreign missionary agents. Christianity was now defined as prohibited propaganda, not by its content, but by the location of its preachers and places of worship.

What began as a rather minor issue about seemingly isolated and ineffectual cases of religious preaching had burgeoned into much larger questions about governing Muslims and Christians and, among Christians, whites and blacks. The Emir seemed to interpret Ari's conversion as more of an offense within the patronage system, and the attempt to demote Ari seemed to be an effort to work within the prevailing system of clientage, not an effort to politicize the matter in the ways that the British authorities had seemed to want. It is therefore difficult to know from which camp the wide-reaching prohibition on public religious activities stemmed, but it was a crucial new step of segregation that seemed more in line with the British efforts to block missions from settling in certain places. While the prohibition, as we shall see, never completely worked, it drove religious activities into more "private" spaces, including houses and places of commerce. Religious fluidity and "freedom" were more easily found within such spaces, rather than in the public. Certainly the wrangling over space intensified personal social interactions as the main mode of religious conversation and conversion.

"BEGGARS CANNOT BE CHOOSERS": CHRISTIAN EDUCATION AND EXCLUSION

Even as Ari's case became more public, the CMS bookshop carried on a brisk business for those interested in Christianity or just reading. Reverend James Cotton traveled home to England in late 1926 as the problems with the Kano authorities were settling down. At about that time, Muhammadu Katsina, a migrant from Borno who had recently arrived seeking work in Kano, brought his ten-year-old son (known by the nickname of Akawu, meaning "clerk") to the bookshop. Back in Borno, the boy's grandfather had been staunch in his refusal to accept the white men's education or employment, but Muhammadu Katsina resisted his own father and "stole" Akawu.[49] On the advice of Sergeant Sule Gumsuri, a mentor who had served in World War I in the British West African Frontier Force, Akawu was not sent to the Native Administration crafts school, where Ari had been a teacher, because only menial trades such as carpentry were taught there. Instead, the Christians "would teach more 'book,'" according to the sergeant.[50]

Akawu's kin were refugees from the Ha'be (pre-jihad) state of Damagaram, which had resisted the Fulani jihad. When the resisters were defeated by the jihadists, Akawu's grandfather and other relatives fled east to seek haven in Borno, where Muslim leaders also did not accept the flag of the Shehu. During the British conquest, the family was brought by African troops to Maisandari, a "liberty village," or freed slave camp. In the opening scene of his memoir, Akawu (later known as John Garba) relates an incident in which local boys of the Kanuri ethnic group chased Akawu and his uncle, calling them *afnu* (Hausa). It was then that Akawu's grandfather told him that his family was Kanuri, but most lately of the bush territories of Hausaland, the area to which they had been chased. Always proud, Akawu's grandfather swore never to be a slave of anyone, either the Fulani or the whites. When his own son, Akawu's father, decided in 1926 to leave Maisandari for Kano with the British West African Force, the old man disparaged his son for

Photo 2.1. *Teaching Soldiers to Read Numbers*, Geidam Barracks, Borno Province, ca. 1913. (Major C. T. Lawrence Collection, Image Library of the National Archives, UK.)

becoming like the "good-for-nothing 'Yan-Soja (Soldiers) and 'Yan-Bariki (de-tribalised elements) [literally, people of the barracks]."[51]

Men like Muhammadu Katsina, Akawu's father, found that the only opportunities for work in Kano were either as laborers for the British authorities or private businesses owned by Europeans, Syrians, or Lebanese, or as African clerks of the government. He began as a "boy" to a clerk but, within a few years, taught himself enough English to be a *tafinta*, interpreter, at the Kano Provincial Office in Nassarawa. Akawu's stepmother, Fatu, did what many urban Muslim women did and sent Akawu out to earn a few pennies hawking cigarettes. In his memoir written later in life, Akawu recalled that it was after Sergeant Gumsuri discovered how Fatu was using him that he was placed in the missionaries' school.

Akawu's story reveals the multiple ways in which ordinary Muslims viewed the Christian bookshop in the 1920s. Literacy was attractive to marginal people of the barracks, as photos from Northern Nigerian military camps from the 1910s show (see photo 2.1). Soldiers taught one another. For a child of new settlers to Kano City, Christian learning meant something else altogether. There is no doubt that Akawu's father, through the sergeant, understood the upward mobility his son could gain from knowing how to read and write as white men did in Kano, where boko literacy was tightly controlled. Akawu's aunt, his father's sister, had been married to a Gold Coast native in the employ of the British in Borno. Akawu's nickname came from this man. The Gold Coaster wielded great influence "beyond his official status" because "he lived in style," with beer, gin, and the like for Christmas and bales of cloth for the big Sallah, the festival to end Ramadan.[52] This wealthy stranger first suggested that his namesake, Akawu, be sent to formal clerks' school in Maiduguri, but his father-in-law, the old patriarch, refused to let his grandson go. Probably through the clerk, Akawu's father got his first job as a contractor for the army.

Muhammadu Katsina was rumored to be a Christian, and eventually he and his wife, Fatu, resided inside the 'dan Agundi gate of the Old City wall, a move that appears to have coincided with his taking employment with the Kano Native Administration. This move was, of course, important to reduce the suspicion the emirate authorities cast upon Africans working with the colonial government. Muhammadu's religious identity shifted in relation to his line of work.

There were other men, including Ari Biu, who were seen as fully Christian. After his dismissal from the crafts school, Ari taught children like Akawu in the CMS bookshop (see photo 2.2). A Zaria convert, Istifanus 'dan Daura, also frequented the bookshop. He was a barber-surgeon who served in World War I and then converted to Christianity in Zungeru, the former capital of Northern Nigeria.[53] 'Dan Daura's principal occupation seems to have been conducting Bible readings in the Kano marketplaces, where learned men came to him to "buy a bible touch."[54] Other adults whom Akawu met at the bookshop had intriguing identities like his father's. George Rufus Atiku, who was a teacher in 1929, "later recanted Christianity and embraced Islam . . . , becoming Alhaji Atiku Kano, even though he hailed from Katsina."[55] He rose to the position of *Wakilin Ma'aikata* (chief secretary) of the Kano local government, then *Wakilin Tasha* (officer in charge of Kano motor parks), and even personal adviser to the Emir of Kano. Christian identity entered the social conscience and material exchange in the form of a crypto-Christian caste of workers who exploited the line between the dual government of British and native authority. It is hard to believe that the ban on public preaching would have had much effect on this kind of "conversion."

What little the British authorities knew of the bookshop school was not accurate. Ari, the former crafts school teacher, was, according to the British

Photo 2.2. James Cotton and schoolboys in Kano, ca. 1927. (Collection of Mrs. Amina Garba.)

authorities, "in charge of [six] small boys . . . of the type of those whose parents have either lost control or touch with. The boys are fed and clothed and are to be sent to Zaria after a short course of instruction."[56] John Garba (Akawu) remembered that his father paid the Cottons thirty shillings per month for his son's instruction and lodging until the boy's fees were waived because of the work he performed for the Cottons.[57] Muhammadu Katsina and Garba himself viewed their relationship with the missionaries not as charity but as employment and schooling. Urban Christian missions had transformed from shelters for freed slave children into business enterprises in the sense that the Nigerian governor Clifford intended in 1919. With the support of this unseen hub of Christianity in Kano, Ari rejected the Emir's offer out of a newfound sense of economic independence.

In Hausaland, the practice of *ri'ko*, or child fosterage, to willingly place one's children in the care of others, including kin and nonkin, was common.[58] However, giving Muslim children to the Christian missionaries was a different and conscious innovation for a new small urban class. Akawu's father and the fathers of other bookshop boys were men who were less well-to-do but aspiring, whose children could access new colonial-era institutions without great risk to their parents' Muslim identity, as the Emirs of Biu and Kano had done with their servants. The rumors of their Christianity remained only that, for these men were consumers of missionary culture, not dependents of missionaries.

The Muslim identity of Akawu, for one, earned him a special place in Christian schools of the late 1920s. Once he learned to read, he began attending the Catholic Holy Trinity School in Sabon Gari where he was one among just six boys from the North, all from the Cottons' home.[59] Moving from Fagge to Sabon Gari, Garba came to understand the geography of Kano as a microcosm of the North and the South of Nigeria. In 1929, Cotton "smuggled" Akawu to attend the World Boy Scout Jamboree in Birkenhead, England. Prior to his departure, Garba had to "earn" his Boy Scout badges quickly so that he would be as prepared as the rest of the Scouts, who were all from the South. Garba prepared his "national costume" and Hausa song and dance to perform, wearing for the first time in his life a turban and learning a religious song from his father. The Scoutmaster did not find the song appealing, so Garba, once he was reunited with the group, was designated "as a minority" and then "attached to the Yoruba group." "Little did the members of our various cheering audiences realise that the whole thing was a mystery even to some of us the actors!" he wrote.[60]

Garba stood out painfully once the troop arrived in England and the children went to church. Writing in a diary was part of his Scout exercises, and Garba wrote in his then rudimentary English: "Out of 24 of us 1 is Mohammedan and three are Catholic and they did not go to church we are going when we come to our domotory [*sic*] the Scoutmaster said that he saw some of our boys sitting laziness in the church."[61] Garba again felt ashamed when he failed the health badge exam because he could not understand English, and the Scoutmaster let Garba take it twice.

Another boy, Joseph Mohammed Sani, who was born in Kano City in 1921, encountered similar difficulties due to cultural distance when his father took him to the CMS Zaria school in 1927 at the age of six.[62] Sani's father worked as a clerk in the Kano Native Administration Survey Department and had attended the government schools for which the Emir handpicked pupils, though Joseph did not say in his reminiscences how his father came to attend these schools. Sani's father chose the Christian boarding school hundreds of miles away over a local Kano school because, Joseph wrote, of a domestic problem. Joseph's mother had died, and his father had taken a new wife, who treated her stepson unkindly. Joseph was sent to his grandmother, who enrolled him, "without consent," in a Qur'anic school. The family objected to the decision to take such a small boy, a motherless "orphan," it was said, so far away, but his father insisted. He took Joseph to Zaria City and left him with Dr. Walter Miller, saying he would come back with sugarcane. "I did not see him again until six months afterwards, when I went home on holidays," Joseph wrote. The missionaries contemplated moving him to the girls' side of the school because he was the youngest in the school and bullied by the boys, but a mile's separation between the dormitories was too great a distance for him to walk to his classes.

Both Joseph and Garba were at the CMS school when it moved from Zaria to Wusasa in 1929 and observed surprising problems of mobility for boys and girls who had received Christian education. Joseph wrote that his first teachers in the infant school, the section where he was placed, were pupil teachers, that is, "they were themselves pupils in Standard V or VI, and they had no intention of taking teaching as a profession, they were only teachers for a short time."[63] The older girls, who were sixteen or seventeen years old, either were finished with the highest class, Standard VI, or were too old to matriculate into that class. They were waiting to marry. Of the two Hausa girls in John Garba's class, one married the school headmaster, a graduate of the school, and the other married the senior nurse at the CMS Saint Bartholomew Hospital.[64] Joseph noted that the boys were "no better," in that they were not teachers but older boys who had no other employment after Standard VI. They had been "called upon to 'help the Missions' before taking jobs under the Government or [private] Firms."[65] Sani was quite critical of the quality of teaching at the CMS school, implying that the constraints of the Christian missionaries' moral and economic expectations lowered the standards of Christian education. Education was clearly not the pathway to mobility that Muslim parents had sought when placing their sons in these schools. The practical problems—of few employment opportunities in the British dual government system, for one—forced those educated in Christian schools to not rejoin Muslim society either by marrying in the Christian faith or by working in the missions.

After finishing at Holy Trinity in Kano, Garba attended one year of classes and then sat for the government Standard V exam. After learning of his passing marks, Garba wrote a letter to his father, who was then working as an interpreter for the United Africa Company in Gusau, that he had "finished the whiteman's knowledge!" Garba then attended Class II secondary school in Lagos and enrolled locally at Igbobi College for Boys, then recently opened in 1932. He passed the Senior Cambridge examination in December 1934. There, at the center of political life and in the most prestigious schools for African students, Garba met Sir Donald Cameron, the Governor of Nigeria, and his wife. "Lady Cameron admonished me," Garba wrote, "to return to the North, and to help my people. In those days discriminating Northern and Southern Nigeria did not cause the raising of eyebrows as it does today. Then it was not only understood, but widely accepted, that there were two distinct parts in the country."[66]

Garba completed his formal education in eight years instead of the usual fourteen. He returned to Kano in 1935, where he reunited with his missionary mentor, Dr. Miller of the CMS, and began teaching eight boys at the bookshop compound in Fagge. The pressure on Garba to remain in "his part" came as a political imperative from the Camerons, and as a religious one from Dr. Miller. When Garba told Miller that since he had passed the Cambridge exam, he wanted to attend Yaba Higher College in Lagos, the highest educational institution in all of Nigeria that had just been opened in 1934, Miller "was extremely furious, calling me selfish wanting more and more for myself while there were so many in Kano and elsewhere in the North who either had no education whatever or just a little."[67]

Garba's employment situation became desperate. Working with the Kano Resident, Miller found a position for him at an outpatient clinic in the area where the Africans' hospital stood until 1929; it was moved into the walled city in the hopes that rather than the "foreign" Africans, more "indigenous" people would use the medical services. Garba declined this offer, and the government turned down a proposal to formally recognize the bookshop school in Fagge, where he would have been the head teacher. Two of Garba's fellow students, Peter Bagudu and Ibrahim Musa, worked for the British Bank of West Africa, which Garba refused to do, and another of their friends, James Jamo, went to the government waterworks at Challawa. Garba also declined to take a post teaching at the American Church of Brethren school several hundred miles to the east in Garkida, where the first Christian leprosarium was established. He was not selected for other teaching posts—one at the government teacher training school in Toro, Bauchi, because he was too young to teach married men, and another in Kano at Holy Trinity, his alma mater, because he could not play the organ and he was not married. Bishop Alfred Smith at St. Andrew's College in Oyo, Yorubaland, turned down Miller's request to take Garba on, suggesting that Garba go into the world and return after finding his "God-given vocation." The bishop believed that Miller was too heavy-handed in his influence, and Garba too young and sheltered. When Garba turned down the bank clerkship, he learned for the first time the saying "Beggars cannot be choosers" from Miller.

Garba's age, only about twenty years, and his bachelor status disqualified him from attaining positions of authority over men older than him. Garba's difficulties in this regard arose from the protectiveness of the Christian missionaries. Describing Wusasa, where he was schooled, Garba wrote, "The missionaries, understandably out of the sympathy for the plight of the women-folk in our traditional Northern Nigerian society (who have been suppressed by, and subordinated to the men-folk for centuries) did all they could to 'protect' them, and to usher in a new social order among the Christians. The girls could not fail to cash in on this aspect of the sensibility of the 'new order.'"[68]

Without a wife and prospects of children, Garba could not become a man, at least in the Hausa sense. Further, Garba's origins may not have been perceived as "elite" within the Hausa Anglican community, because his father was not a "real" Christian nor was his family a locally established Muslim family. The problem of Christian boys not being "good enough" has lasted into the present, with some Wusasa girls remaining unmarried into old age.[69] Joseph Sani, on the other hand, committed to a path of teaching and was married in the Wusasa Church to a granddaughter of Audu, the pilgrim who converted in the early 1900s. He eventually recanted Christianity before his death.

It appears that there was some suspicion about Garba's own religious qualification. Bishop Smith believed that he was not following a genuine calling from God. He had no Christian wife and no apparent desire to remain contented as a teacher in a Christian school. Christian missionaries questioned the piety—a quality with ever-shifting definition—of many African converts, particularly ones of humble origins, because they were wary of their opportunism, but many Africans came to the missionaries precisely for the benefits of a kind of education that was restricted and largely available only to Sabon Gari residents as Southern Nigerians who were Christians. Few of the options open to Garba really allowed him to gain authority among Hausa Muslims, the community he wanted to still call his own. Urban enclavism in Muslim cities like Kano had begun to restrict the mobility of Western-educated Muslims and crypto-Christians, whose opportunity to enhance their authority was severely curtailed by their inability to have social dependents and clients, like wives and students, as Ari had tried to do.

CONCLUSION

Garba went on to have a successful career. He was a Nuffield Scholar at the London School of Economics. He held high political positions such as the executive directorship of the World Bank. His education in Christian institutions and his identity as a Northern Christian played no small part in this rise. He worked in the Nigerian Pilgrim Office in Khartoum, alongside an esteemed Sudanese sheik who had worked at the Kano School of Arabic Studies. Both technically were in the employ of the British Embassy. Like

Inusa before him, Garba maintained Islamic and Christian ties as part of an ambiguous or plural religious identity in public life that helped him professionally. He married a Muslim wife, which could be seen as an act of defiance against the missionaries as well as a statement of his regard for both Islam and Christianity as his religions. Even in its exceptionalism, the social and political acceptance of Garba shows a fluidity of religious identity continuing and the perception that Christian Hausa could facilitate colonial cross-cultural mediation even as the political authorities attempted to circumscribe Christian mission activities.

Christians' activities were accepted in certain spheres, such as translation work, but in others, such as teaching, they were increasingly circumscribed by Muslim authorities. Christian missionaries like Walter Miller tried to keep Christian youth within the mission ambit. Quite unintentionally, these two powerful forces together succeeded in separating and segregating Christian education. Yet education in Muslim areas, particularly for girls, continued to be hotly debated.

Most white Christian missionaries wanted the British and Muslim authorities to allow them to open schools in Muslim areas, but this strategy was in some ways counterproductive for the religious side of missions. While gaining ground as a secular skill, Christian literacy was beginning to lose the religious authority that Inusa had attempted to find through his preaching and writing. Unlike Inusa, both Garba and Sani wrote their private papers largely in English, not in Hausa, signifying the importance of literacy learned in Christian settings to enter the colonial and mission bureaucracy. They were converts of the CMS, whereas Inusa, who used his literacy to preach, was a convert of the SIM; the two missions had very different philosophies concerning what education was and should be used for. Christians like Istifanus 'dan Daura, who used the talismanic quality of writing to sell Bible touches in the market, found yet another use.[70] This seeming commercialization of Christian identity in Northern Nigeria provoked an evangelical reaction that shaped the course of Christianity's growth from the 1920s forward.

3 ⇝ A Christian Feminist Freelance
Policing Propaganda and Piety, 1920–1935

THE KANO MOTOR CLUB, located in the Bompai section of Kano, is a concrete room with a porch. The club now and again holds a weekend morning race, but mostly it serves English breakfasts and drinks to expatriates and a few Nigerians who deal with foreigners in diverse businesses, from petroleum to prostitution. Patrons know nothing of the history of the unpretentious house, which was built by the Emir of Kano, Abdullahi Bayero, for Ethel Miller, the freelance British missionary turned local historian and librarian. She was also the author of the incendiary pamphlet *The Truth about Mohammed*, discovered by British authorities in 1926 at the height of the controversies surrounding Christianity's penetration into officially prohibited areas.

The present commerce at the club would surely have displeased both the Emir and Miller, a self-proclaimed Christian fundamentalist and prohibitionist. The idea that these two very different people would have shared any common purpose would surely surprise many. Yet Ethel Miller was, in many ways, a pioneer of modern activism on behalf of Muslim women in Northern Nigeria. As in other parts of the colonized world, Christian missions were crucial in framing the gender relations of indigenous societies as part of Euro-American salvationism.[1] Ethel Miller was unique, however, in many respects. She was one of the first white women to go to Northern Nigeria for the Church Missionary Society (CMS), but she left the mission fold, objecting to its increasingly male and secularist focus, which was calculated to stay in the good graces of the British authorities. Second, when she was outcast by Christian missionaries and the British authorities for authoring a pamphlet demeaning Muhammad, the Emir of Kano took her under his protection as an act of piety if not surveillance. The provision of a house for Miller was a strategy to contain her religious dissent. At the same time, the relationship between the Emir and Miller in the midst of white men's intense opposition to her reveals a shared moral commitment that the missionaries who rejected her sought to use to forge productive political engagements with Muslim officials.

After the largely female-oriented freed slave homes were opened in the 1910s, no Christian mission for Muslim girls and women emerged. Part of the reason for this lay in the increasing evangelical competition within missions, as women missionaries overtook men in numbers in Northern Nigeria from the 1910s onward. Neither secular nor missionary men liked the growing power of Christian women, yet they came to depend on white women as symbols of Europeans' moral superiority over Islamic society. As Ethel Miller and J. Lowry Maxwell of the Sudan United Mission (SUM) had pointed out, Islam offered women more opportunities for mobility than Christianity in Northern Nigeria. Ethel Miller argued that Christian missions, rather than offering women more material advantages, should recognize women as evangelicals and reformists, a radical vision that did not sit well in the political climate in which missionaries sought greater cooperation with Muslim and British officials. Euro-American gender dynamics were growing more contentious.

The "female question" thus became a gauge of moral authority among Christians themselves, and between religious and secular whites, Christians and Muslims, Africans and Europeans. The colonialists' own politics, in the case of Ethel Miller, worked against women's reform work, under the cover of supporting Islamic gender norms. The provision by the Emir of a house for Ethel Miller, however, shows that those Islamic gender norms were much more intricate than British discourses of native sensibilities admitted.

WOMEN MISSIONARIES AND THE HALFHEARTED ABOLITION OF FEMALE SLAVERY

When British authorities handed over the freed slaves home to the SUM in 1908 and parceled children out to other Christian societies, the low numbers of women missionaries in Northern Nigeria became immediately apparent. The SUM called for more women missionaries, and in 1909, women from Britain and South Africa arrived. Though the Sudan Interior

Mission (SIM) and CMS had had women work at their stations earlier, illness and death reduced their numbers. Ethel Miller, who arrived at the CMS Zaria station in 1907, then under the direction of her brother Dr. Walter Miller, herself became invalided within a matter of months and had to return home.² Two of the first SIM women missionaries died in 1910.³

White men, too—missionaries and others—died of sickness in Northern Nigeria, but colonial officials cited the vulnerability of white women caused by the "female condition" and the supposed threat of physical violence by Africans to women missionaries. Sir Percy Girouard, High Commissioner of Northern Nigeria in 1908, agreed with his predecessor, Frederick Lugard, that the missions could operate in areas outside Muslim rule but complained about the presence of unmarried women missionaries. "Some of the dissenting missions are quite impossible," Girouard wrote, "and the members chosen most unwisely: the mixture of unmarried men and women is hopelessly misunderstood by the natives and not unnaturally has ended in one poor girl being married in a great hurry immediately going home only to die of childbirth before reaching Plymouth—the man being the recipient of condolences. I intend to have him turned out of the country."⁴ Perhaps because he was a Catholic (the Catholic missions employed only male missionaries in Nigeria at this time), Girouard blamed nondenominational Protestant missions for hiring single women and causing embarrassment to European moral authority. These nontraditional missions preferred single women, assuming they could act like surrogate mothers to Africans, but Girouard considered them unacceptable for they would invariably marry their male coworkers and then become pregnant and die from pregnancy-related conditions. Allowing a white woman to die in West Africa for the apparently futile mission of evangelizing Muslims seemed the height of fanaticism.

Lugard, who was less antagonistic toward Christian missions than Girouard, felt that Christian missionaries were better off marrying one another, lest problems arise with interracial unions. He advised Girouard that G. W. Webster, a long-serving colonial officer who married a black woman, "should be cleared out at once."⁵ Lugard seemed to appreciate the value of white women in maintaining the prestige of white men. Africans eyed unmarried white men with suspicion. When a British Resident complained about the SUM's request for entry permits for single lady missionaries for the freed slaves home, blaming "native" impressions that they would be seen as extra wives for polygynous white men, the missionary J. Lowry Maxwell angrily dismissed it as "simply gratuitous hindrance, capricious and tyrannical. I'd advise the SUM to simply ignore it."⁶ According to Maxwell, Africans believed that white men, government officials in particular, wanted to keep black women for themselves, more often as mistresses than as wives, and Maxwell himself was approached by an African man offering his daughter. "I pointed out that I might possibly meet someone at home whom I should want to marry," Maxwell wrote. "He said that I should marry the two!"[7]

Even as Christian missionaries tried to promote the necessity of their civilizing influence in Northern Nigeria, it was becoming clearer to many, particularly women missionaries, that Islam was not the problem Westerners made it out to be. Polygyny offered benefits: co-wives with whom to share company and work. Senior wives earned the right to delegate to junior wives, who, in turn, looked to the time when they might enjoy the labor of their own subordinates.[8] Even slavery, whether a woman was a concubine or had a slave working for her, had its benefits, and children born of concubines were, by Islamic law, free. After leaving and returning to Nigeria in 1911, Ethel Miller published in *Muslim World* magazine an essay titled "Things as They Are: The Problem in Nigeria," to disabuse Europeans of the notion that Muslim women were somehow captives held against their will. She wrote: "The colours of this country do not lend themselves to the painting of dark pictures of unhappy, shut-up women, or thinking men hungry-souled for that which Islam cannot give. For the most part these are a happy, sunny people, and of them the Moslem is the best-housed and best-clothed. It is only we who know that they are alienated from the life of God through the ignorance that is in them."[9] She, of course, considered Christianity as morally superior, for it had the potential to make its believers "living temples," testaments to the power of spirituality over materialism.

Ethel Miller admitted to advising runaway girls who came to her to return to their fathers' homes if they could, instead of staying with the Christian missions.[10] Missionaries would pay bride-prices or other sums for such girls and then, like fathers, marry them off. Miller, as a single woman herself, found Christian mission marriages to be particularly problematic as the only promise held out to freed slave girls. Her article, reflecting on the meaning of Christianity in a Muslim society, questioned what being a missionary meant for Christians and for Africans. Her Christian conscience chafed against different standards between the two.

CHRISTIAN WIVES AND WOMEN WORKERS IN THE SERVICE OF MEN'S MISSIONS

Missions, finding themselves divided between the purposes of raising the first generations of Christians and of pressing their case to the government

Photo 3.1. Maikwando, evangelist's daughter, and babies at Wushishi orphanage. (Collection of SIM International Archives.)

to enter and evangelize in the Muslim territories, formed a common association in 1910. At their first meeting in Lokoja, attended by Ethel Miller and other women, notable on the agenda was the group's commitment to making a more concerted effort to reach girls and women.[11] Coupled with this was the agreement to lobby colonial government collectively to give missions "a large measure of liberty in location of unmarried Lady Missionaries."[12] Many items under discussion at the conferences, which continued until the 1950s,[13] were concerned with setting careful boundaries between each mission's spheres of activity. The marriage of girls and the labor of boys were high on the missions' collective agenda. These two matters reflect the ways in which the Christian societies sought to engineer indigenous convert communities.

Women missionaries, for their part, took an ad hoc approach to girls and women. At Wushishi, Zaria, and other stations founded early in the missionary movement in Northern Nigeria, a kind of generational bureaucracy arose. Older freedwomen, who were few, assisted the head missionary matron at Wushishi and cared for children while girls were in school (see photo 3.1). A girl named Biamuradi, who came to the SIM from the government freed slave home as an older teen with no known origins, preached at Wushishi in the late 1910s and 1920s, and became a trusted helper to the missionary in charge, Emily Clark. She later married Inusa Samuila, the lay evangelist and convert from Islam.

At the CMS station in Zaria, classes began to be held for girls after an outbreak of sleeping sickness orphaned many children.[14] A few older girls and women became evangelists. Upon her arrival in Zaria in 1907, Ethel Miller and Lahami, the sister of a Christian convert named Malam Fati and formerly a second wife of a Muslim,[15] visited Muslim women in their homes and taught several of them to read Roman script.

Missionary men tended to do more grassroots evangelism, and, as African men and their wives began to undertake more public preaching,[16] missionary women were increasingly kept at stations to conduct classes. In Zaria, Ethel Miller and her colleague, a Miss Paddon, challenged their placement in the classroom. They complained to the CMS secretary about teaching and "offering what one may call the 'bait of education' to those whom we desire to bring under the Mission influence." Miss Paddon had written of her interest in "individualistic work," including tutoring students one-on-one, itineration, and other activities. She disliked having to leave an inquiring student to teach a class.[17]

Voicing this dislike of service in Christian schools was unusual within Northern Nigeria, where missions struggled politically, but it was a part of the wider conversation throughout world mission in this period concerning the relationship between evangelism and social service. The definition of missionary women's work in relation to the social gospel was a central question.[18] At the conference on missions to Muslims held in Cairo in 1906, Dr. Emmeline Stuart, a missionary doctor practicing in Ispahan, Persia, argued that medical missions, a form of the social gospel, broke down barriers to evangelization by opening the way for theological discussions about death and salvation. She saw no separation between medical and evangelical work, as many critics in the Christian community did. Christian medicine could challenge Islamic fatalism, in her view: "The only comfort [Islam] gives them is the assurance of the Prophet that women who die in childbirth go straight to Paradise." Nonetheless, she questioned the viability of any mission built largely on the poor, sick, and outcast women; education or other programs had to support the effort.[19]

A coworker of Ethel Miller, Dr. Frances "Daisy" Wakefield, came to Zaria with the Church Missionary Society with the same kind of evangelistic goal to combine healing and preaching, but she left to join the SIM after conflicts with the leadership.[20] She was instrumental in encouraging Inusa Samuila, the SIM evangelist, to bring his detention by the Sokoto and British authorities before the International Missionary Council, headed by Joseph Oldham, the Christian ecumenical leader. This challenge was not just to the political authorities but also to the SIM heads, for they did not take seriously Inusa's story, according to his diary. Wakefield herself wrote that she had been threatened with arrest if she evangelized women in Sokoto.

Ethel Miller and Daisy Wakefield attempted to "internationalize" the religious problems of Northern Nigeria. Their frustrations led both to eventually abandon formal missionary affiliations. Daisy Wakefield followed in the footsteps of Charles de Foucauld, a Swiss aristocrat-soldier turned independent missionary, into Algeria. De Foucauld became an ordained Trappist monk and mystic, and died at the hands of brigands in 1916, shortly before Wakefield's arrival. In 2005, Pope Benedict XVI, in a gesture toward historical religious tolerance amid the backdrop of conflicts in Iraq, Afghanistan, and the Middle East, beatified de Foucauld, citing his teaching of universal brotherhood and associations he inspired across religious and secular communities, lay and clerical.[21]

Ethel Miller resigned from the CMS in 1914 and left Nigeria to serve in Egypt at a wounded soldiers' home. After the war, she returned to Nigeria, boarded the train to Kano, and got off at Challawa, a village outside the city, where the engine stopped to draw water. She lived there until the early 1920s, when she was forced by British officials to move into Kano's European business district at Bompai, where the Emir built her a house that later became the Motor Club. Ethel Miller and Daisy Wakefield, leaving the missions, could go where no established missions could—to Muslim villages they chose. Their preference for a more spiritual mission ran counter to the tide of missions' movement toward social service, especially medical work. While most English and American women missionaries retained formal affiliations, Miller and Wakefield chose evangelical work precisely counter to British colonial opposition to missions among Muslims. In so doing, they marked themselves as outsiders. Around the time of the departures, the SIM, in its 1916 pamphlet for new missionaries, warned: "Do not tell Government officials anything disparaging about missionaries of your own or any other society. Remember that we are a Missionary Family and outsiders do not need to know Mission affairs."[22]

SHUNNED BY MISSIONS, SHELTERED BY MUSLIMS

When Ethel Miller came to Northern Nigeria in 1907 as one of the first white women in the region, she was nearly thirty years old. She had left England for Canada, then left Canada for the Anglican mission in Nigeria, then went to Egypt during World War I. After returning to Nigeria in the early 1920s, she spent nearly forty years in Kano as an independent missionary. She described herself as a revolutionary even before coming to Nigeria: "I am a Victorian. I was in Toronto teaching Canadian girls to speak English when Queen Victoria died. I have scrambled on to horse busses going up to Ludgate Circus, and have gone mafficking as mad as any. I was a pioneer in Women's hockey, and among the first to ride a fixed gear bicycle in long skirts. So I find it difficult with my Victorian outlook to sum up the changes." However, the far-off days of the early 1900s were better than the 1950s, she said: "They were spacious, they were safe."[23]

Many of Ethel Miller's compatriots marveled at her and other missionaries' "pluck" but also mocked their "foolishness."[24] She herself relished being a pioneer. For her, abandoning the mission for life in a Muslim village was to answer a religious calling. From her earliest CMS days in Zaria, trekking and itinerant evangelism thrilled Miller. In a letter she wrote in 1907, she described an encounter with several Hausa men on one bicycle trek: "We had some very friendly greetings. One man saluted us with his fist (the way they greet 'kings') saying 'Giwa, Giwa' (which means elephant). I might have been offended at the salutation, only they always salute the Emir as 'Lion'!" She went on, "It is such a mistake to class these people with the half naked heathen who have no past behind them. One almost feels one could trace these men back to Abraham or Jacob with his flocks and herds!"[25]

The honorific "Giwa" showed that Ethel Miller, as a white woman, had the authority and attendant mobility that "native missionaries" did not. Her physical presence was also commanding; she was tall, nearly as tall as her manservant, Salihu, who accompanied her around Kano. She was an arresting sight, bicycling along the newly constructed roadways to visit hamlets surrounding Kano City and nearby towns.

With only her bicycle, her necessities for living, and her books, she had few tools of evangelism. She treated the wounded in her home or trekked to them, but with modest supplies. "I and my small comrades, now in good jobs in Kano," she recounted, "would walk miles with our bandages, 'pot permang,' and iodoform to answer a call, and if a cure was effected the villagers firmly believed I received £5 from the King of England. Who else would pay me?"[26] She could do little more than disinfect wounds with potassium permanganate and wrap cuts and ulcers with bandages and gauze.

By abandoning the institutional structure of missions, she rendered herself her principal tool of evangelism. She presented herself as poor to counter the widely held perception that Christian missionaries worked for the colonial government. Even today, the older men of Mariri, a hamlet of Kano where she regularly stopped, tell a revealing story. Ethel Miller had gathered curious children around her, on the pretext of teaching boko, but she spoke about Jesus and also, somewhat later in the colonial period, about the importance of vaccination campaigns. Most fascinating of all to her young listeners was her story of black and white. "Black and white, we are all the same," she told the children. "A black goat has white milk, and, if you cut its flesh, its blood is red. Blood, it is the same for you and us."[27]

The reference to shedding blood, and the example she hoped to show through her own life, was sacrifice. The story of Ethel Miller's mission in Mariri conjures images of the "Book without Words" or "Wordless Book,"[28] used by Miller herself and widely circulated by SIM missionaries who came to Kano after her.[29] The Wordless Book showed colors to tell a story: sin (black); Jesus' crucifixion (red); cleansing (white); and heaven (silver), illustrating Christian life and death in the simplest terms. Miller improvised two critical points. First, Muslims sacrificed rams and goats for Id al-Adha, the Muslim festival to commemorate Abraham's sacrifice of his son Ishmael. Though different from Christian belief of God's sacrifice of his Son, blood as sacrifice was an image Ethel Miller evoked to skirt a key controversy between Muslims and Christians, the divinity of Christ. Second, the theme of racial equality ran through her messages, even as a challenge to her listeners. She often used the image of blood running red, even if the person's skin was black or white. According to a government source, she once told villagers that "they were behind the times and that they allow foreigners, such as the Syrians [shopkeepers and merchants] to take bread from their mouths."[30]

While infusing her itinerant preaching with class and racial politics, Ethel Miller also began a more public campaign of writing and translating. Through the 1920s, she published a number of pamphlets: *Hausa Heroines* in 1923; a Hausa translation of the life story of Apollo Kagwa—the Prime Minister of Buganda in East Africa and the first African to be knighted by the British—in 1924; a Hausa translation of the life story of Marshal Feng, the Christian warlord of China who led the Beijing coup in 1924; an English-language pamphlet, *The Truth about Muhammad*, around 1925; and *Women Count*, sometime thereafter. The stories of Kagwa, an Anglican, and Feng, converted by American Methodists, were adapted from mission publications and clearly intended for Nigerian audiences.[31] Both of these converts were prominent Christian figures of 1920s mission publications.

Ethel Miller's other writings were aimed at Europeans, Britons more specifically, and obviously intended as moral lessons about the plight of girls and women.

Several of the tracts unfold in the tradition of Christian conversion stories, centering on the life stories of individuals. *Hausa Heroines* is special for its ethnographic quality and decided focus on female fortitude—Christian and Muslim—in a society dominated by men, with marriage the sole expectation for girls. Conversion is a less important theme in *Hausa Heroines*. Each of the five stories is named for its protagonist, beginning with Diji, a Muslim girl who first married at fourteen as *sadaka* (given charitably without brideprice) to a member of the elite and then traded with the harem. It ends with Jimai, injured by telegraph wires as a girl, and married off multiple times because of her worsening physical condition. The three other stories are about girls who found their way to Christianity by running away, by escaping slavery, or through a husband. Only the stories of Rakiya and Hawa, two Christians, end happily, indeed, tenderly. "I once taught an African mother to kiss her little girl," Miller wrote, "but Hawa has learnt it from her own loving heart." The third convert died in the influenza epidemic of 1918, three years after coming to Christianity. Jimai's story ended without resolution. She was forced to recant Christianity on threat of expulsion from her home, had "neither husband nor guardian and when she falters a prayer, before even she asks for her daily bread she says, 'Lord, bring me a husband from North, South, East, or West.'"[32]

Ethel Miller appeared in each of these stories as a helper, though she never represented herself or Christianity as complete escape. The passion in her writing came from the bonds, in some cases thwarted by Muslim men, between her and the Hausa women. The friendships, as well as references to Gimi, the community established outside Zaria with the help of Ethel Miller's brother Walter, and some details about male characters, suggest the basis of the stories in actual life histories. Jimai's story contains the line: "People said strange things of the white lady who refused the houses offered her in the city and lived just like themselves in a hut on the farms."[33]

Lady Maud Selborne wrote a note of appreciation for the pamphlet. The wife of the former High Commissioner of South Africa, she was herself a suffragist and influential conservative social reformer in England. "Of course I am not a judge of how far they are an exact representation of the social conditions of Africa," she wrote, "but they give one the impression of having been sketched from life. The atmosphere of opinion is often better conveyed in a story than in a more formal account."[34] Ethel Miller was politically astute in sharing her views with an influential figure like Lady Selborne. While Miller had separated from the missions, she took the opportunity to make connections to powerful Europeans through her expertise as a rare witness to the lives of African Muslim women.

It is not clear how far *Hausa Heroines* reached through suffragist and imperial networks, but letters between Ethel Miller and the British Resident of Kano, E. J. Arnett, around the time of the pamphlet's publication reflect a heated exchange about various topics—the presumed insubordination of Hausa Christian converts toward Muslim authority, abuses of the Muslim courts, and the type of Islamic marriage contract in which Diji had been given, which Ethel Miller believed to be a form of slavery. In a subsequent letter to Arnett, presumably to answer his questions about her intentions, she reaffirmed her loyalties and vowed to stay out of the "court of justice." Like other British women who employed writing for reform in this era, Ethel Miller's challenge to British men to take a hard look at themselves appeared as disloyalty to their race and as undermining of imperial authority.[35]

Miller's *The Truth about Muhammad* gained the greatest notoriety because of its strong anti-Muslim content. Subtitled *An Appeal to Englishmen in Nigeria*, this pamphlet drew on the works of published scholars of history and religion to attack the Prophet Muhammad's character and the moral relativism of Englishmen who considered Islam a civilizing force in Africa. Miller cited her own credentials, honors in history and classics and membership on the Board of Experts from the University of London, and complained that "when a missionary ventures to express an opinion on religion he is dubbed a fanatic, which if an astronomer writes about the stars he is deemed an expert."[36] She admitted that she did not intend the pamphlet to be a collection of facts or views even. "It is a long pent up ebullition of convictions, and of indignation at the trifling knowledge that displays itself too frequently in praise of Muhammad." Its vehemence stood in stark opposition to the tone of *Hausa Heroines* and of her relations with Muslims in daily life. It was an open insult to the many Christian missionaries and British officials who believed that Islam had "civilized" Africans. Miller wrote: "It is the founder of a religion not its followers that must be brought to the bar of our judgment; and even if I have to concede that a Muhammedan is often as good a man as a Christian, that will never convince me that Muhammad is as good as Christ, or even as *a substitute for Him*. When a soul needs Saviour I am taking no risks either for myself or for *others*. At such a crisis I do not compare systems or successes, (for that matter the devil had had the best success of any), but I make a comparison of persons, and I find Christ incomparable."[37]

Yet she did not call for conversion to Christianity. Echoing the famed historian Edward Gibbon, she concluded that the demise of Christian spirituality began with the political power of Christians under the convert Constantine. "The true Church must always be looked for in the obscurity of contempt or the glare of persecution," she claimed. While Islam contained rites unattainable to many "owing to sex, status or sphere," she wrote, in Christianity, only two rites were important—baptism and the Lord's Supper (the taking of communion).

Miller used her anti-Muslim, reformist Christian, and pro-women stance to challenge secularist and other apologetic British discourses. Her pamphlet *Women Count* targeted the British squarely. "In pursuance of legislation which he [Muhammad] enacted in the Koran," she wrote, "Christian women and girls were sold at 1 pound apiece and distributed to men in the year of our Lord nineteen hundred and twenty-one. In the same year the writer was in Egypt. Nationalist processions blocking the streets of Cairo were common, and on one occasion a motor containing an educated Egyptian woman (a Moslem) was held up. She stood up in her seat and addressed the crowd from her motor on current political topics. A Moslem gentleman remarked, 'We didn't know they had it in them.' Exactly, nor do Englishmen." In her parting shot, Miller asked Englishmen to step out of the way. "You may admire Muhammedanism as a political or social system, and enjoy its picturesque accompaniments, but at least as a reasonable Englishman you will repudiate it as a *religion*, and even if you do not mind going to hell yourself at least give men and *women* who do a fair chance to save their souls."[38]

Miller mailed *The Truth about Muhammad* and perhaps other writings to British Residents in various parts of Nigeria. It was suspected that she also sent them to India and North Africa. The administration in Nigeria discussed with the Colonial Office in London possible criminal charges against her for insult to religion, an approach that, in the end, they abandoned. They did initiate an investigation of missionary activities in Kano, finding other independent missionaries, including Dugald Campbell, who worked extensively with medical missionaries in Hawaii, but focused mostly on Miller and a Mrs. Pomeroy and her daughter, about whom very little is known.[39] Within a few months' time, news of "converts" surfaced— including Ethel Miller's protégé, Audu, who lived in Mariri and came to learn to read and write with her three times a week.

Although the authorities claimed that Muslims were insulted by Miller's pamphlets, there is little evidence to corroborate this. The Christian missionaries were generally convinced that the British officials exaggerated Muslim rulers' resistance to Christianity. An incident in 1927 seemed to confirm this. The British Resident of Sokoto learned that the heir to the throne of Gwandu, Emirate in Sokoto Province, had purchased Bible tracts at the CMS bookshop in Sokoto, and was nearly persuaded to become a Christian. His brother, then the Emir of Gwandu, did not seem to mind, according to Resident G. W. Webster, because of his affection for his brother. According to Webster's report, the Sultan of Sokoto himself considered a man's religion his personal affair, except in the case of persons who were *sarakuna*, the ruling elite. Rites did not matter if one's heart was impure. The sultan believed that commoners would not mind the conversion of the Gwandu heir, but that the *ulema*, the clerics, would interpret all misfortunes as a consequence of their leader's apostasy. Furthermore, the sultan warned, it was the literacy of the young man that led to his conversion and that would lead the Muslim clerics to see Western schools as a negative influence on the minds of young people. A former British official wrote years later that certain missionaries along with British political officers used the sultan's logic to compel the would-be heir to the throne to recant his conversion.[40] This case set a precedent that converts to Christianity had to recant and become Muslim in order to accept positions of authority in the Native Administration, a very different situation that obtained with the offer of continued employment, albeit with a demotion, that the Christian convert Ari received from the Emir of Kano (see chapter 2).

While the sultan and the Emir of Gwandu showed sympathy for the convert, casting blame instead on the clerics of their own religion, missionaries from this point began to police Christian "propaganda." Andrew Stirrett of the SIM wrote that the work of his mission was "construction rather than pulling down. You will find I feel sure that we extol the excellences of Him whom we serve feeling assured that once Moslems get a proper sight of Him they will do the pulling down themselves."[41] Bishop Melville Jones of the CMS wrote to the Chief Secretary of the Colony that his mission did not engage in open-air preaching, though Ethel Miller herself had trekked on a bicycle while in CMS employ. Dr. Miller in Zaria, Jones claimed, was "strict that women should only enter women compounds." "What may have been done by 'free lances' like Miss Miller, I cannot say, but I fear we suffer from their indiscretions."[42] These male missionary critiques of Ethel Miller cast her attempts to witness as a public representative of Christianity, a role they claimed for themselves, as outside the proper conduct of missionary evangelism.

The British authorities struggled for several years to contain Ethel Miller. She made visits to Had'ejia, a neighboring emirate of Kano, to the palace of the Emir himself. In 1930, the authorities contemplated strategies to deal with her, from letting the Native Administration handle her to attaching "female attendants or special policewomen to Miss Miller's person as guards." "Such action, apart from the possibility that it might bring obloquy and ridicule on a European lady, must inevitably tend to exacerbation of religious and racial feeling which there are always influences to exploit," warned the Secretary of the Northern Provinces. In his view, any strategy, especially prosecution in court, that risked creating a "cause célèbre" in Nigeria and England, had to be avoided.[43] By 1937, the British, after claiming that the Muslim administration disliked Ethel Miller, reported that she "has been in Kano so long that many of the City Moslems, both official and non-official, pay her friendly visits and although the Emir and Council refuse to allow activities on her part within the city walls they are at the moment building her a small room in Fagge (about a half a mile away) in which she hopes to start a library for English speaking Moslems."[44]

"NO CRYING EVILS": SURRENDERING WOMEN'S WORK FOR MISSIONS' FREE MOVEMENT

Ethel Miller wrote an article titled "Defence Mechanism or Protection?" published on August 18, 1934, in the *Nigerian Daily Times* newspaper, complaining of discrimination against Christians:

> I am the oldest resident in Kano. I am a University woman and an educationalist by profession, yet in spite of repeated requests, I have not been allowed to go inside the School for Moslem Girls provided by the Government in City. Yet I know of no tourist even, *man* or *woman* (it is a "purdah" school) who has been denied entrance. And my request to be allowed to go to Palace to congratulate the wives of the Emir on his safe arrival from England was similarly turned down. Why? Because I have a reputation of an active Christian and might contaminate them. If I were a Moslem I would not be proud of such protection.[45]

Because she was independent, Miller could not be barred on the grounds of any government policy against missions to Muslims. Rather, by her account, she was the victim of governmental discrimination on the basis of her religion. She suggested that anticolonial Southern Nigerian Christians might find this episode significant. Whether the restrictions on her movements came from the British or the Muslim side, that she, a lone woman, could provoke such a reaction on the part of Muslim or British powers, she wrote, was a sign of Islam's weakness in Northern Nigeria. At the very least, it was paternalistic on the part of the British for preventing the African from "standing up to the fight, to receive as well as give blows, to be wounded." "Not till then," she wrote, "will he enter into Life, abundant, satisfying and blessing others." In government correspondence on the article, the Resident of Kano, H. O. Lindsell, admitted that he prevented the school's assistant mistress from taking Ethel Miller as a Hausa language interpreter on a visit to the Emir's palace. He added that Miss Fegan, the school's headmistress, "understands the position" and "feels that Miss Miller has been trying most unfairly to use a new recruit to the teaching staff to obtain access to the Emir's Compound." He claimed that the Emir did not want her to visit him or the school.[46]

As the conflicts between Ethel Miller and the government continued, they began to focus more on secular reforms for African girls and women. Lindsell's struggle to explain the incident suggests that he had indeed blocked her as a potentially radical influence on non-missionary British women working for the colonial administration. The tensions between Christian and secular Europeans—no longer just between men and women but now between secular women like Miss Fegan and Christian women like Ethel Miller—spilled over into debates surrounding girls' education.

The origins of government girls' schools—opened first in Kano and Katsina and, later, in other emirates—are shrouded somewhat in mystery, or at least in misperception. While the colonial administration introduced Western education for Muslim boys in 1910, they found it difficult to convince Muslim elites to offer up their sons and proceeded cautiously at first to train workers for the Native Administrations. Muslim girls' education received no serious consideration. In contrast, the CMS school in Zaria, then Wusasa, had, as Ethel Miller herself knew, a strong girls' education component.

Around the time of the CMS move to Wusasa in 1929, Eric R. J. Hussey, the first Director of Education for Nigeria—the North and South combined—suggested that two girls' "centres" be opened in Muslim territories. They were officially called centers, and not schools, until 1935.[47] Why girls and why centers? The explanations advanced until now have neglected the gender dynamics of colonial Muslim Nigeria. Historians have interpreted the origins of the government girls' schools variously as part of the efforts by the British government to control education as a way of keeping a firm hand on Muslim indirect rulers or as a response to the government's difficulties with missionary societies. In 1927, the British administration had to contend with pressure from Christian missions and from an educational reformer concerned with African colonies.[48] The mission societies working in Northern Nigeria collectively enlisted the help of Joseph H. Oldham, head of the International Missionary Council, to lobby the British government to allow Christian societies to enter Muslim areas. Oldham and representatives of the missions wrote a letter jointly to Graeme Thomson, Governor of Northern Nigeria, making the case for the importance of mission institutions in Muslim areas as colonialism brought rapid social and economic changes; they promised in turn to undertake their efforts "in a wise and discreet manner."[49] At a meeting in London, Thomson promised Oldham and the mission representatives that the British government would educate the Emirs in religious tolerance as preparation for missions' entry into the emirates. In the same year, Thomson asked Alec Fraser, an expert on education in the Gold Coast (Ghana) and Oldham's brother-in-law, to undertake a study of the educational system of Nigeria.[50] Fraser produced a scathing report accusing the British government of failing to provide education and of standing between Muslims and missions, which might have otherwise provided social services. The report was suppressed.

Education of Muslims in "religious tolerance" by introducing formal education for girls, for which no real precedent existed, could hardly be seen as a good political strategy.[51] It seems, rather, that at the heart of new girls' schools was a desire to refute Fraser's implicit view, shared by like-minded social reformers, that Islam disempowered women and that Britain had disempowered women by empowering Islam.[52] In 1929, the Lady Superintendent of Education in Lagos, Sylvia Leith-Ross, undertook nearly nine months' research in Ilorin Province about the prospects for girls' education among Muslims. Focusing on urban, mostly elite Yoruba women, Superintendent Leith-Ross concluded that girls and women in Ilorin were not suffering from lack of formal schooling; instead, school made them rather "uppity" in their refusal to marry men who were not clerks or somehow in the ambit of colonial or modern institutions. Unless Muslim Yoruba women were deceptive, Leith-Ross argued, they were content, and the Native Administration was noncommittal in suggesting that they would not oppose girls' schools but would reserve judgment until they saw the results. She found that young children "unconsciously" reached out for something—creation, mastery, growth—but she doubted if this interest was anything more than a short-lived phase. There were "no crying evils that need remedy," just poor hygiene. She seemed unsure about what to recommend, ultimately suggesting that the Montessori method be adapted to local environments, or that there be "no change until the women cry out for it."[53]

The government's establishment of "centres" for elite girls in the Hausa emirates, following Leith-Ross's rather uninspiring recommendations owing to her Yoruba experience, was a response to criticism posed by Ethel Miller and other women's reformers, including Maud Selborne, and less to Alec Fraser or Joseph Oldham, who represented the missions. Just twenty years prior, the government had decided that philanthropy was not part of its mandate and turned over the freed slave homes to missions; by 1930, it had started creating institutions for girls modeled after Christian freed slave homes. The girls' centers had single-sex classes taught by European women for girls between the ages of four and eleven that included play, childcare, domestic science, and hygiene. Girls left the schools when they were married, not unlike mission institutions, though elite Muslim girls tended to marry at younger ages than Christian girls and poorer Muslim girls.

According to British sources, Muslim leaders requested these schools and demanded that their design accord with Muslim norms of domesticity and piety. The Emirs and their councils were made to pay for them. When the British administration claimed that it did not have the funds to pay the European women teachers needed to staff new schools in Sokoto and Birnin Kebbi, the Native Administrations covered the costs. If they had not, they would have had to acquiesce to the proposal made by Miss Fegan, early in 1932, that girls in the younger classes join the boys' elementary schools.[54] Just as some in the British administration obstructed the entry of white women missionaries into Northern Nigeria even after the turnover of freed slave girls to Christian societies, the colonial authorities were now complicating Muslim girls' education even after Emirs themselves had accepted it. Cost was no doubt a factor since the Great Depression had set in, but the political resistance had preceded this by many years.

With too few women teachers and chronic underenrollment, the government girls' school foundered well into the 1940s. Emirs and other Muslims who had supported the school seemed to lose interest. Keeping girls in school and increasing their numbers proved difficult because of the relatively early marriage, sometimes as young as eleven, of elite Muslim girls. The British showed little interest in providing schools for poorer girls, even though the Resident of Kano wrote in 1938 of the disappointing progress of girls' schools in districts outside the urban centers: "There have been new entrants but marriages, deaths, or unsatisfactory attendances have accounted for many dismissals. It has been carefully pointed out that no obstacle will be placed in the way of marriage but suspicion appears to die hard. Rather more than half of the girls, too, are of the upper classes who marry earlier than the '*talakawa*' [the commoners]."[55] With the worldwide economic depression cited early in the report as the conditions for such institutions, the cost of maintaining such a school was a burden. In the wider context of education in Muslim Northern Nigeria, even the boys' schools filled slowly as compared to schools across colonial Africa.[56]

The explanation, or rather the blame, for the halting pace of the modernization of schools has always fallen upon the Muslim elites, with their preference for girls' early marriage and, more generally, for their purported resistance to Christian missionary and secular Western education; colonial officials, scholars, partisans of religious and political groups, and development workers have either joined this chorus or accepted its conclusion without question. Yet when one examines female education across Muslim and Christian spheres and across different kinds of institutions for girls in colonial Northern Nigeria—mission and government—the evidence does not support the Emirs' opposition as the primary reason for failure, though it certainly may have played a part. British officials were aware of the high numbers of white missionary women entering Northern Nigeria and were not prepared to hire them into the government. The government supported the separation of African girls from the lower social orders away from boys and away from towns, on moral grounds, in contrast to Miss Fegan's (not serious) proposal to coeducate Muslim girls with boys in government schools.

A lingering ambivalence about African girls—Muslim and Christian—and their education—moral and intellectual—carried over from the earliest days of the freed slave homes and across mission and government spheres. Whether intentional or not, the practical effect was that social hierarchies and religious differences were entrenched within institutions for girls—missionary and government, which intersected through freed slave home collaboration. As late as 1926, the government sent poor and non-Muslim girls to mission care. The SIM Wushishi station, which formally became a girls' "training centre" in 1922, received girls and money for their upkeep from the British government. Dr. Andrew Stirrett sent a bill to the British Resident in Niger Province, where the Wushishi mission station was located, for the care of seven girls at a rate of two shillings per day for each. Six of the girls stayed with the SIM for nearly a year, while the seventh left after eighty-eight days because she was married.[57]

Writing sometime in the 1930s or 1940s, missionary Faye Moyer, an education expert who worked for the CMS before she came to the SIM,[58] wrote to the director to complain that the girls she saw at Wushishi were "aimless—are they here for marriage or school?" She recommended that the SIM drop the idea of a school altogether and instead call the institution an orphanage.[59] Schools for girls, both mission and government, lacked purpose in the eyes of white men and women, secular and Christian, because African girls were bound for marriage. Dame Margery Perham, famed writer and political commentator who visited Kano and Katsina in 1931–1932, dismissed the government education for girls as playing house, writing, "Education as yet is a matter of washing, of looking at pictures, and playing with coloured Froebel dolls."[60] Watching the girls in the Katsina school, Perham measured her own freedom against their apparent entrapment: "I felt a wild bird indeed, looking into that cage, and though Calder [the Resident] rallied my gloom by saying, 'They like it all right. They don't know anything else,' I wonder how long it would take them to cross over to where I stood, and remembered with a more instructed satisfaction about the Emancipation which happened of late in Turkey."[61]

Some twenty years earlier, Miller and Wakefield had expressed a similar fatalism about education. By the 1930s, the government girls' school became a symbol of the impossibility of "modernization" in Muslim Northern Nigeria. For Perham, Leith-Ross, and Fegan, their tendency to separate themselves from African girls and women was different from Ethel Miller's view of relationships with Muslim and Christian African girls and women, reflected in her reminiscences and pamphlets like *Hausa Heroines*. Though she might agree with her compatriots that Islam had disempowered girls and women, she emphasized African female individuality and knowingness, dwelling on their ignorance as a lack of knowledge of Christianity because of the British denial of the possibility of reform, not Muslim opposition.

Muslims and Christians, though they had grown "closer" in some respects, were growing further apart when it came to gender politics; the fault lines were drawn between religious and secular Western feminism. Perham visited Ethel Miller in Kano, and the two women shared certain points of reference in their writings; both wrote with enthusiasm about the women's movement in Turkey. Yet they understood their relationships to their government and their civilization quite differently. Perham felt protected by the British spirit of secular modernity and therefore safely outside what she considered the "drama" of the British in Muslim Africa. After she visited Ethel Miller, she described "the old missionary women" in theatrical terms:

> a tragic comic figure, all links lost with England, living in a dusty little one-roomed shack, too poor, I was told, even to afford a servant. She was busy tearing up the illusions of a lifetime with almost exultant bitterness. She had lost belief in missions; as for the black

man, he was black inside and out; he hated us and we hated him, and it was all very well for officials out for a few years on short tours and getting only smiles and obedience to take a different view. Let them live alone among the blacks, poor, with no holidays, and speaking their language as only she among the Europeans can speak it![62]

An admirer of Lugard, Perham had no sympathy for any of what she saw now in Northern Nigeria: from colonial favoritism toward the Muslim elite, limited education, to the cautious pace of British efforts to "modernize" Muslims. Yet she also despised Ethel Miller's evangelical zeal and took pleasure in the blows that failed mission work had inflected on her. Such scorn was not reserved for only a Christian missionary. Of the Emir of Katsina, Perham wrote: "A year before he was a wild priest, 'an eater of nuts,' professing some mystic brand of Mahdism, with dreams of the second coming and of the extermination of the infidel." By the time of her trip, he had become a willing supporter of the Girls' Centre, among other British innovations. Perham speculated that the Emir's trips abroad had likely tempered his religiosity, and she added, "I can't help believing that the admixture of negro blood [to his presumed Hamitic or Semitic racial stock] acts as a sedative."[63] To her, Ethel Miller and the former Mahdist occupied the same place, on the fringes, with no role to play in the secular reforms that the British imperial government wanted to bring to its colonies. What would become of attempts at reform in Northern Nigeria?

Until lately political officers on occasions veiled their own wives in deference to Mohammedan embarrassment; net curtains have been hung over the gallery holding European women at public events; no political officer evers [sic] allows his wife to appear in the house when the Native Authorities come; if an Emir or other notable encounters a white woman by accident invisibility is assumed on both sides. But it is not only the question of women, but also of dogs that appears on the files.... Meanwhile, though the Emir is treated with the greatest deference, and all action is nominally taken by him—the European officer never acting directly himself—he may be a man put in by our choice after our deposition of his predecessor, in administrative matters must be partly, and may be entirely an automaton in the hands of his political officer. Indirect rule is, indeed, a kind of inversion of the constitutional trick we have learned in England; the autocratic Emir retains nearly all his powers in theory while in practice, behind the curtain, he is checked and propelled, not by a ministry, still less by a democracy, but by an unobtrusive, kindly, middle-aged Englishman who derives his authority from the military power and wealth of Great Britain.[64]

Whereas Perham plainly saw British power over Muslims as resting in the material, Ethel Miller grounded it in the moral realm. Missionaries in an earlier time shared Miller's view but increasingly had become more politically expedient.

Missionaries, too, had sided against Ethel Miller and, with some exceptions, gave up on serious efforts for the spiritual conversion of girls and women. The costs were too high, and the souls of women less important than the "crying evil" of poor hygiene. Many Christian missionaries had given up the idea they once held that women's conversion was key to keeping men and children in the church, but Ethel Miller, propelled by her own unmarried and iconoclastic life, tried in vain to persuade Christians to see the value of females' souls for their own sake.

CONCLUSION

Ethel Miller failed to "speak for" Northern Nigerian women, and she spent many years in penury in the small concrete house built by the Emir in the Bompai section of Kano. She came to spend her final days at a nursing home in Brighton on the south coast of England, though she had declared she wanted to die in Nigeria. She was forced out, according to Ladi Joe, the granddaughter of Malam Fati, the CMS convert who had left behind all but his first wife upon conversion. Ladi Joe had known Miss Miller since she was a child because her father, Ibrahim Bawa, worked on the Hausa Bible translation team, and she lamented how the elderly woman's story ended: "We would have taken care of her. She was our mother." For women like Ladi Joe, Miller represented the end of any measure of Christian missionary autonomy from political power. Her legacy lived on in African Christian women's devotion to teaching Muslim girls, which Ladi Joe and other former Wusasa undertook in the 1960s. Male reformers, Muslim and Christian, have since unwittingly copied at least one of her more public acts of religious resistance. Ethel Miller staged a public spectacle in Kano, "a vivid temperance lecture [in which she visited] all the beer-shops, buying drinks at all of them and pouring the pints down the gutter."[65] Pro-shar'ia activists did the same in Kano in the early 2000s, in fact at Miller's former home, the Motor Club.

Few alive today remember Ethel Miller and, in one written history about her, she is characterized as an oddity used to catch "bigger fish," her brother and other male missionaries seeking to enter Kano.[66] Her story, of course, is much more than this—in her personal transformation, she had a catalyzing effect on her community. She used the cause of Muslim women and girls for her own purposes,[67] not unlike more modern secular Western feminists. She also rejected the cultural relativist mode of different standards for Africans and for whites. She wrote:

> People often say to me, "Your converts are no better than the Muslim." Maybe. But do we help them to be? Too many, I admit, just slide into being Christians by learning to read or getting a job at the mission. They are attracted by the apparent prosperity of the missionary, good houses, cars; he [the missionary] is to him just another aspect of the white man, another department, poorly paid perhaps, but still a job. I remember a Katsina College boy with whom I used to talk; he was drawn to Christianity by the domestic blessing of a missionary he saw; an obedient wife, plenty of children, peace in the home![68]

Though Ethel Miller was exceptional among missionaries in her openly hostile stance against elements of Islamic culture as they affected women in Northern Nigeria, she had, ironically, a much more intimate relationship with the Emir of Kano as his dependent. Thus, it is striking that it took the case of Ethel Miller for British officials to appreciate the benevolent and paternalist capacity of Northern Nigerian Emirs, a mode of power and surveillance that was crucial to the institutionalization of formal mission-Muslim cooperation in which the Native Administrations effectively adopted Christian missions as a wing of their government in the 1930s.

PART II

Followers of the Word

4 ⮎ Christian Medical Missions as Muslim Charity
Paternalist Alliances, Maternal Alienation, 1928–1942

THE PROBLEMS RELATED TO MISSIONS in Kano in the mid-1920s—the conversion of the crafts school teacher Malam Ari Biu and the question of women's social and religious welfare—opened a new era of engagement between Muslims and Christians. Together, British colonial authorities, Christian missions, and Muslim and non-Muslim Native Administrations turned their energies to medical work, specifically the creation of leprosy treatment centers and rural dispensaries. This institutional cooperation became stronger by the late 1930s, effectively shutting out freelance missionaries like Ethel Miller while creating standards by which Christian missions were judged in their conduct toward local populations and in their utility for the indigenous and colonial governments. Yet the cooperative medical scheme was more than a political bargain. It was a new social experiment that brought Muslims and Christians together as patients and practitioners, clients and patrons, using public health as a mechanism to manage religious relations.

Missions had doctors on staff and had run informal clinics in markets in Northern Nigeria before the 1920s. The CMS St. Bartholomew Hospital built in Wusasa in 1929–1930 was the only mission hospital built in any Muslim area before the establishment of Christian provincial leprosariums in 1937. Missionaries in other fields, such as Egypt and India, wrote about the medical mission approach,[1] but the societies in Northern Nigeria had focused much greater attention on conventional evangelism and Bible reading to that point.

British officers' views about the value of Christian missions in relation to medicine changed from the 1920s to the 1930s, along with the growing British colonial interest in Africans' health throughout the empire during this period.[2] Dr. N. A. Dyce-Sharp, of the West African Medical Service, writing about epidemics in the mid-1920s in West Africa, made a special example of relapsing fever, which his epidemiological survey revealed had arrived with Senegalese soldiers returning from World War I and spread south down the Niger River from French Soudan (Mali) to Lagos, leading to deaths in the six figures over three years.[3] Although West Africa had been known as the "white man's grave" for its many infectious diseases, it was virgin territory for this particular fever, according to Dyce-Sharp. He felt sure it was the first disease to spread southward from the less-populous and drier North to the more humid and densely settled coasts.

Dyce-Sharp echoed then prevailing sentiments of colonial medical authorities that modernization wrought by colonialism was sickening Africans,[4] but he offered new evidence and proposals. Using an approach different from that of many medical officers, he gained information about ethnicity and disease from African political authorities, who he claimed were "fully as capable of making a correct diagnosis of [relapsing fever] as is the medical officer, hampered as he so often is by a complete absence of history and by lack of time."[5] Further, Dyce-Sharp viewed modern education as detrimental in making coastal Africans more cognizant of symptoms of cancer, labor pains, and tuberculosis. He viewed the majority of Africans and missionaries alike as passive transmitters of disease.

Citing the Emir of Gwandu in Sokoto Province of Northern Nigeria, Dyce-Sharp laid blame for local outbreaks of relapsing fever on the Zabarmawa, whom he described as compromising "a large number of clans for the most part on both banks of the Niger." The Emir referred to them as *kalakala*, "traveling beggars," and Dyce-Sharp noted that they came south during the dry season to work as drawers of water and hewers of wood. "One would not be far wrong in describing them as the gypsies of Nigeria."[6] A supposedly "warlike" people, the Zabarmawa were also found in good numbers in the French and British militaries. Dyce-Sharp noted that statistics of relapsing fever fatalities from as far west as Accra showed that a large proportion of victims were Zabarma migrants.

Along with these Africans, Dyce-Sharp blamed Europeans for bringing to the West African coast "diseases of civilization," including cancer, gastric troubles, and painful childbirth, reportedly learned by coastal African women from "education," and for allowing Muslim missionaries to bring their diseases to healthy pagans. "Syphilis seems to follow faithfully, if impartially, the Cross and the Crescent," Dyce-Sharp observed. New drugs such as Salvarsan could readily cure syphilis and relapsing fever, but colonial medical officers were neither numerous nor mobile enough to effectively spread the medicines. Meanwhile, he issued a warning about African carriers: "If we assume, as indeed we may, the incrimination of the Zabarmawa as the vectors of one, and perhaps two, new and deadly diseases into parts of British West Africa, the relations of these people with the natives of the Gold Coast and Nigeria must become a matter of profound sanitary importance."[7]

Ten years later, Dr. Ernest Muir, the Medical Secretary of the British Empire Leprosy Relief Association (BELRA), offered a very different vision. He proposed a scheme to marshal political agents of surveillance and the very kinds of carriers that Dyce-Sharp criticized into a large-scale public health effort. Muir, who worked with Sir Leonard Rogers in India, sought in the African colonies to achieve voluntary separation of leprosy sufferers.[8] Leprosy, a chronic infection caused by the mycobacteria *leprae* and the more recently discovered *lepromatosis* (related to the agents causing tuberculosis) and affecting the skin, nerve tissues, eyes, and other organs, has a very long incubation period and has been called the "least infectious" disease."[9] Yet only recent research has confirmed this quality of leprosy. Eighty years ago, Muir argued that leprosy should be a focus of public health work because of its stigmatizing physical effects and the potential efficacy of education about it.

Muir's scheme involved both native and colonial authorities, missionaries, and migrants in creating central leprosariums and satellite communities. After receiving missionary care, ex-patients would establish clan-based villages offering outpatient treatment and medical education. Muir called this the Propaganda-Treatment Survey (PTS) method and highlighted a successful example from Bengal, India, that he recommended be implemented throughout Nigeria.[10] Given that no medical consensus existed on the utility of new medicines in curing leprosy or preventing its transmission, Muir's plan departed from precedent in proposing residential segregation as only one phase of a campaign to mobilize leprosy sufferers themselves.

The ready religious association of leprosy with the Bible was important for Muir's justification for missions acting as the bridge between clinical and compassionate care,[11] but, during the previous ten years, colonial medical thinking had become increasingly preoccupied with who had control over disease and health care. For Muslim Northern Nigeria, the purpose of producing Christian mission-trained "medical auxiliaries" was to provide an occupation for members of a religious minority who had struggled to find a place in Muslim areas. In a complete reversal of earlier efforts to segregate Christians from Muslims, the leprosy scheme proposed mobilizing Christian missionaries and their wards as healers of Muslims. The plan would unfold under the supervision of Muslim Native Administrations.

The cooperative leprosy centers and dispensaries reflected a new confidence—in medicine, African participation in public health, and the ability of British and Muslim authorities to contain and control Christian missions. Over several decades, the scheme produced positive results. For one, voluntary participation grew and, with it, appreciation of new medicine. Medicine began as botanical oils and home remedies from the largely American missionaries, but modern pharmaceutical therapies like the sulfa drug dapsone for leprosy and penicillin for yaws followed. The prevalence of leprosy appears to have declined, although the statistics from early in the twentieth century are not entirely reliable for comparison.

The successes of the cooperative medical missions scheme, however, obscure a complex situation of competing priorities and unexpected disaffection, particularly among women patients and many African Christians who did not share their missionary leaders' interest in collaboration with Muslim authorities in medical work. In sorting out the relations forged within the leprosariums, perhaps ironically, the evidence suggests that cooperative medical work in the end failed to consolidate either religious or medical power and instead fractured and decentralized it.

GROWING CONFIDENCE AND CONSENSUS

Leprosy had emerged as an imperial cause among political and medical authorities by 1867,[12] even before much of Africa was brought under colonial rule. The disease captured the public imagination in Europe and the United States following two signal events: Armauer Hansen's discovery of the leprosy bacillus in 1873 and the death in 1886 of Belgian Catholic missionary Father Damien, who contracted the disease when working on the island of Molokai in Hawaii. The scientific community at first did not accept Hansen's theory that a bacterium, not heredity, caused leprosy. Influential men of science, including the leprosy expert (and Hansen's father-in-law) Daniel Danielsson and public health pioneer Rudolf Virchow, opposed Hansen's theory.[13] Even after its general acceptance, the promotion of segregation was highly contentious.[14] Yet Father Damien's death galvanized new vigilance against an old disease, uniting traditional foes like Catholic and Protestant crusaders, while stigmatizing certain migrants, including Norwegians in Europe and Chinese in the United States.[15]

At the First International Leprosy Conference in Berlin in 1897, Phineas Abraham, a British dermatologist born in Jamaica who became the Medical Secretary of the British National Leprosy Fund, cautioned against "emotional outbursts."[16] Yet political forces began to outweigh practitioners like Abraham who argued for a more conservative approach to leprosy. In the United States, Congressman Joseph Ransdell pressed his government to establish the first national leprosarium in his state of Louisiana at Carville in 1916.[17] Carville and US-supported leprosariums in the Philippines became centers of research and drug development that influenced the formation of a global campaign. In British India, the region considered by medical experts to have the highest incidence of leprosy, clinical research led to new drug therapy trials and engendered an intense debate over the medical utility of segregation. Overcoming resistance from some medical experts, secular and Christian activists, and Indians themselves, the authorities established Christian and secular segregation facilities.[18]

In Northern Nigeria, British medical officer Dr. J. M. Dalziel undertook the first research into leprosy distribution in 1910, after the Second World Conference on Leprosy.[19] He found high prevalence in some areas, like Sokoto, and the *Official Gazette of Nigeria* cited his report and others to suggest that leprosy was "more common among Mahommedans than among the Pagan tribes."[20] Dalziel himself wrote that religion could explain the greater mobility of some carriers, who received alms (*zakat*) from Muslims obligated to support the less fortunate, but he did not see any connection between religion and treatment of prohibition on sufferers. His survey turned up a variety of practices among Muslims, including a prohibition of sufferers marrying noninfected people. Although he argued that large leprosy facilities were not yet feasible in Northern Nigeria, his discussion with the Sultan of Sokoto led him to think that the British could subtly suggest segregation of sufferers as a method of prevention. The sultan asked that titled officials, *sarakuna*, who had leprosy not be bothered. For them, Dalziel recommended that "a little tactfully offered advice or persuasion on regard to modified isolation within their own ménage, cleanliness of person and houses ... etc., would probably not alienate their sympathies from the proposed measure."[21]

From the very earliest colonial interventions in leprosy control in Northern Nigeria, class determined the extent to which sufferers were affected. The 1910 Lepers Proclamation, which took effect throughout the region, established two different actions—effective segregation and absolute segregation—to be taken in cases of suspected leprosy sufferers.[22] Newly created lazarets, shelters providing food and other aid, were established using Native Administration funds in various emirates to support absolute segregation.[23] The proclamation was mostly symbolic but created a new space of interaction between alms-seekers and almsgivers, where, before, leprosy sufferers were generally not physically separated, only avoided in some social interactions. The law formalized the use of the Native Administration's zakat collections for this medically sanctioned purpose.

Though quite meager, these government actions toward leprosy control in Northern Nigeria appear to be unique among other British territories in Asia and Africa. Elsewhere, Christian missions took over leprosy control relatively early in colonial history because of governmental disinterest or accord with Christian missions, the ready association between Christian healing and leprosy, and medical missions' relatively abundant resources.[24] Missions were more limited and otherwise preoccupied in Muslim Northern Nigeria. Though several medical missionaries worked in Northern Nigeria, some avoided medical work because of ongoing debates on what mission evangelism should be and a personal feeling of impotence in treating tropical diseases.[25] Dr. Walter Miller of the Church Missionary Society (CMS) in Zaria, as early as 1903, wrote to friends back home: "We get only chronics, like sleeping sickness, total blindness, quite hopeless, and so on; all other cases they keep to themselves. There are no hospital cases; they are not the sort of things one sees in these countries; people get queer pains in their backs, which if you don't cure at once they look on you as hopeless and no good."[26]

Andrew Stirrett, a pharmacist who spearheaded much of the Sudan Interior Mission (SIM) work in cities like Minna and Jos until the 1920s, took more of an ad hoc approach to medical work. Stirrett detailed simple treatments that Christian missionaries could provide in the course of their other mission work in a small pamphlet titled *Cerebro-Spinal Meningitis and Relapsing Fever*.[27] Beyond the clearing of dust and keeping free of lice, his main advice was to pray: "[Relapsing fever] is a very dangerous disease and has killed very many." Christian missionaries had few medicines to offer other than some antiseptics and painkillers. As in other parts of Africa, surgeries for cataracts, removal of teeth, and the like were more likely to raise the esteem of missionaries than their then rudimentary medicines.[28]

The discovery of new botanicals presumed to be useful in combating leprosy in the 1920s elicited a new hope among colonial authorities and missionaries. The seeds and oil of the *hydnocarpus wightiana* tree, also known as chaulmoogra, were identified in Indian and Chinese medicine as treatments for leprosy. Colonial researchers experimented with mixtures of oil esters with sodium hydnocarpate (Alepol), potassium iodide, or other compounds.[29] In 1922, in the Malay States, a Chinese method (known as Tai Foong Chee) of administration of a powdered seed mixture directly by mouth was touted as a major improvement over injections.[30] According to Dr. E. A. O. Travers of the Kuala Lumpur General Hospital, the mixture of two different kinds of hydnocarpus nuts with hemp seeds kept several of the Chinese patients virtually symptom-free. Travers explained:

> The patients collect round of the attendants (a leper), who is provided with a pail full of the powder and a little aluminum measure. . . . He measures a dose into each leper's hand. . . . As the attendant gives each dose he shouts the name of the patient, and another patient makes a mark against his name on a large paper. The steward (a leper) stands by, to see that each dose is swallowed, and the number of doses taken each month by every leper is registered in a book kept by the medical officer. The Chinese lepers have become so extraordinarily quick and efficient at this work that over three hundred and fifty doses are given and registered in under half an hour.[31]

A circular about this method went out to the colonies in 1925, and authorities throughout British colonies and protectorates began seeking to import seeds with which to start local plantings. Trinidad began growing hydnocarpus plants in the Port of Spain botanical garden in 1922, and, following Travers's research, Governor Graeme Thomson of Nigeria, along with leprosarium authorities in Basutoland and a representative of Albert Schweitzer's mission in Ogowe, French Equatorial Africa, sought to replicate the Trinidad farm. They argued that they could produce fresher medicines locally and weather any shortage in seeds, given that demand was increasing.[32]

Leprosy had already piqued the Nigerian governor's interest by the time the Scottish United Free Church Mission Society approached the colonial authorities for land in southeastern Nigeria for a leprosy settlement.[33] The missionary Dr. Macdonald began helping a handful of sufferers in late 1926 and, by March 1927, the number of patients had swelled to nearly three hundred. His request had first been for land, then materials for housing, and, finally, general assistance. Governor Thomson was so pleased with the cooperation at Itu, what became the Scottish mission leprosarium, he used it as a model for encouraging the Colonial Office to contemplate a campaign throughout Nigeria.³⁴ He recommended that the expansion occur under a representative of BELRA.

Thomson argued that Itu was so successful that medical mission-government cooperation could extend to education and general medical care, if the government did "all possible to avoid suspicion that Govt [sic] is subsidising alien religious propaganda."³⁵ The Secretary of State for the Colonies recommended tighter control over missions to avoid the precedent in Southern Nigeria, where Christian educational institutions commanded "drastic power."³⁶ Part of the power of missions, argued J. E. W. Flood of the Colonial Office, was their effective use of free services. He wrote: "The Medical Department are inclined to be jealous of the medical missionaries who don't charge fees but who do get at the people. Dr. Adam as an ex-missionary has no sympathy with this attitude and he has converted Dr. Alexander."³⁷

Ever fearful of "propaganda" in Muslim areas, the Colonial Office recommended that medical missions first be let into "pagan" areas of Northern Nigeria, where they could prove their trustworthiness to native and British authorities and then later be rewarded with sites in Muslim areas. British provincial residents were regularly to inspect these sites. The Kano authorities already had their guard up as a result of Ethel Miller's publications and the local converts' lodging within Kano Old City, and they were concerned with missions' "misusing" approved sites for ulterior purposes.

In 1928, the British authorities accepted a proposal from the American Church of the Brethren, a Mennonite mission, to work with native and British authorities in establishing a leprosy colony at Garkida, in a part of Adamawa Province that was largely non-Muslim with Muslim communities nearby.³⁸ Garkida was also an experimental farm; on the five hundred acres given by the Native Administration for leprosy sufferers, the Brethren introduced new crops, such as strawberries, and new species of cows.³⁹ A school was opened. Within two years, patients released as "arrested cases" settled on the periphery, where they were taught reading and writing and simple health care. This arrangement satisfied the government that the Brethren mission was producing productive and healthy people who remained "obedient" to the Native Administration.

Satisfied that he had found a pragmatic solution to the political problem of missions in Muslim spheres and to the social "backwardness" that the British were accused of letting fester, Thomson left the business of expanding the model to his successor, Sir Donald Cameron.⁴⁰ Cameron endorsed it, urging representatives of Christian missions to wait patiently for their chance to enter the emirates at an interview in 1931. He responded to the

SIM's complaints that they had been refused a site for an ordinary station in Garko in rural Kano by referring to the short time since 1927, when his predecessor, Thomson, promised to "educate Emirs in tolerance": "Four years [is] a short time in which to inculcate in Mohammedan rulers ideas which were foreign to their own training and that of their ancestors. We couldn't seat them in a row, put a pistol to their heads and educate them."[41] Cameron advised that missions should try to succeed in places like Garkida, on the margins, and then the people themselves in the central Mohammedan areas would invite them in.[42] Confidence in the Emirs and the missions ran high. No one anticipated how African patients themselves would respond.

AN UNRESTRAINED ENTHUSIASM: THE MISSIONARY DOCTOR AND THE ANGRY MOB

A political thaw allowed Christians to obtain certificates to occupy sites in Muslim spheres between 1931 and 1937, even before the Christian missions officially entered into the cooperative leprosy agreements with Native Administrations in Kano, Katsina, Bauchi, Niger, and Sokoto Provinces.[43] Better British feelings toward Christians among Muslims grew with the missions' provision of social and medical services for Africans and with the Emirs' support of social welfare investments, more generally, in their domains, although the missions still had not obtained plots for schools. In Kano, girls' and boys' elementary schools, in both Arabic and boko mediums, increased in number, thanks to Native Administration funds, and older pupils of these schools were sent to train as nurses in the Native Administration hospitals.[44] Trainees were sent to Kano from other emirates.[45] Yet Kano City Hospital could not serve the needs of patients from even the immediate environs, and the Colonial Office received reports that the Emir had voiced his desire that only urban "citizens" use the City Hospital.[46] The British Resident of Kano disputed this, but the process of admitting patients, ascertaining their area of domicile, and then getting on to the business of treating them all made clear that the medical institutions could not meet growing demand.

The government's decision to give the SIM its first station in Kano Province at Garko, in the rural southeast, was clearly in the interest of promoting medical work. SIM was also given a site in Kano Township as a forwarding station from which it could conduct business at its stations in French Niger.[47] The CMS, despite the animosity among British Residents toward Dr. Walter Miller, was granted a plot in Fagge for a church for African Christians and given sites in southern Katsina Province, at Bakori and Funtua, where clinics were established. The Emir of Kano and the Resident, acting in conformity with the earlier ban on public preaching, sought to isolate the missions' proselytization to these specific sites by explicitly banning market and roadside preaching in the first certificates of occupancy.[48]

In 1935, when leprosy work was still confined to the existing Native Administration lazarets, Will Lambert arrived. Lambert did not work for any of the Christian missions already in Kano or any in the Northern Provinces, for that matter. He was affiliated with Toc H, a mission founded by World War I British army chaplain Tubby Clayton.[49] BELRA asked Toc H for volunteers for Africa in 1934, and Lambert, after taking a twelve-month medical course at Livingstone College, London, arrived first at Itu and then went to Kano.[50] Lambert initially worked with another doctor, Carlton Howard, and then on his own for several months. He took two dozen leprosy sufferers selected from the lazaret four miles outside Kano City to a new site at Sumaila, twenty-three miles away, where the patients labored to turn "Nigerian bush into farmland."[51] In addition to starting farms for food crops and cotton to spin into bandages, Lambert found a blacksmith and potter among the leprosy sufferers who "came drifting in."[52] A well was dug, and every man and boy had a farm. Lambert taught reading and trained six nurses in injections. The Tai Foong Chee oral administration method was never practiced in Nigeria, but the methods of administration described in the Malay States were. By the time he left in November 1936, Lambert noted that the "healthy" villages might have envied the leprosy settlement's farms.[53]

The Sumaila settlement was working well when Ernest Muir of BELRA undertook his tour and proposed his scheme, but he needed to secure the cooperation of Christian mission societies that were larger than Toc H if he was to expand the missionary investment in leprosy segregation. Dr. Miller of the CMS, about whom Lambert spoke very highly, turned down Muir's request to join the effort. He wrote to Muir, dismissing the prospects for collaboration with the Native Administration: "Islam has looked upon the leper as a man or woman to give alms to, not to cure or help. The Native Administration is passively opposed to segregation and british [sic] treatment, and resents the removal of people who as recipients of alms help the pious moslem [sic] go to Heaven."[54] Miller was, by now, thoroughly alienated from the British and native political authorities, his sister Ethel Miller, and SIM missionaries. The latter were especially peeved because the British authorities informed them that Walter Miller's attempts to move from Zaria to Kano had resulted in heavier scrutiny and delays on all Christian missions' applications for sites throughout Muslim areas.[55] Miller disparaged the SIM as crude: "a strong driving force; working with the usual American mass tactics, and efficient even from a commercial point of view. Men and women will be sent in platoons; money will be poured out—not always wisely."[56]

The American factor proved important in the SIM's negotiations for five leprosariums in the Northern Provinces and the eventual overshadowing of BELRA, the sponsor of Garkida and Sumaila. American research into leprosy was as advanced as British research, and the American Mission to Lepers (AMTL), which supported the Brethren at Garkida, had on its board influential wealthy spirits distillers who had switched to pharmaceutical work during the era of Prohibition in America.[57] Dr. Albert Helser, a Canadian who came to Nigeria in 1922 with the Church of Brethren and supervised the Garkida Leprosarium for nearly ten years, joined the SIM to become its superintendent of leprosy work in 1936. Helser reportedly had had a falling-out with the Brethren, a mission he considered too "modern."[58] Although the Brethren warned the British authorities about Helser's fundamentalist Christian beliefs,[59] Helser had strong secular credentials, including a PhD in education from Columbia University, where he studied with the anthropologist Franz Boas and with Mabel Carney, a pioneer of rural education in the American South and South Africa.[60] Both of these mentors wrote approvingly of Helser's use of folklore of the Bura people at Garkida as a basis for adapting Western education for Africans,[61] a topic that Americans had influenced through the Phelps-Stokes Commission, which promoted an agriculturally oriented educational scheme as the solution for black poverty in the American South.[62] In a 1940 review of Helser's book, *Education of Primitive People*, Eric Hussey, director of education in Nigeria from 1929 to 1936, appreciated Helser's efforts to "induce a higher scale of values," based on Christianity, without the need "to fulminate against pagan beliefs and practices."[63] For his magnanimous personality, Helser acquired the nickname Asharomo (meaning "let one drink broth" in Hausa), by which he was commonly known around Kano.

The American SIM also had the added advantage in availability of doctors and other staff that resulted from the Italian expulsion of American missionaries from Ethiopia in 1937.[64] Dr. Thomas Lambie, an American SIM missionary who worked as the personal physician to Haile Selassie, traveled to Nigeria to help SIM negotiate the leprosy takeover.[65]

After the negotiations were concluded in 1937, SIM trained three doctors—Cecil Morris, William Jotcham, and Edwin Harris, previously in Congo—at their Hausa language school in Minna, and then sent each to his assignment. Harris took over Sumaila (Kano), the largest, while Morris went to Sokoto and Jotcham to Katsina. SIM celebrated the new openings with a photo spread titled "Peaceful Invasion of the Northern Emirates of Nigeria."[66] Yet, Harris, in his self-published diary, described this period as much more difficult than SIM narratives suggest.[67]

He took up his post just as the rainy season began, but, though the rain had come to nearby villages, Sumaila remained dry for two long weeks. Muslim teachers told the people that the arrival of Harris, with his family, and Harold Saul, the administrative manager, delayed the rains. The villagers held prayer vigils night and day, to no avail. A mob then came to the dispensary with clubs and swords, chanting "Muna bukata ruwan sama!" (We need rain). A woman approached Harris and, stopping at the door to the dispensary, showed Harris a knife. The doctor's Hausa was rudimentary, so his African factotum Paulo, from Garkida, translated: "She says that you have prevented rain from coming, and so their crops will fail and they will starve. She also says that she has inherited this knife from her father who was a butcher, and that it is very sharp, and ready to use."

"May Allah give you all wellness," Harris answered in Hausa. She answered, "Amin," and left, telling the crowd what had happened. The mob dispersed. Harris wrote that a few hours later the rains came in torrents, blowing roofs off many villagers' houses.

After the rains came and the villagers seemed too busy to come to the mission, Harris and the other missionaries decided to "show" themselves to the people. Accompanied by a zealous young man hanging from the running board of their Ford sedan, shouting out that the whites could heal anyone, the missionaries had their car stoned in one town. In another, they were completely surrounded in a market by people "actually crushing each other against the car." Harris admitted that he did not know what to make of it at the time and only later began to see that he was not prepared for the people's need or their "unrestrained enthusiasm."[68]

The SIM could not have predicted the volatility their "peaceful invasion" caused. The white missionaries now had freedom of movement, whereas, until this time, African evangelists and other Christian converts often took great care to be ambiguous in their public identifications. The white missionaries, on the other hand, came with promises of plenty, in this case promises of health for leprosy sufferers. The power of rainmaking was celebrated and sought in both indigenous African religions and Islam in many parts of Africa,[69] and what seemed to threaten the Sumaila and surrounding villagers most was losing the apparent abundance Lambert had left. Moreover, they appeared to be suffering for having the missionaries among them, as compared to their neighbors, who had rain and no strangers around. The SIM's main argument for moving the leprosarium from Sumaila to Ya da Kunya (meaning "cast off shame"), closer to Kano City, was irregular water supply, in spite of Will Lambert's previous successes.[70]

Despite the difficulties, the SIM made a good friend in the District Head of Sumaila, 'dan Darma. The manager, Harold Saul, presented him a Hausa Bible and visited him regularly, declaring 'dan Darma to be a Christian. After the SIM moved the leprosarium to Ya da Kunya, Saul returned to Sumaila, where 'dan Darma reported that he was still a Christian but that Muslim leaders persecuted him so severely that he had to hide his true belief.[71] Harris wrote, "There were some so called 'professional' missionaries who told me that they seriously questioned 'dan Darma's conversion because, they said, he had never been baptized, nor ever became a member of an established Church. To this I say, remember the thief on the cross beside Jesus? He believed, and was saved yet he never was baptized, nor came off his cross to become a member an established church. . . . I am sure I'll meet 'dan Darma in Heaven when I get there."[72]

Missionaries began to write more of "secret believers," comparing them to Nicodemus in the Bible (John 3:16), a well-to-do Pharisee who could not in this lifetime confess his belief in Christ, or else he would lose his position. But he was born again in death for his belief. The discourses of secrecy and rebirth in death eased the ways in which SIM missionaries approached their cordial but uncommitted hosts.[73] The missionaries thus set a certain standard for influential Muslims out of pragmatic concerns while expecting very different kinds of behavior from ordinary people, particularly those in the leprosarium context.

Cooperation with Muslim leaders continued after the missionaries moved the leprosarium to Ya da Kunya and in Katsina, Sokoto, and the many regular mission stations that opened throughout rural Hausaland. The village head of Ya da Kunya married his son to the granddaughter of the Emir of Kano, and the wife of Dr. Harris went to "pay her respects" to the new bride.[74] Offering gifts of Bibles and invariably receiving requests from Muslims for more reading materials and the opportunities for religious discussions, the missionaries' activities were increasingly tied to political leaders, even as conversion among leprosarium patients increased the Christian fold considerably.

DYNAMICS OF THE LEPROSARIUM

SIM medical missionaries spent a great deal of time recording and reporting on their efforts to major donors like the American Mission to Lepers

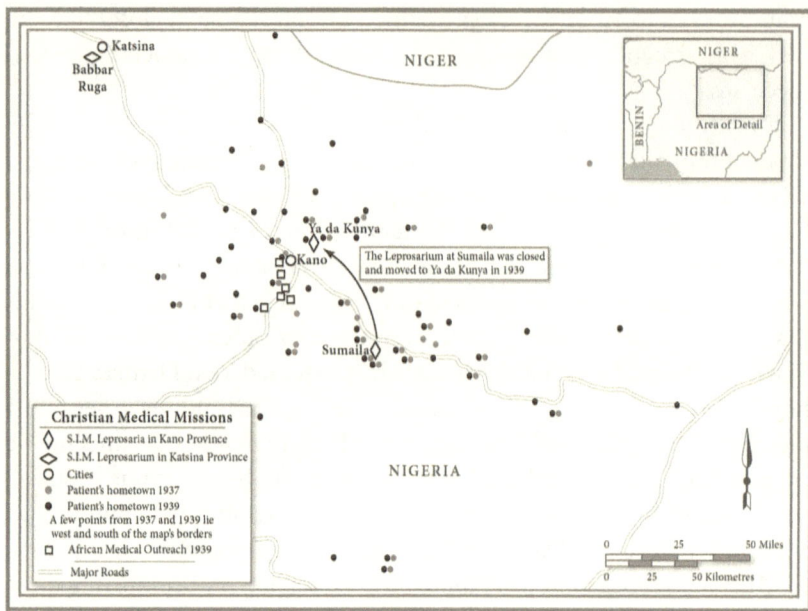

Map 4.1. Patients at the SIM Kano leprosarium came from a long distance. African Christians undertook itinerant medical work to establish outposts beyond mission control, 1937–1939. (Drawn by Gerry Krieg; developed from SIM patient lists and station reports.)

and to congregations. Dr. Harris noted that charts on every patient needed a significant amount of detail as to the diagnosis and treatments patients received. His job became complicated after Dr. Jotcham at Katsina died from cerebrospinal meningitis in late 1937. Harris had to travel between Kano and Katsina and make field visits to villages and the Kano City prison to investigate suspected cases of leprosy. He acknowledged that much of the day-to-day documentation on all of this activity was lost.[75]

Two surviving documents, one from Sumaila in 1937 and the second from Ya da Kunya in 1939, list names of all leprosy sufferers and their towns or villages and districts. They show the growth of the total number of patients, from 190 to 346.[76] The more central location of Ya da Kunya helped draw patients from a wider geographical area of Kano Province, whereas previously most patients reported they were from Sumaila (see map 4.1). The leprosarium population was mostly Muslim. In 1937, just four patients hailed from Sabon Gari Kano, the aliens' enclave, and, of these, one patient, Audu, had a Muslim name. In 1939, the three Christians from two years earlier—Zakirai (Zachary), Margaret, and Boye Kete—were still under SIM's care, along with Isaiah, James, and Cyril. The proportion of Christian patients, if gleaned purely by name, was very small.

The cadre of Christian African medical workers remained small at first because Dr. Helser wanted to make sure the SIM had "full control" of the leprosariums before sending "native missionaries" anywhere.[77] When the takeover was complete in Kano, the SIM sent Adamu Kano and another former government leprosy worker to the Kano City Native Hospital and brought on men like William Mafobi and Joel Shellem from outside the area (in this case, Yorubaland and Adamawa).[78] Youngsters in mission stations like Wushishi learned, almost as a rite of passage, to mix medicines, administer nose drops, and dress wounds to prove their preparation for being sent into the emirates, but single or married males were preferred over unmarried girls.[79] Not all young men saw medical work as an opportunity, however. African Christians did not feel that they stood to gain the same respect that foreign Christian missionaries gained from Muslims, particularly the elites, as a result of medical work. Because of the reticence of local Hausa Christians to take on medical work, which involved giving intramuscular injections, former leprosy suffers from Garkida and other non-Hausa areas arrived to work in the Hausa areas. The opening of new mission stations and the continued expansion of the leprosarium in Kano created demand for skills like masonry.

Native evangelists were expected to be supported by their congregations, which were small and poor.[80] The material rewards were not the same for African Christians as for white missionaries, who worked, according to one Christian Northern Nigerian woman, for *lada*, a word meaning anticipated reward or merit for good works done on behalf of God or a wealthy benefactor.[81] Christian workers in the day-to-day operations of the leprosariums did not stand to gain as much as leprosy sufferers, for whom Muslim Native Administrations supplied land. The average-size plot was half an acre, parceled out to able-bodied men and boys, and those who could work larger plots received as much as two to three acres.[82] The leprosy sufferers also had more spacious housing, about five houses per eight occupants, as recommended by government doctors.[83] Dr. Daly of the Katsina Medical Department emphasized the importance of this ratio on a visit to the Katsina leprosarium in 1938, after an outbreak of cerebrospinal meningitis led to fatalities surpassing the previous year's mortality.

Christian missionaries stressed literacy for leprosy sufferers and worked closely with government officials to produce Hausa instructional reading materials.[84] Now, in addition to religious texts, the SIM was involved in the production of medical texts. The detailed Hausa language primer on leprosy, *Kuturta*, was produced by government printers in the 1930s and rereleased in the 1950s. Expanding literacy among the leprosarium populations meant a new kind of authority for people previously unconnected to Roman script. The instruction in the leprosariums was very much restricted to men and boys. In Sokoto, for example, two "dispensary boys" taught two classes for boys and men, one for beginners and the other for more advanced readers. The classes covered print and cursive, and "special classes in numbers are held for the leper nurses to teach them how to read the thermometers and keep their charts."[85]

At the Sokoto leprosarium, just four women received instruction, in the hope that they would teach others.[86] Women left their children to play in the picture room (*da'kin foto*), where images of children playing, flowers, and animals on cardboard were hung from string across the walls. In addition, stuffed animals and a beanbag kept the children busy because as, Helser noted, they "are not allowed to come in . . . while the women are learning to read." None of the camps had many young children. Helser noted that "a woman may bring her husband but in Hausaland they usually leave their families at home."[87] The population of every leprosarium, from the Brethren-run Garkida settlement in Adamawa to Sokoto in the west, tended to be mostly male. Early on, in December 1938, females accounted for almost half of the population at Kano, but within six months, the male population nearly doubled and became two-thirds of the roughly three hundred patients.[88]

Though the leprosariums were residential institutions, their records show the emerging distinctions between *maganin asibiti* (hospital medicine) and mobile medicine. While males took advantage of the leprosariums, Muslim women took advantage of the mobile missionary medical assistance that the SIM provided while they "trekked in search of lepers" or to advertise their new dispensaries. Pauline Guyer, a nurse in Malumfashi, Katsina, described treating many women in their homes and, in one, she was brought a six-month-old baby weighing about four pounds. As family members watched, she showed them how to give the baby feedings of milk from a spoon. "At my suggestion," she wrote, "they were arranging to get a goat to milk so that the little one could have the nourishment it needed."[89]

In Ruma, in Katsina Emirate, the wife of the missionary in charge, John Vander Schie, arrived at the house of the chief to find his senior wife "all dressed up in velvets and brocades." A child's doll was the main attraction. "Women came from everywhere and nowhere and each one had the privilege of holding it. They passed it from one to another like a baby, careful to hold one hand under its neck and another under its back. We enjoyed this pleasant visit with the women in the compound, and Miss Hooge [an SIM nurse] and myself were invited back the next afternoon. We found, incidentally, that the chief's wife is a daughter of the Emir of Katsina." The chief's distant demeanor melted the next day, and he "confided to John [Mr. Vander Schie] that his wife had 'evil spirits' every afternoon." The missionary records: "Nurse Hooge decided the woman was suffering from high blood pressure, as she was unusually stout, and suffered from terrific headaches during the heat of the day. She was given a dose of salts, and told to rest during the heat of every day with wet leaves on her head."[90]

Later that same day, the chief came to fetch the missionaries to report that more medicine was needed. "There were suddenly many in his town who were ill, and his wife had not had an attack of evil spirits!" The house was decorated "with tapestries and brilliant hangings of every description. . . . There was a strong smell of burning incense. Mats and tapestries were laid on the floor to sit on, although two native made chairs were also available. The scene was quite oriental, and we were reminded again of Bible stories. As we sat visiting, showing pictures, and having a nice time together, we were constantly fanned with ostrich feather fans in the hands of some of the black servants."[91] Meanwhile, the chief gathered the town's leprosy sufferers to send with the missionaries back to the Katsina settlement.

More elite women seemed to take greater advantage of the missionary mobile services than less well-to-do women. At the leprosariums themselves, the most notable mention of an elite patient was a sister of the Emir of Kano who lived at Ya da Kunya and enjoyed painting. Women's literacy and medical training were not promoted except for inquirers seeking religious construction. The idea that women did not want for much held over from the struggles over education in the 1920s (see chapter 3) and gave the SIM little reason to invest specifically in women's health.

White women medical missionaries, furthermore, did not command the authority of male missionaries. Nurse Martha Wall, while at the dispensary at Jega, in Sokoto Province, met a boy who had been bitten by a rabid dog. Wall and Dr. Titus Payne, the medical director of the Sokoto leprosarium, recommended that the boy go to the city where serum was available.[92] A man arrived to say that the boy's mother refused. "I protested that that was ridiculous, that she was callously asking her son to give up his life for her selfish whim," wrote Wall. "Furthermore, I added, the boy was old enough to judge for himself as he was fully grown. 'What can we do?' countered the older man. 'You know what women are like?' I ignored the thrust at my sex and told him [the son] to disregard her. I pled with them almost tearfully.... I even told the older man he should be held responsible if the lad died.... Fools! We had offered them life—there was no money involved, even the trip to Sokoto was free. Yet they had chosen death, walking away without hesitation or wavering. Fools!"[93] Wall would likely have had no access to any patients if Dr. Payne were not present. Some women missionaries reported that they could never enter a compound when male heads of household were present.

African women's avoidance of the leprosariums made young men the mainstays, a demographic bias that was a direct result of the social dynamics of the leprosariums and mobile medicine. While missionaries and Emirs recognized this disparity in the population, it was rarely acknowledged to be a problem. Harold Saul, manager of the Kano leprosarium, told a story of one young man, whose difficulties in maintaining Christianity were due to the pressure of a girl whom he sought to marry: "This has brought to our attention that we must lay this before the Lord that he will bring either Christian girls to the camp or else pagan girls who will not be influenced by the mallams and who will become Christians so that our unmarried boys may be able to find wives."[94] The sex ratios in the Christian leprosariums were exactly reversed from the days of the freed slave homes in the early 1900s. While the leprosariums served the political purpose of cooperation and the medical and social interests of an increasingly narrow group, the medical work began to change the nature of Christian conversion, which no longer readily held out the promise of a wife or remunerative occupation within the missions. Religious debates and reading from the Bible, activities by which Christians once distinguished themselves, also became less important in the leprosariums.

NO IMPREGNABLE WALL

Between 1938 and 1939, the SIM grew in influence. In Jega, in Sokoto Province, the missionary in charge, Howard Borlase, received a shipment of medicine on August 7, 1938, and, the next morning, found that thieves had broken in. Dusting powders, ulcer powders, and aspirins were strewn about the floor. Borlase wrote, "It was pitiful to hear the remarks the patients made as they came one by one. Some even cried to see their good medicine all wasted on the ground. The most general remark was, 'We've been cheated, we've been cheated.'" The thieves had been interested in only a few small things: aprons, little dishes for washing ulcers, and two tins of ointment, one boric and one menthol Mecca brand. The local district head, the Sarkin Kebbi, was considered a close friend of the SIM, a secret believer. He felt so badly upon hearing the news that "he seemed to feel that the offence was as much against himself as us," wrote Borlase. The missionary asked the Sarkin Kebbi not to tell the British district officer and instead handled it through the Emir of Gwandu, whom the missionaries considered a secret believer. The key suspects were young men "connected with the local Native Administration dispensary."[95] Some patients reported to Borlase that they preferred the mission medicine—*maganin Almasihu* (literally, medicine of the Messiah)—over the Native Administration's *maganin banza* (worthless medicine).

A few months later, in 1939, the missionary John Vander Schie at Malumfashi in Katsina was "startled" to learn that the district head and *galadima* (another titled official) of the town were virtually at war with each other.[96] The missionaries had realized, from the time of their 1938 arrival in Malumfashi, that the town was embroiled in a moral competition because of the presence of Muslims, non-Muslim Maguzawa (pagans), and clerks from Southern Nigeria, described by the SIM as "living for the devil."[97] The district head disclosed that the galadima had come to the mosque only four times during his eleven years of holding this important title. No one ever observed him fasting at Ramadan, and it was rumored that he ordered his *malamai* (clerics) to kill a ram, bury it within his compound, and hold meetings on this mound. The district head carried the secret of this *tsafi* (magic) and did not tell the Emir of Katsina. But he confided in Vander Schie, who thereafter better understood why he had never faced any censure for preaching in public. "While the Mohammedans stick together as one, it is not the impregnable wall here that I once thought it was." One Bamaguje (pagan) youth, interpreting the Muslims' weakness before the Christian mission, happily told Vander Schie that he had learned from "beggars [lepers and blind people] that a special place will be reserved in heaven for the Maguzawa and they will have all the beer they can drink. He said he could give up anything but his drink!"[98]

Vander Schie did not, of course, approve of this version of Christian eschatology, but the missionaries' success often came at the cost of losing control over their messages. As the SIM's influence grew, the Emirs of Katsina and Kano complained to the Chief Commissioner of the Northern Provinces about "proselytization in connection with the Leper Camps and dispensaries."[99] The commissioner worded his account of the Emirs' view carefully—they wanted to prohibit any religious instruction to children, but, "should any adult Moslem of his own volition, and not as the result of being 'called' (i.e. persuaded) by a Mission, wish to learn something of the Christian Religion it would not be proper for any Moslem to interfere."[100]

The Emirs complained that the SIM was using medicine to proselytize and convert sick and vulnerable people to Christianity.[101] The British began to worry that the cooperative scheme was at risk. The British, as brokers between the Emirs and the SIM, could give neither side enough control to satisfy them. The Chief Commissioner and the Secretary of the Northern Provinces debated the possible designation of the missions as independent contractors so that aggrieved individuals did not take up complaints with the Native Administrations, but instead with the British authorities. Yet the commissioner, Adams, questioned whether this plan would provide for sufficient governmental oversight of the missions.[102]

The British authorities also discussed adding clauses to the leprosarium agreements to define the primary purpose of the missions as medical and prevent them from undertaking educational work. But some others worried that such a measure would lead to accusations that the colonial government was disinterested in African social welfare.[103] The wrangling continued into 1940, when the British government authorized the Colonial Welfare and Development Act as a way to answer critics who accused the imperial government of not doing enough in Africa.[104] An amount of ten thousand pounds for medical work was discussed, and the SIM let it be known that this amount was not enough for the Northern Provinces to go about medical work on its own, threatening to pull out of the agreement.[105]

The more interesting debate was not about whether or not mission-Muslim collaboration should continue but rather about how to define the age and autonomy of children. The SIM refused to agree to the insertion of a clause prohibiting the teaching of children under the age of eighteen. The Emirs viewed age as measured not in years or by physical puberty (*balaga*), but, instead, by a young person's discretion and relationship to elders. As they continued to debate, Chief Commissioner Adams referred to children of Muslim parents as "protected." Children of "pagans," he noted, were not.[106]

What prompted this protectionism, this new category of child debated in legal and biological terms?[107] The fosterage of children by Muslim Emirs and missionaries had never been questioned before, and the practice of removing youngsters from mothers infected with leprosy was the accepted standard. This discussion was not about very young children, however. Instead, the debate concerned those on the cusp of adulthood, on the imprecise line between self-determination and dependence, whose religious education and mobility came to be a matter of concern in the competitive religious environment brewing in the SIM leprosariums and stations. The effort to police youth was an effort to police the influence of Christian religious and medical proselytism.

Two young men were arrested in 1941 and brought before the Emir of Kano, the district officer, and the Resident for peddling medicines and Bibles. One of these men was Ibrahim, a former patient of the Katsina leprosarium who apparently had shown no interest in the Bible while a patient, according to a missionary source, but later took up evangelism at Matazu, a village known as a haven for Isawa dissidents (see chapter 1).[108] Missionaries in Zaria had already evangelized the Isawa as early as the 1910s, but now, in Kano and Kazaure Emirates, Muslim teachers appeared to be using Injil, the New Testament, in Arabic script to lead their own prayer groups within and near the leprosariums. Adams claimed that the men had native drugs, penicillin, and other materia medica, whereas Playfair of the SIM claimed it was simply iodine and quinine, like the kind available in Kano stores. Playfair denied the SIM's authority over them, referring the authorities to the British Foreign Bible Service (BFBS).[109] The BFBS, for their part, reported that they had given the texts to the men, but not the medicines, which had to have come from the SIM. These lay evangelists, if they may be called that, had clearly found that medicine and books were attracting many Muslim inquirers. At the Roni SIM station, the missionary in charge reported that "the government or native administration has removed all who cannot read our English script from their positions so it has stirred up a bigger interest in learning to read. A rather sharp division has come amongst them [the *malamai*], entirely on their own part with some wanting to learn to read the Bible and test out its truth with the others stubbornly refusing."[110]

The SIM attributed the "problem" of youth to the Emirs' fear of the growing success of Christianity, but it is likely that the pressure came from Muslim scholars within and near the leprosariums. The SIM suspected that Muslim jurists from Egypt and Sudan, whom the British had brought to Northern Nigeria to teach law and Arabic, were advising the Emirs of Kano and Katsina. The SIM contrasted these more "radical" Emirs with the Sultan of Sokoto and the Emir of Gwandu, who had worked very well with the missionaries, the latter nearly converting to Christianity.[111] Missionary education had escalated competition over knowledge of all kinds but also increased debates between Emirs, shar'ia experts, and scholars of theology over the proper lines between Muslims and non-Muslims. The leprosariums, more specifically, shaped a new definition of education. Christian missionaries began to speak of it as a "right." The British authorities, who formerly controlled education tightly, by the 1940s saw schools as necessary for "public health" and, in places like Gold Coast and Southern Nigeria, vital to political negotiation with African nationalists. Now, Muslim elites, who had long worried that mission or government education would encourage insubordination among youth, began to view education as a competitive political reward.

Adams remarked, "One has got to remember that Emirs are quite as keen to give children of Christians Mohammedan teaching as the missions are to give children of Mohammedans (Christians in embryo) Christian teaching."[112] He recommended that professing adult Christians be required to appear before Emirs to secure permission for their children to receive Christian education. Adams wanted Christian adults to appear before the Emir in a kind of public confession that had no precedent aside perhaps from Ari's situation (chapter 2).

The situation threatened to break apart the cooperative agreements. A compromise was reached in 1942 when new clauses were inserted into the agreements. The Native Administration would operate a building for the care of children under the age of five as well as a mosque that would serve as the center of religious instruction.[113] The administrations would also appoint African women to oversee the crèches, although finding suitable Muslim girls from the Native Administration schools was a problem that often resulted in the hiring of Christian girls from Southern Nigeria, since many Northern Nigerian Christian girls did not want to do this work.[114] The minimum age for religious instruction was eighteen. Thus, the remedy was to situate Islamic religious institutions within the leprosariums, thereby creating more surveillance of and social pressure against Christian conversion. The strategy ensured that Muslim religious instruction would be available alongside Christian mission education, rendering the leprosariums religiously competitive fields.

CONCLUSION

The cooperative medical work had profound effects in popularizing Christian mission culture and making it more available. Since conversion to Christianity was not mandatory and could be secret, Muslims could participate without costs, monetary or loss of prestige, as far as we can tell from the available sources. This situation produced a good many "Muslim Christians," a status that unsettled the more devout members of both religions.[115] It did not help that many of these half-converts were young men.

Evangelism became more democratic as Muslims and Christians broke with Emirs and missionaries who were in charge of the leprosariums. By

1940, it was rumored that Emirs were discussing the possibilities of sending "Moslems among Pagans."[116] The target of this evangelism is not clear. Were the Emirs seeking to compete with the white missionaries? Were they responding to the fact that "pagans" had achieved authority among Muslims through medical training and conversion to Christianity? In the SIM's annual review for 1941, the mission celebrated the increase of Hausa literacy among Christian converts from pagan communities. These new Christians began taking monetary collections in churches for "foreign missions," mostly meaning for the work of migrants in the emirates.[117] Neither the missionaries nor the British or native rulers appreciated the competitiveness of the lay Christian networks connecting the leprosariums to rural areas.

5 ⤚ Joining in the Melee
Soldiers, Youth, and Rural Revivalism,
1945–1950

IN 1941, Sudan Interior Mission (SIM) missionaries met with representatives of the Kano Native Administration and the British Resident and colonial medical officers, as they did regularly to discuss progress at the provincial leprosarium. The conflict over the teaching of children in the leprosariums had abated with new clauses stipulating the minimum age of eighteen for "religious instruction," but a new problem had arisen in Kano. The Sarkin Kutare, the "chief" of the leprosy sufferers at the settlement who had been given a title created on the model of the political bureaucracy of the emirate system, had kept order among the four hundred–odd residents.[1] Now, the authorities were contemplating dismissing him for proclaiming to his people, "Black man's medicine is better than the white man's."[2]

The missionaries had previously reported on resistance from Muslim clerics who complained about the Christians' preaching before treatment and from women who refused to be separated from their children. This new confrontation was different because it concerned the efficacy of the medicine itself, even though medical and mission authorities had acknowledged for some time that the existing remedy of tree oils did nothing to treat or cure leprosy.[3] Whatever words the chief used to express the difference between African therapies—*maganin gargajiya* (medicine of our forebears) or simply *maganin namu* (our medicine)—and the foreigners' medicines (today, most commonly called hospital medicine, *maganin asibiti*), the available sources do not say. It is clear, however, that the authorities perceived a call for racial solidarity from an "authority" recognized by the Native Administration. The situation was threatening for both the missionaries and the emirate government.

The Kano leprosarium, though a medical site in a suburban village outside Kano City, was not isolated from the increasingly contentious racial and anticolonial politics in West Africa during World War II. As thousands of African soldiers fought for the British (and French) in battlefields as far as Burma, agitation for African political participation and autonomy grew in colonies like Nigeria and the Gold Coast. These activists mostly were trade unionists, soldiers, and students of Western-style schools. Among other strategies to contain dissent, the British government passed the Colonial Welfare and Development Act in 1940, hoping to appease Africans pushing for more investment in indigenous welfare.[4] About the emirates, Nigeria's Governor Bernard Bourdillon, serving in 1943, wrote to British Residents: "If properly energised and guided the traditional dignity and respect for authority which are inherent in the North can exercise a powerful restraining influence on the ebullience and loose-thinking which are, I fear, too common characteristics of the Southern politicism. But if that influence is to be felt—and at the moment it is practically non-existent—the North must step down from behind the plate-glass window through which it surveys disdainfully the antics of its plebeian neighbour, tuck up its long sleeves and join in the melee."[5]

Bourdillon was anxious that, paradoxically, the relative conservatism of the North might prove more dangerous than the conflicts between "ancients and moderns" that erupted regularly in the South. "In the North the habits of discipline and obedience to authority ingrained in them by their religion will tend to keep feelings of discontent underground until they reach the point of becoming really dangerous. I regard the task of inducing the Emirs to realise the existence of a young educated class that is beginning to think for itself, and the necessity of allowing them to say what they think instead of bottling it up as one of the most important and one of the most difficult tasks that lie before you."[6]

Meanwhile, in London, Abubukar Imam, a representative of this educated class and editor of the main Hausa-language newspaper, *Gaskiya ta fi kwabo* (Truth is worth more than a penny), warned Lord Lugard not to underestimate Northerners: "Today we the people of Northern Nigeria are like patients, and the Europeans are like doctors. If the doctors really want to cure us [sic] our diseases, it is necessary for them to make us feel so confident of them as to show them frankly what parts trouble us. If the doctor refuses to listen to what the patient says is hurting him, the patient feels that he does not really want to cure him."[7] Imam's analogy of paternalist medicine for political reform is an intriguing choice because health was precisely the area in which Muslim elites had developed alliances with Christian missionaries and British officers to enhance their authority over new kinds of political subjects—Christians, Muslim and pagan children, and women patients.

Conflicts at mission sites in Muslim Northern Nigeria never rose to the scale of workers' strikes in West Africa that led to many deaths and forced the French and British to negotiate with African political leaders, but they were simmering "underground," to use Bourdillon's word.[8] The war prevented the movement of foreign missionaries across the Atlantic from North America to West Africa, and, as a result, the SIM's reliance on figures like the Sarkin Kutare as well as indigenous Christian workers increased. At the same time, new political priorities created the impetus for the opening of more clinics, dispensaries, and schools, not only in cities like Kano but increasingly also in rural communities. Christian missions received grants in aid from the British government, and the SIM opened its eye hospital in Kano Township in 1943 with financial assistance from a British philanthropist. The missions were conduits for the new surgical practices and medicines developed during World War II, particularly chemotherapeutic sulfa drugs to treat diseases such as syphilis, yaws, leprosy, tuberculosis, and pneumonia.[9]

The Sarkin Kutare, chief of the leprosy sufferers, represented a new political constituency, not often seen in the historiography of late colonial-era resistance, focused as it is on soldiers and workers. Christian evangelists and some Muslims within Christian missions began to use the language of Africanness, blackness, or indigeneity to define themselves in opposition to or separate from white missionaries and one another. The push for autonomy and preoccupation with cultural authenticity—on the basis of religion, ethnicity, and natal origins—were growing more insistent in parts of Muslim Northern Nigeria but often in localized ways that seemed disconnected from wider political movements.

THINGS OF WONDER:
BRAILLE AND A BLIND REVOLUTION CONTAINED

The leprosy campaign showed Dr. Albert Helser of the SIM the potential for an eye hospital to expand his mission's reputation and presence in Northern Nigeria. In *Glory of the Impossible,* published in 1940, he explained: "Missions and Government feel [Eye Work and Hospital] to be an urgent need, not only to help those already blind, but to cooperate with scores of Government and Mission doctors and nurses in saving many thousands from ever becoming blind."[10] Cataract surgery was already performed at the leprosariums, and infections of the eye like trachoma showed good prognosis with penicillin treatment, which missions had increasingly on hand. In a new twist on the missions' tradition of emphasizing literacy in Hausa areas, in 1938, Helser arrived in the village of Dass in Bauchi Province looking for a blind teacher to return with him to Kano to begin acquiring the means to build an eye hospital.[11]

The SIM missionary Charles Beitzel, who had established the station at Dass in 1922, was a braille teacher, and introduced Helser to two blind students, Bete Gagare and Sabo.[12] Bete began learning braille in his village of Polchi, not far from Dass, in 1934 with a Nigerian Christian evangelist, Mato Wandi. It is unclear whether braille writing or oral memorization was the initial basis of Christian evangelism to the blind, but the fact that this area had suffered from river blindness, leading to the impairment of many youngsters like Bete, suggests that indigenous Christians like Mato Wandi found a strong purpose in Dass and other areas of the Bauchi Plateau.[13] Mission publications report that the first formal blind school in Northern Nigeria was opened in 1955, at Gindiri on the Jos Plateau, by the Sudan United Mission.[14] Mato was not blind himself but took Bete under his wing and then brought him to the SIM station at Dass to continue his studies with Beitzel. Under the care of Musa Tsakani, one of the first Northern Nigerians to be ordained a reverend,[15] Bete walked and then hitched rides with passing lorries to make the several-hundred-mile trip west to Kano.

According to SIM histories, Bete became something of a legend in Kano: "Dr. Helser took him to see the Emir [who] tested him, hearing him read, saw him write with the Frame and the mats, knitting that he had done. He gave us his permission to enter the old walled City of Kano."[16] The SIM rented a house in the Dala ward, where explorers in the nineteenth century had reported on the existence of an organized blind almseekers' quarter.[17] Two white women missionaries, Anne Wooding, recently arrived from England, and Leona Kibby, who worked in Ethiopia before the Italian occupation in 1935, began to hold classes.[18] Their first student, according to Wooding, was the Sarkin Makafi, the chief of the blind, who, like the Sarkin Kutare at the leprosarium, was the leader of the community. Wooding remembered that the chief of the blind was himself "sighted and elderly with a long beard."[19] At first, she doubted he could learn any braille but was surprised by his aptitude in picking up some words quickly. He then allowed Bete and the missionaries to begin teaching.

The classes continued for only about nine months. Missionaries later wrote that the outbreak of World War II was one reason, although Wooding in her memoir separately blamed the resistance of "Mohammedan Malams."[20] Malam Bete remembered the events another way: "The blind became hostile and rebelled, asking that the Emir give them their own chief with a title. The Emir said no."[21] Bete recalled that the blind people turned violent, destroying public works such as the water pipes. The Emir still refused and then turned out the missionaries, forcing them to set up their blind school far to the north of the Old City near Sabon Gari.

The missionaries chafed at their placement in Sabon Gari, which they characterized as "immoral" because of the sale of alcohol and other activities they associated with Southern Nigerians.[22] The mission sought to maintain its moral authority through its avoidance and disavowal of "troublemakers," which included Southern Nigerian Christians. Bete lamented that the blind people at Dala only wanted political recognition, to "elect their own leader,"[23] a desire that had undoubtedly grown because of the attentions of the white missionaries and the Emir. Bete, barely twenty years old at this time, felt the thrill of politics and the power of being an evangelist.

Amid these emerging divisions, the SIM Eye Hospital was opened in 1943. Dr. Marion Hursh, the first ophthalmologist who arrived in 1940, worked at the Kano leprosarium until construction of the eye hospital was completed.[24] He noted the shortage of building materials and money caused by the war. Galvanized iron for the roof, for instance, was impossible to find. "You [could not] get any out of the U.S., it [was] all allocated, but somebody found some in a Brooklyn yard that hadn't been discovered and got it out there in time and so we opened with twenty-five beds, . . . equally divided, shall I say, twelve and twelve, men's ward and women's ward, one private room."[25] Indeed, it seems the Emir of Kano stifled progress on the hospital, but Lord John Scott McClay, a major donor who was a Scottish shipyard owner and Parliamentarian, insisted that his funds be put to use quickly for the hospital.[26] The Emir and his retinue appeared at the opening ceremony, along with British officials and McClay (see photo 5.1).

Dr. Hursh kept busy with surgeries for African patients on certain days and refractions for Europeans the rest of the week.[27] A school for the blind occupied one room of the hospital, and, under Hursh's direction, Malam Bete and other blind students evangelized in the hamlets surrounding Kano.

Photo 5.1. Opening of the SIM Eye Hospital, Kano, 1947. (Collection of SIM International Archives.)

They took along books they'd produced themselves and, when it became available, used microphones to preach on the roadside and in markets to gathered crowds.[28] Malam Bete became the best "advertisement" for SIM in hamlets like Mariri, on the main paved road going southeast out of Kano.[29] According to oral histories in those villages, if the white Christians came to the villagers to preach or disseminate medical information, parents hid their children, whereas if Bete or another blind man came to read, crowds gathered. No enforcement of the prohibitions on public preaching—either from the 1920s or from the leprosariums—was reported.

Like the Emir, the villagers marveled as the blind reader ran his fingers lightly over the pages marked with small bumps (*tozo*, literally, hump of a camel) and began to read aloud Bible passages. His fingers became his eyes, Mariri residents remembered, who did not know his name but called him Makaho Mai Kyan Kai (blind man with the good head). They described him as a black man, not of Hausa ethnicity but Hausa-speaking, from somewhere in the city, where he worked as a "boy" of the Christian mission. The villagers remarked on how the Christian missionaries brought "black people we had never known before." Irresistibly drawn to these wanderers, the children had to endure their parents' admonitions: "You had not better follow the Christians."[30]

The blind students, Dr. Hursh remembered, were "terrific" preachers who became revivalist-types invited to indigenous Christian congregations looking for an infusion of fresh life into their worship.[31] Bete had a reputation as a performer, retelling his dramatic story about losing his eyesight when smothered by a swarm of flies. Along with his eyesight, he lost the attention of most of his family members, for whom he became just a mouth to feed.[32] His extemporaneous performances for Muslim and Christian Africans became a much greater draw than the braille books that he and other students spent much of their time making when they were not trekking.[33]

Christian Nigerians' interest in Bete's performances reflected an appetite for the evangelical and exhortatory uses of literacy that coincided with the newly formed African Missionary Service (later Evangelical Missionary Service) in 1943. This group within SIM included Christians like Bete, who are considered in Northern Nigerians' oral histories to have planted the church in Kano and other Muslim areas.[34] Bete much preferred evangelism to teaching blind students braille, and he considered the vast majority of his students, who were beggars from the Old City to Sabon Gari, to be opportunists in whom investment was wasted. He felt that Christianity was becoming secondary to its advertisement, and, with this change in interest, white missionaries who prioritized the medical work were missing an important transformation. Their authority diminished somewhat among Muslim and Christian Africans. Neither the emirate authorities nor the missionaries tried to stop or change the itinerant preachers' practices because, it seemed, "public health" trumped all potential threats in proselytism.

The eye hospital steadily grew, particularly as Hursh was able to secure more antibiotics and successfully treat many cases of conjunctivitis, a major complaint of patients of all ages.[35] Untreated eye infections were quite contagious and brought a steady stream of patients to the eye hospital.[36] Reporting in 1944, Hursh noted that the number of beds for inpatients had increased from 25 to 28, but the vast majority who came to the hospital were outpatients from within one hundred miles.[37] The outpatients walked, often with the help of relatives, to stand in line for hours. Gradually, the SIM's medical work connected its urban and rural work beyond the leprosariums. Various agendas were operating within these networks, which the eye hospital's faltering start showed, and neither Christian missionaries nor political authorities could control them.

NEW ENTICEMENTS TO WANDER

By 1941–1942, the Sudan Interior Mission in Kano township began to report that evangelism among "the Forces" in newer settlements of the township was taking up virtually all of its nonmedical missionary resources.[38] The neighborhood of Tudun Wada, a reservation similar to Sabon Gari but settled by Northern "strangers" in Kano, Zaria, and other cities, was close by the airfield and the staging area for troops' exercises. The missionaries reportedly were seeing good success in church attendance among soldiers and "transients" in these neighborhoods, where street services as well as tennis, baseball, and football games were part of the newly invigorated urban evangelism campaign. One missionary described children's evangelism, using "felt-o-grams" and a "gramophone with Hausa records which adds [to] the attraction and propagation of the Word." Wives of evangelists had the special role of bringing children off the street and into homes or rented quarters in which to offer instruction. Using their houses as schools and prayer meeting rooms, residents of Sabon Gari, Tudun Wada, and other neighborhoods were brought into the growing evangelical campaign.

Among the soldiers and transients, the missionaries noted the presence of "Sara boys" from French Equatorial Africa.[39] The Sara, migrants from southern Chad, were known in Kano as soldiers of the French army. Given the worse reputation of the French army as compared to the British army among Africans, no doubt some of these newcomers were deserters. The British colonial government looked at demobilization generally with great apprehension, though it did not expect Kano to have as great an influx of ex-soldiers as towns like Bauchi and Potiskum to the east, closer to the border with Chad.[40] Ex-soldiers from French territories could not draw benefits from the British government, but the British authorities did not want to send them back, as they would take with them their purchasing power of surplus commodities, which became a new economic priority for the colonial government.[41] The British government also worried about the northward movement of Southern Nigerian soldiers, who, owing to their military experience, would be prone to nationalist tendencies.[42] What would such migrants do, the authorities wondered, fearing "the prospect of ultimate pauperization or a criminal career."[43]

While the Lagos Resident suggested "settling" soldiers into new neighborhoods with housing built on the model of medical quarantine facilities to combat sleeping sickness,[44] in Kano, no such planned communities were constructed. The local British authorities instead expected that "religious duty," presumably meaning alms for soldiers' support, would be forthcoming. The Kano Resident, E. W. Thompstone, clarified: "There are no special arrangements for the relief of the destitute or disabled other than the pensions and gratuities to Military, Government or Native Authority pensioners and a recently constituted Scheme for the relief of destitute ex-soldiers. It is a social—and to some extent a religious—obligation among the Hausas to look after the aged and infirm, and the sick and lepers who are indigent are cared for in the hospitals and leper settlements."[45] Throughout Nigeria, the British authorities expected the involvement of "civil organizations" in demobilization. In the north-central and north-western provinces, Christian missions became a magnet for demobilized soldiers without jobs, housing, or land.

In 1941, a man named Hassen, who worked as a colporteur for the SIM, took twenty-eight shillings' worth of books and set off from Kano to trek southeast into rural districts. He returned empty-handed, claiming that he had sold the tracts to the chief of Dutse, and then left with the first deployment of soldiers from Kano to work as an interpreter. The SIM missionaries soon after learned from the Dutse chief that he never bought any tracts from Hassen. Because of Hassen and the arrest of two Bible sellers in a rural southwestern district, the Kano Resident asked the missionaries to stop allowing "boys to go out selling Bibles." "This is the thing which must be taken up later perhaps when the war is over," the missionaries noted.[46]

Unemployment, malnutrition, lack of kin—poverty by different names— led wanderers who became soldiers or were veterans into the SIM projects—medical and nonmedical—through the 1940s. Soldiers appeared as a new category of patients on SIM leprosarium rosters,[47] and the government authorities made a deliberate effort to link disabled veterans with missions.[48] The government gave the SIM small subsidies for veterans' care at the leprosariums. Yet they may have not had leprosy but instead other ailments or no other place to go.[49] Higher rates of leprosy in South Asia may have meant more infection among African soldiers who fought in those theaters, but the mission reported treating a host of other diseases, including tuberculosis, pneumonia, and syphilis, increasingly with antibiotics.

The arrival of newer kinds of patients at the leprosarium in Kano coincided with the start of trials with sulfone drugs administered by oral delivery and injection. Just a year earlier, in 1943, Guy Faget, director of the Carville leprosarium in Louisiana, used sulfone in the treatment of tuberculosis.[50] The SIM was in close contact with the American leprosy research community via the American Mission to Lepers. Sulfone, considered to be the first class of modern "miracle drugs," was also used to treat meningitis, epidemics of which occurred in various parts of Northern Nigeria in the 1940s.

Sometime during this wave of official and unofficial demobilization, a soldier named Musa found a young boy named Ishaku Bello outside the 'dan Agundi gate on the south side of Kano Old City. Musa took the boy

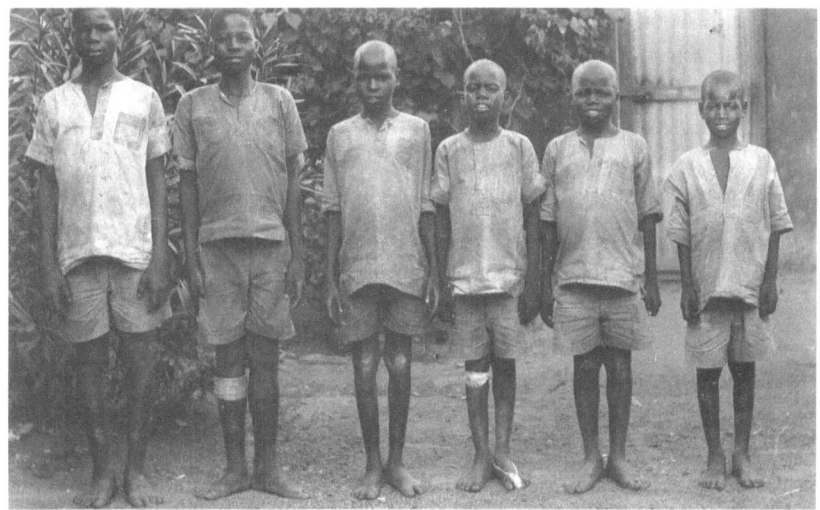

Photo 5.2. Waifs from Kano City bound for SIM Boys' Home, Roni, ca. 1946. (Collection of SIM International Archives.)

north across town to the SIM compound.[51] Ishaku, a boy about ten years old, was from a village called Wailari in Kumbotso, an area south of urban Kano. The SIM compound, where the eye hospital stood, seemed to him halfway across the world. His parents, Fulani Muslims, died while he was still very young, and he wandered aimlessly until he met Musa. Ishaku said Musa was from Chad. Ishaku stayed either at the SIM's compound in Kano or in Tudun Wada for some time before he and a group of boys were sent to the SIM's station at Roni, a town to the north in Kazaure Emirate, where the SIM established an industrial school for waifs and orphans (see photo 5.2).[52]

Other Sara men, Alhamdu and Gin Magari, were the first evangelists and founders of the Maraba and Air Force churches in the Tudun Wada and Brigade enclaves.[53] Ishaku recalled that these men were attractive because of their uniforms, their "news of the world," and their kindness. The so-called Chadians, many of whom must have been Sara, represented another wave of African evangelists, following Bete of the blind school and others who had come just a few years earlier. The Chadians were different because they were not "mission boys" from other parts of Northern Nigeria but were mostly Sara, that is, belonging to an agglomeration of ethnic groups in Southern Chad who were raided for slaves by the Hausa, Bagirmi, Kanuri, and other Muslim groups in earlier centuries.[54] In Chad,

Joining in the Melee ⇒ 103

many Sara spoke Hausa and were practitioners of indigenous religions who increasingly converted to Christianity during the colonial era.[55] In Kano, using Hausa language and sometimes claiming Hausa ethnicity, the Chadians joined mission networks and undertook independent evangelism to attract young clients in order to assimilate as Northern Nigerians.

When the British authorities discovered the waifs in Christian care, they reacted strongly against the white missionaries because of the earlier problems of the leprosariums.[56] Dr. Helser of the SIM explained that the children were a mix of orphans and children of Christian and Muslim workers for the mission who gave their consent to mission fosterage. John H. Carrow, the British Resident, confirmed their status by undertaking interviews: "All the orphans have been placed in the care of the S.I.M. by authorised persons, e.g., guardians. One was accepted at the request of the Police and another at the request of the Chief Alkali [Muslim judge]. . . . Six voluntary members are children of ex-soldiers, ex-commercial and ex-Government employees, mostly from Tudun Wada section."[57] The alkali's purported request raised some eyebrows, but Carrow accepted it on the grounds that the boy was reportedly suspected at first of having leprosy. After internal deliberations within the British Colonial Office and the Native Administration, the authorities ultimately accepted mission institutionalization for the boys. Carrow knew that the boys were going to leave for the proposed SIM industrial home in rural Roni.[58]

With the help of the Chadians (working between the Kano, Katsina, and Sokoto leprosariums and rural mission sites), Ishaku Bello and several other boys were taken to Roni in 1946. The facility was known as the Kano Boys' School, though it was in Kazaure Emirate.[59] The curriculum at Roni included the "three R's," based on the Bible, *Pilgrim's Progress*, and biographies of David Livingstone, with a heavy dose of agricultural and Boy Scout training. Through Roni and its girls' equivalent at Kabo opened in 1949, the SIM offered Christian instruction, despite the fact that in 1946, "a ruling was made in some parts of the district, that no child under eighteen years of age will be allowed to go to the Mission for reading and writing and Bible study."[60] Other than those, the Catholic school, Saint Thomas, which had been in Kano Sabon Gari for some time, and other Christian schools were permitted to continue, about five government-recognized schools in total.[61] They were seen as serving the Southern Nigerian Christian minority of Kano and Katsina. The colonial authorities approved the SIM's two new schools primarily because they would relocate urban youth to rural areas. These youth, with adult transients, left the cities and found farmland in the rural areas. Using lay medical and religious networks begun by the foreign missionaries of Sudan Interior Mission, Chadian soldiers and their wandering youth recruits found new identities and new occupations.

FAMINES AND EVANGELS OF BRIGHTER VILLAGES

Roni and other rural stations that the Sudan Interior Mission opened after the war and into the 1950s were not randomly selected. Roni, Malumfashi, and Matazu were surrounded by large homesteads populated by non-Muslim Hausa (Maguzawa). The British and emirate authorities believed these villagers to be the "only pagans" remaining in Kano, Katsina, and Kazaure Emirates and, implicitly, accepted Christian evangelism among them.[62] At Roni and Matazu, which missionaries learned was known as the Medina of Katsina,[63] Christian missionaries found members of the dissident reformist sect Isawa (see chapter 1). They lived in scattered homesteads, satellites of villages they reportedly left because of persecution. Local residents tell stories of the "pure bush" that the Emirs granted as sites to the SIM. The Roni mission station, for one, was situated atop a rocky outcrop that was said to be a place of spirits where no one (before the missionaries) had attempted to farm.[64] The SIM was given detailed population estimates of Maguzawa, presumably from tax records. The emirate officials in Kano and Katsina may have thought the Maguzawa would resist Christianity as they had also resisted Islam.[65]

In the 1940s, when rural Hausaland suffered drought and famine, the tensions between rural populations and the emirate authorities became acute.[66] The catastrophe was known in Katsina as 'Yar Dikko (literally the daughter of the Katsina Emir Dikko). In Sokoto Province, people called the event 'Yar Gusau, referring to an administrative center, the seat of political power. According to accounts of SIM workers in Malumfashi and the Church Missionary Society's (CMS) Dr. H. A. Kelsey in Zaria, the famine caused mass mortality from 1941 until after 1945. Starving children were abandoned in village marketplaces and even dropped into wells.[67] In suicidal protest, survivors refused to plant anything because it would all be taken in taxes. The Emir of Katsina, a friend to the British administration and backer of the SIM leprosarium in his jurisdiction, was popularly believed to take peasants' food and whimsically distribute it to others.[68]

An outbreak of cerebrospinal meningitis followed the famine. In the dry season of 1944, the mission site, the leprosarium at Babbar Ruga, Katsina, was struck.[69] In Malumfashi town, the SIM reported that 160 died from the infection in January alone.[70] The district office led the relief effort, but the mission also took in some patients. When another epidemic struck the town exactly four years later, in the dry season of 1948, the SIM supplied drugs, and the government provided for isolation units and recruited male nurses to tend the sick.[71]

Dr. Kelsey of the CMS reported that all the "famine grain," typically collected through obligatory alms and kept for emergencies, "was sold to the soldiers some time ago."[72] Villagers told SIM missionaries that chiefs' messengers entered granaries ostensibly to assess whether farmers had paid enough in taxes, then stole their food.[73] When the SIM asked the Kano Native Administration for increased rations of maize to feed leprosarium patients, though, the Emir's office reportedly replied that the market was "sticky."[74]

Whether or not the accusations against the native authorities about their collusion with the soldiers and the British were true, they reveal a resentment among the peasants, the "underground" about which Bourdillon had warned British Residents some years earlier. Rural folk did not share the British colonial authorities' hope that African soldiers, if properly trained, could be beacons to "their people." The Kano Resident J. R. Patterson, in 1944, wrote of demobilization: "We should make the maximum possible use of the opportunity of having this large number of men under discipline to give them all the lessons that are available in literacy, hygiene, forest utilisation improvement in the standard of their agricultural practice and anything else that is likely to enable them to bear the evangel of brighter villages back to the country with them."[75]

As the famine raged, the SIM was reputed to have food, as revealed by the records of the treks of the missionary couple Harold and Eugenie German with their children. Eugenie wrote:

> The children are a great attraction to everyone. . . . Many women call me aside and want to know if we have any medicine to help them have children. They marvel at the size of the children for their age. They think it is because of the medicine we give them. We tell them it is because of proper food that makes them grow. Many come to see them eat and they realize our children eat food like theirs such as the guinea corn, etc., only that it is cooked differently. The drinking of fresh milk is such a new thing to them and they think it a most unusual thing that the children do not nurse from the breast longer than about 8 months.[76]

Mrs. German learned only later that villagers were resentful of the missionaries not only because of the possibility that they possessed some trick for feeding their children, but also for perhaps being the "canteen traders" who had paid them too little for their raw materials, their cotton and peanuts.[77]

Hungry adolescents were, however, interested in mission life for the food and cash to be had. At the Katsina leprosarium in the 1940s, the missionaries conducted an experiment that ran for ten weeks to test children's comparative weight gain with supplements of indigenous herders' milk versus Nestle condensed milk. If children failed to report for their daily eight-ounce ration, they were fined. While the data on children's weight were entirely useless owing to the missionaries' inability to control the children's diets, one "positive" outcome was recorded: "At first those taking the canned milk did not like it and would not take as much as they should have taken; however once they got use [sic] to it they liked it very much and would nearly fight over what was extra."[78]

The famine resulted in the proliferation and dispersal of unattached children. For institutions such as the Muslim Native Administration schools and the Christian mission schools, it was an opportunity to increase influence. In Kano Province, through the late 1930s and early 1940s, Native Administration elementary schools increased in number, but not all children were wanted. After "a thorough combing-out of children who were malcontents or suffering from undernourishment or any other considerable disability, whether physical or mental, nearly 100 children [were] dismissed through this sacrifice of quantity to quality."[79] While the Muslim schools passed on such children, Christian mission schools aimed to create incentives for Muslim children to join, often with missionaries supporting the "Hausa and Fulani" children by offering to pay their schools fees and clothing costs.[80]

Northern Nigerian youth were identified increasingly as delinquent.[81] The anxiety over them was rooted in the increasing competition between new migrants like the soldiers vying for clients, and new institutions such as Christian mission and Muslim Native Administration schools. Garba Bako, a Fulani from Tafawa 'Balewa, Bauchi, was a Muslim child who attended mission school for about six years beginning in the late 1940s.[82] Around the age of ten, he asked his parents, who were poor farmers, to send him to the Native Administration school with his age-mates. They refused because of the cost. He approached Fred Whale, "the head of the missionaries" in Tafawa 'Balewa:

I explained myself to him. That I wanted to go to school, but my parents refused to pay my school fees. He asked me, "Which school did you want to . . . did I want to?" I said any type of school. So he asked me, "Can you join a missionary school?" I say yes. I had something which I had my interest in. There's a something which missionaries used to do when they want to go to preaching, either . . . for the local areas. They had Boys' Brigade. And Girls' Brigade. That's Boys' Brigade, we called it BB. Then Girls' Brigade we called it GB. So his wife was heading the women. He himself was heading the men. They used to go to market and preach God to any type of local government. They're going there and preach. So I was very, very interested to join them. He asked me; I said, yes, I will do it. Then they gave me the uniform, and every year leave we go and take examination. They have different type of badges. Yearly you will go and take examination. We go together. I was a model.[83]

From as early as the 1930s, the children's brigades were the connective force across the various mission societies spreading into Northern Nigerian villages. An early brigade leader, the Anglican missionary Dr. Norman Cook, born in Uganda, arrived at Wusasa, Zaria, in 1930.[84] Cook reported that sickness led to youth wandering when he met two boys who walked from Malumfashi to Zaria after contracting sleeping sickness. Cook took them in and formed a brigade unit to march in Maska, on the main road south and east from Malumfashi to Zaria. "By the end of the third day, thirty-nine bandages were walking proudly round Maska, the first Christian witness in a Moslem city."[85] Cook himself died from septicemia just three years after his arrival in Zaria, at the age of thirty. The Maska dispensary he founded became a "branch hospital,"[86] and a dispensary built in nearby Bakori was named in honor of Norman's brother Bertie, who took over.[87]

The brigade movement grew, with the SIM beginning chapters first at Kano and then at Roni (see photo 5.3).[88] The boys performed tasks—washing, weaving, bush clearing—together. Around 1950, boys from the leprosariums at Kano and Sokoto formed the first companies for youngsters with leprosy in all of Nigeria.[89] That year, thirty boys from the Sokoto company rode 350 miles by truck and joined thirty-two Kano boys to make yet another trek to the village of Tasa, twenty-five miles outside of Kano. A Christian community had grown there since the late 1930s through the aegis of Malam Idi, who converted as a result of the touring work of a Nigerian evangelist reportedly known as Elijah even before the opening of the leprosarium.[90] The village soon had its own religious instruction, without any white missionary

Photo 5.3. Boys' Brigade, SIM Company 2, Kano, July 1947. (Collection of SIM International Archives.)

Photo 5.4. Christian villagers at Tasa, Kano Province, led by lay evangelist Malam Idi, ca. 1947. (Collection of SIM International Archives.)

(see photo 5.4).[91] When the Brigades got there, villagers quickly harvested their peanuts and made space for the boys to camp and prepare food.[92] As they finished their meals by campfire, the boys sang gospel hymns and other devotional songs. Crowds turned out for the songs, and, again the next day, to watch them perform signaling and drills.

Joining in the Melee 109

Alhaji Garba Bako remembered that Fred Whale came to Northern Nigeria, following his position with the SIM in French Niger, to coordinate the brigades. He believed that these youth clubs were important rites to "replace the many pagan practices which a boy must give up on becoming a Christian."[93] Physical training suitable for a growing boy, including drills, swimming, handicrafts, and first aid, were, according to Whale, the best way to give boys "a week away from degrading heathen circumstances." Dry season camps were organized throughout the country, and, in addition to the leprosy companies, a company for blind boys was planned. Whale's description of the plans was businesslike and targeted: the goal was to train moral leaders for independent Nigeria. He believed such boys could be the answer for a "continent in ferment."[94]

Though he never renounced Islam, Bako toured extensively as a brigade boy until 1954, the year of Queen Elizabeth's visit to Nigeria. When her entourage passed through Jos, he claimed he was there with his Bauchi company waving a flag. His great interest remained the uniform and marching in formation. Garba later joined the police force.

The fate of Christian children with whom Bako and other Muslims schooled was different. A pagan Hausa youngster from Musawa recalled in Katsina that he, along with his sisters, went to SIM schools in Kano, but they were unhappy: "It seemed they had gathered only useless children. . . . The one whose room I was put in, the one in charge of the room, at night he would take a knife and take our food and money; if we didn't give it, he threatened to cut us!"[95] The Bamaguje youngster begged the local missionary from his village, Mr. Cox, to take him back to his father's farm, which Cox did, but the boy found that the only way not to become a farmer as his father was to return to the missionary school, study, and become a pastor in the SIM leprosariums and then in rural outstations.

Bako, on the other hand, went into the employ of the government and, when he started to earn wages and give some money to his family, his father said, "Okay, let me forgive you. Sorry." Bako recalled of his father: "He did not know the school would make me benefit like this. Out of this school, which he did not allow me to continue in, now I had some money and I take small money and I come and give him. In all my brothers, none took a penny and gave him. Yes, he told me he was sorry, *yi ha'kuri*, have patience. Since those days, if I got work, if I got small something, I buy cloth for my father, I buy cloth for my mother. If I don't buy them something for one month, the second month, I must buy it."[96]

Rural youth who went to the Christian missionaries could make something of themselves through their education, and many kept links between their families and their mission lives. Yet the schools took in many kinds of children, and the reminiscences of African Christians and of the missionaries confirm that the SIM took in some opportunistic exploitative boys. Two boys, Sani and Idi, came to the Malumfashi SIM station after living on the streets, peddling sweets or some woven goods.[97] The missionary Jessie Whitmore wrote, "One night after Miss Jantz and I had retired these three boys led by an older male patient entered the women's compound—and acted up terribly. After much prayer and guidance I was led to dismiss Ana Ruwa and Idi—but to give Sani no. 2 another chance."[98] Such complaints about youth are different from those of the early 1900s, which were preoccupied with maintaining social and ethnic hierarchies at the freed slave homes. By the 1940s, concern over wandering youth had shifted from non-Muslim girls to Muslim boys, who were seen as violent and predatory.

The Christian schools were rough, and missionaries sometimes wondered about the purpose of the institutions. Were they charity for Muslim scalawags from the city or a means to educate young Christians? Christian Northern Nigerians—young and old—grew disaffected and resentful. African Christian parents received reports from their children who boarded at Roni and Kabo that food rations were meager and infested with maggots and their water contaminated.[99] The parents were shocked that the white missionaries never asked them for school fees. Many would have readily paid money to have their children fed better, and many Christian Africans felt that schooling as charity attended a loss of prestige.

SELF-SUFFICIENCY AND SPIRITUAL LEADERSHIP

In 1947–1948, the British authorities laid out a ten-year scheme to develop Nigeria's educational and medical institutions by greater decentralization in order to foster indigenous participation and greater control over Christian missions and other voluntary agencies that were to fill in where native resources lacked.[100] For the North, the Deputy Director of Medical Services, Dr. R. L. Cheverton, defended continued SIM leprosy work in collaboration with the Muslim Native Administration on several grounds:

> Western Democratic ideas are derived mainly from the ethical teaching of Christianity and it is not a question of limiting mission work to religious instruction but rather that the work should be reinforced by personal example. Therefore, the Sudan Interior Mission does exemplify this way of life by service to the community and as such this service can be considered to be a demonstration in

training for citizenship in the best sense. The social significance of Christian ethics and the question of proselytizing the local inhabitants in order to convert them to Christianity is of minor importance as compared with the ultimate good being done by example and the actual effect on leprosy itself.[101]

The Emirs saw the issue of citizenship differently. Writing about the SIM, the Emirs of Kano and Katsina contended that

no application by the Mission to establish a School or a dispensary will be approved by the Native Administration as it is entirely the responsibility of the NA (and not the Mission) which collects money from the peasants in order to help them in such ways. When these peasants become more civilized, there can be a possibility of them criticising the NA for failing to spend public money for the welfare of the public and leaving such responsibilities to the Mission who only afford to do so with subscriptions collected in a foreign country (America) where there is enough money to carry out such proposals.[102]

Muslim leaders reminded the British authorities that indigenous systems of aid existed and that their political reputations suffered for creating native dependency on foreign aid. The cooperative relationship between Christian missions and the Muslim Native Administration was limited by the Emirs' fears of popular discontent with leaders' failure to spend alms to help their subjects. Contrary to the view of Governor Bourdillon, the Muslim ancien régime was well aware of the rising political tensions.

Within missions, independence movements were spearheaded, though they were cast in religious terms. Men like Musa and Umaru Layi, another Chadian who was popularly credited with expanding Christianity in Roni in the late 1940s, founded their evangelical outposts in rural areas of Kano, Katsina, and Sokoto Provinces.[103] The community of Kagadama, meaning literally "do as you feel," was a leprosy segregation village founded by Umaru Layi, who was trained at Ya da Kunya. This village attracted women leprosy patients who avoided the big leprosarium at Kano. Such villages did not require the separation of mothers and children, and women had the chance for closer relations with charismatic male religious leaders, as compared to the more "policed" affairs of the leprosariums. Mission work spawned its own peripheries where religious and social autonomy seemed more possible.

Both Christian and Muslim charismatic entrepreneurs gained legitimacy in rural areas with credentials gained in urban centers. As the eye hospital director Dr. Hursh described it, his interactions with indigenous medical practitioners actually increased the clientele of his competitors. Specifically, he met a local practitioner of couching, a procedure to dislodge cataracts described in India from 500 BCE and practiced in rural Nigeria by itinerant Fulani surgeons:[104]

> He practiced right there in Kano, and he wanted to watch me work and so I said, "Fine." Now, it so happened that just before that, the government had come to me and said, "Well, we need help in getting this practice stopped, stamped out, and so you must report to us anyone you know of who is doing this operation." Well, I reported but I didn't count on them acting so fast. Well, he . . . after the day he watched me work he said, "You know I want some of that medicine that you used to make them lie still." He said, "I have to have two people holding mine down." Well, I said. "I can't give you that, but I'd like to watch you work now that you've watched me."[105]

Hursh subsequently informed the medical authorities and then met the coucher again:

> He said, "We have to go and see the [Muslim] judge, the *Kadi*." I said, "Oh?" He said, "You reported me, didn't you?" I said, "Yes, I had to." "Well," he said, "I can't do the work now." So he went to see the judge and I tried to not . . . get him to . . . to . . . to not prosecute him. So, he says, "Now I am going to have to leave the country, because this is the only occupation I have. I'll go across the border to French country." He said, "I can work up there." I said, "Well, you can if they'll let you." "Well," he said, "I'll need a . . . a paper, a recommendation from you." Well, I was on the spot. So I wrote it out on letterhead and, of course, it was . . . I wrote it in English, so he didn't know what it said anyway. I said, "This man is forbidden by law to practice his art of couching in Nigeria," and I signed my name. He came back two years later, very profuse thanks, saying that "you . . . your letter's gotten me much business up there. All I had to do was show them this Kano Eye Hospital and they thought I was one of yours." So it backfired.[106]

The Fulani practitioners would eventually become "nomadic" and "rural" with the increasing uptake of hospital medical services within Kano township.

The establishment of medical missions in both urban and rural areas clearly shaped the social perception of difference—between indigenous and foreign medicine and charity, ethnic categories, and religious hierarchies. The interactions of Northern Nigerians from very different parts of the region, despite their ability to communicate in Hausa, produced new kinds of challenges. Dr. Hursh noted the practice of *'bori*, or spirit possession: "The women who we had operated . . . their eyes were covered and so forth. And they would start, in their own language, of course, start talking in a way . . . you see, they never stopped, just go on and on, and that's very unusual for them. . . . And more than once I had people that I knew had no contact with white people before, talking to me in English, not even knowing what they were saying. . . . So I would call the church elders. This is early days, but we had some Nigerian Christians then. And they said, 'Oh, this is the devil, this is evil spirits, no question about it.'"[107] The only thing that worked, Hursh said, was praying, invoking Christ's power over Satan, over possessed people. Hursh accepted the Africans' explanations of *iskoki*, spirits, as the cause of "irrationality" and even physical misfortune, but African Christian workers, not Hursh, led these prayers and cultivated a kind of prayer healing that even Muslims seemed to appreciate within the medical practice of the mission.

CONCLUSION

Africans developed networks and practices within medical, social, and religious institutions and beyond them. This independence was indeed celebrated by some progressive foreign political and social observers of African affairs in the late colonial era. For example, Sir John Foster Wilson, a blind lawyer and activist who founded the Royal Commonwealth Society for the Blind in 1950, described the Kano blind "syndicate" as the only example he could point to in which the disabled "came together to find an answer to their problem within the framework of native society":[108]

> Twice, in Northern Nigeria, I have visited the blind beggars of Kano. There are some 800 of them—blind men with blind wives and often blind children—and they live as an exclusive guild in a part of the city traditionally reserved for the blind. In the morning they make their way, often with almost baffling skill, through

the cobbled twisting streets to the mosques, the markets, and the houses of wealthy traders. In the evening they return and their takings are shared out by the Treasurer in accordance with the ancient rules of the guild. If you talked to the blind chief of the community—Sarakin Makafi (The King of the Blind) as he calls himself—he would tell you, with courtly sincerity, that his guild serves a vital function in the city. . . . If all the blind became craftsmen, to whom would the faithful give alms? As we left, we asked whether we might take a photograph of the blind elders. After much consultation the interpreter said: "The King will allow you to take his photograph so long as you don't use it to restore his sight. Allah has made him blind; it is not for men to interfere."[109]

It is not known whether the chief described here was the same person whom the missionary Anne Wooding taught braille. In any event, the blind community's interactions with the Christian missions, beginning with the efforts of Bete, catalyzed a certain "nationalist" discourse. The desire for belonging emerged in many quarters at this time, not always expressed in language that fit into the secularist narrative of anticolonial agitation that colonial authorities identified. Similar to Wilson's observation that "you do not see [the blind] until you do something for them,"[110] youth, too, became a more visible category through mission and Muslim competition over their loyalties. The invisibility of Christian Northern Nigerian networks helped the Chadians, but, at the same time, the grassroots character of Christian communities posed a challenge as Northern Christians sought political recognition in independent Nigeria.

6 ⁓ Security and Secrecy in the Era of Independence, 1950–1975

As Nigeria prepared for independence from Britain in 1960, indigenous political leaders from various parts of the colony met to negotiate the specifics of regional integration into a national framework, the terms of the future constitution, and the postindependence role of voluntary agencies, including Christian mission societies in education and medical work. Northern Nigerian political leaders made public speeches celebrating religious cooperation in their region, singing the praises of the Sudan Interior Mission (SIM) and other Christian agencies. The SIM reproduced passages from notable politicians' speeches in its pamphlet *Independence Year Report*.[1] The prime minister, Alhaji Sir Abubakar Tafawa 'Balewa, acknowledged in his "Motion for Independence" in January 1960 the Christian "missionaries who have done so much . . . in the field of education and by the provision of medical facilities for so many of our people." Alhaji Sir Ahmadu Bello, the Northern premier, spoke at the SIM headquarters in Jos, describing the missionaries as "devoted to the welfare of people" and about the good relations between missions and government. He reflected back on colonial-era cooperation but looked to the future: "Our Government is a Government of Northerners, both Muslims and Christians; we wish to allow all men to practice their religions as they wish." A third quote appeared, from the Igbo leader named Sir Francis Ibiam, who was an ordained elder of the Presbyterian Church. He echoed the appeal for future cooperation: "All true Nigerians look forward to the day [of independence] with the most inexpressible pleasure and thankfulness in their hearts."[2]

The speeches themselves reveal the symbolic and real significance of Christian missions for Nigerian leaders as they ushered their people through transition to independence, reminding citizens not to reject entirely the useful elements of the colonial past, on some of which, of course, the Nigerian leaders' authority depended. The SIM's editorial decision—to include these particular leaders together, with their photos—reveals a slightly different project for brokering peace. The mission aimed to show that religious difference was not central to political conflicts over what independent Nigeria, with its very distinct regional differences, would be. 'Balewa was a Hausa leader hailing from humble origins in Bauchi Emirate. In the 1950s, he achieved fame as a teacher who made his way through the ranks of the Native Administration. His farmland bordered the SIM Bauchi leprosarium, which he visited. Bello was the great-grandson of Usman 'dan Fodio, founder of the Sokoto Caliphate. Ibiam, the son of an Igbo chief, would later become Governor of the Eastern Region and support the secession of Biafra through the Nigerian Civil War (1967–1970). The two Northerners belonged to the Northern People's Congress (NPC, the conservative party of the region), while Ibiam belonged to the National Council of Nigeria and the Cameroons (NCNC). SIM was witness to the contests between political parties over independence and tended to victims of violence that broke out mainly between Hausa and Igbo in Kano Sabon Gari in May 1953, following disagreements between Northern and Southern leaders over constitutional negotiations.

Christian missions and Northern Nigerian Christians shaped the path toward independence and, with independence, the North's uneasy internal relations and its relations with other regions of Nigeria. Political negotiations between the three regions—North, South, and East—over the time line for independence were informed by the North's limited "modernization" relative to Southern Nigeria,[3] with Northern leaders arguing that their region's populations had not achieved the same levels of education and training as Southerners and hence were less prepared for self-rule. While other histories have focused on the political consequences of this argument, and regional divisions of Nigeria after independence, this chapter explains how Christian missions and Christian Northern Nigerians were rendered invisible during these debates. Ironically, foreign missions were more numerous and influential in the North than in the South, where Christianity had a longer history.[4] Indeed, in parts of the South, missionaries were rivals of indigenous churches. For example, Dr. Nnamdi Azikiwe's

National Church of Nigeria and the Cameroons rallied against the "tentacles of religious imperialism."[5] Ahmadu Bello, in borrowing from missions and indigenous Christians, particularly their evangelical strategies and emphasis on public conversion, made different political use of religion.

Missions framed nationalist politics of the late colonial period in Northern Nigeria in several ways. Christian Northern Nigerians constituted an educated class ready to take government posts in a Nigerianized civil service, but they had no clear political identity since so many were migrants, or were perceived to be, without any institutional power. They shared language, cultural priorities, and social spaces with Muslim Northerners but were awkward allies with Southerners when it came to religious politics. Christian Southerners seeking work in the North were actually competitors to the small minority of Western-educated Northerners, both Muslim and Christian. To find a sense of Nigerian nationalism, religious, class, and political affiliations were made and remade in this era when greater emphasis was placed on indigeneity, self-determination, and freedom from foreign powers.

SIFTING TIME

Through the late 1940s and early 1950s, the SIM described a veritable explosion of interest in Christianity in urban and rural areas of Muslim provinces. Part of this impression came from the increasingly independent initiative of African Christians, mostly converts from "pagan" communities but also some former Muslims, who plied the SIM network of stations and smaller sites that had emerged connecting urban leprosariums and hospitals with rural clinics, dispensaries, and segregation villages. The African Missionary Society (AMS), formed by leading indigenous evangelists, including the demobilized Chadian soldiers, effectively tapped these networks. Further, the Nigerian Evangelical Churches of West Africa (ECWA) emerged as the independent body out of the SIM in a process that unfolded between 1950 and 1954.[6] The recognition of this independent church coincided with the adoption of a revised constitution in 1954, named after Secretary of State for the Colonies Oliver Lyttleton, which divided Nigeria into three regions: North, South, and East. The regions would be united under a federal framework in 1960.

ECWA leaders aimed to establish their independent vision, emphasizing two particular aspects: being born again (receiving baptism after childhood); and the Lord's Supper (public confession). ECWA would not baptize anyone under twelve years of age, and all baptized members had to take the Lord's Supper (the bread and the cup). If they did not participate in the Supper, a public display of religious commitment, the congregation deemed it a sign of unrepentant sin.[7] The church described the process: "When a person is put under water it is like being buried. He shows that he is burying his old life of sin and wickedness and that he considers himself dead to those things of the past. Then when the pastor lifts him out of the water again it is like the resurrection."[8]

Emphasis on these public rites increased in the precarious environment of the majority Muslim mission field in the 1950s. White missionaries and African Christian leaders noticed the fickleness of Christian commitment, even as they expressed excitement about the apparent groundswell of interest in Christianity in previously unreached or uncommitted areas. In Malumfashi, in Katsina Emirate, the pagan Maguzawa attended church, but, during the abundant harvest season, beer flowed and feasts were all too tempting.[9] This "sifting time" in farming communities made the missionaries despair that "the Maguzawa almost worship the land."[10] The Hausa pagans in southwestern Kano, where they lived in close proximity to Muslims, seemed susceptible to pressure from their neighbors; their attendance at reading classes organized by a native evangelist in the district of Dutse, where the SIM hoped to gain ground, waned because of Muslim gibes.[11]

Agricultural life may have brought a certain seasonality to religious identity, where, in urban areas, the problem of recantation of Christianity was emerging among male heads of households "returning to Islam." In 1951, the case of a young girl named Binta came before the Kano City district officer. Sale, Binta's father, had placed her in the SIM girls' school and orphanage at Kabo, in Katsina, but then he claimed that the missionaries refused to return her to his custody. His association with the SIM went back to 1945, when he and his wife worked for the Christian missionary in charge of Fago, a rural station to the north. Sale's wife was struck by tuberculosis, and Sale brought her to the native hospital in Kano City. She died six days later, and Sale returned to Christensen, left his young daughter with the wife of the missionary's "boy," and traveled east, for reasons unknown. A year later, he returned to Kano, settling in the Tudun Wada neighborhood with a new wife and a job as a builder. He tried and failed to get his daughter back, who had in the meantime been sent to the SIM orphanage at Kabo. In response to Sale's complaint, which the district officer forwarded to Albert Ter Meer, the missionary in Kano Township, the SIM claimed Sale's story was more complicated because his new wife was in fact the wife of another man who lived in Fago.[12] The mission claimed that Sale was an apostate and an absconder.

Sale's relationship to the SIM is unclear, particularly given that he did not take his first wife to the missionary doctors at the Kano leprosarium; most "people of the mission" did so. Second, the SIM claimed they had approached him several times to take back Binta, but he refused. The government apparently allowed the SIM to keep Binta, for the next year, her name appeared on the SIM's roster of girls at Kabo.[13] They reported to the British authorities that her mother was a Christian at the Kano leprosarium and that her father was dead. The death of a father made a child an orphan under Islamic law, making it easier for the SIM to justify her fosterage. Whether this was intentional deception by the SIM in reporting her father as dead is not clear. Perhaps the government, in accepting this version of events, was tacitly in agreement with the missionaries about the best result. While before such contact over a child may have ignited a political furor, the British authorities now seemed to prefer nonintervention in these kinds of domestic disputes involving indeterminate or short-lived conversions.

In 1952, John Tafida Omaru, a member of the royal family of Zaria and a Hausa convert to Christianity, was appointed the treasurer of the Zaria Native Administration. Two days before he took his post, he converted to Islam.[14] Omaru's renunciation shocked his friends and his wife, to whom he was married in 1927 in the Anglican Church inside Zaria City. Until the day of his recantation, he vowed to remain a Christian. After, he gave the impression he would take more wives and remove his five-year-old son from the Anglican Church Missionary Society (CMS) school in Wusasa and enroll him in a Muslim school within Zaria city. These were the fears of his wife, who came to the social welfare officer in Zaria. The officer, in turn, asked the Crown Counsel whether Omaru had to get a divorce before marrying other wives and what, if any, rights the wife had.

The government authorities did nothing. In the Omaru case as in Binta's, their inaction left the daughter and the wife and son in the care of missions while effectively allowing the men to abdicate responsibility for their Christian families. The British authorities professed "sympathy" for Mrs. Tafida (Omaru) and the plight of "her child having to be brought up in a faith which was alien to that which they had both professed at the time of their marriage."[15] In practice, the Muslim authorities did not have to acknowledge Christian marriages, even those backed by secular or magistrate law, after 1960, especially if the conversions could be shown to have been coerced or undertaken by a child, a minor who was not responsible.[16] Omaru converted as a child, and Sale never seems to have received baptism. Such men could exploit the legal and ritual chasms. The social welfare officer wanted, for his part, to read up on the law because he anticipated at least two more cases similar to Tafida's occurring at the Wusasa mission.[17] Legal, political, and even mission forces continued the process of sifting Christian converts, and, indeed, making male recantations relatively cost-free.

While domestic cases were handled informally, the official relationship between missions and government was changing. The Colonial Office began to locate clear divisions between voluntary societies and government in the provision of medical services in the late 1940s.[18] By the early 1950s, Christian leprosariums were shrinking in size because of the introduction of the drug dapsone. Grants for the segregation centers were drying up, the crèches were being closed, and mission institutions were accepting only very debilitating cases.[19] The missions facilitated the segregation of patients during outbreaks of meningitis, a disease that was spreading, according to some long-serving SIM missionaries in rural areas.[20]

The missionaries' medical work was, in fact, becoming less medically advanced or of a lower standard as new drugs became cheaper and more widely available. In 1951, in an unprecedented case, the British authorities contemplated bringing charges of manslaughter against workers at the Church of the Brethren Garkida Leprosarium, where some patients died after being administered the wrong drugs.[21] The Northern Region Medical Services director pointed out that Garkida was not a registered site for nurse training, which effectively set a high bar for all of the medical missions other than the CMS hospital in Zaria and the SIM Eye Hospital in Kano, where white medical doctors performed almost all the nondispensary work. Indigenous medical workers had taken on increasing responsibilities, not always with official certifications. Government scrutiny also increased.

In 1950, the government decided that no new missionaries to Nigeria could work in the provinces of Adamawa, Kano, Katsina, Sokoto, Zaria, Borno (except Biu and Bedde), or Bauchi (except Dass, Tangale, and other pagan areas).[22] The British had to be careful, however, to articulate restrictions on missionaries in terms of public safety and sensitivity to religious freedom, as the United Nations, upon its formation after World War II, adopted the 1919 Saint-Germain-en-Laye Treaty of the League of Nations that enshrined missionary freedom, ostensibly for the conduct of medical relief.[23] Nigerians themselves wanted missions to provide more than religious instruction, even outside majority Muslim regions of Northern Nigeria, in mixed areas along the Niger River such as in Kabba Province, once held by Christian missions and colonial officers as "pagan" fields ripe for evangelism. In Idda Division, the opening of a station by a small church organization, Christian Missions in Many Lands, led to concerns that missionaries would focus on religious preaching over the practical "social gospel." According to the governor, a missionary reported: "The general feeling was that, whilst the people might have considered an application by the Church Missionary Society or by a Roman Catholic Mission, there was little benefit to be derived from the purely religious teaching which Mr. Dibble had to offer. The people wanted a school or a dispensary but wanted both to be Native Authority institutions."[24]

As religious evangelism was coming under more intense scrutiny, the SIM made a point of maintaining good relations with Muslim Native Administrations in order to partake in new fields of educational work that had previously been off-limits to Christian societies in Muslim areas. The Native Administrations stipulated that religious instruction and literacy classes could not constitute formal schools, even if they had more than ten students, which was otherwise the minimum number for a formal school.[25] Yet, at the same time, the Native Administrations sought the support of missions to conduct informal literacy classes and, most importantly, to disseminate pamphlets and other print materials in support of its adult literacy program undertaken in 1953. The efforts came under the umbrella of *Ya'ki da Jahilci* (war on ignorance), and the SIM disseminated a number of publications in rural areas.[26] In this literacy push, the Native Administration produced its own papers that the SIM passed out along with its own materials, and at least one local newssheet sprang up.[27]

Demand for tracts and copies of the Bible in both Roman and Arabic script was high in the villages. In rural southeastern Kano, the chief traveled to the nearest SIM mission station asking for a Bible.[28] Another man, Usman, came to purchase a Bible to replace one that was supposedly stolen from his dead brother. In 1950, the SIM opened its Bible training school in Tofa, the most populous area of rural Kano Province. While the rural and heavily Muslim location for this theological training school could not have been selected with the expectation of many conversions, the opportunities to attract Muslims with reading materials was likely more determining, as well as the lack of space in urban Kano. The only other major Christian school to be opened in a Muslim area during the independence period was the Catholic Saint Louis Girls' School in Kano.[29] That institution, opened by Irish nuns in 1948, served elite Muslim and Christian families. Most of the Catholic families in the North were from Southern Nigeria, while Northern Christian families were poorer ECWA evangelists whose work lay in the rural hinterlands. The strength of the Saint Louis School's academics was an alternative for elite Muslim families to the weak Native Administration girls' schools that the British authorities allowed to founder.

At the forefront of ECWA's rural movement were men like Alhamdu, a Chadian who began his career with SIM first by moving between the main Kano church and the leprosarium.[30] He was the first African pastor ordained by SIM in Kano. In early December 1951, "the [Kano] church held their first organizational meeting, electing elders to work with the Pastor [Alhamdu] and Evangelist [Adamu Dogon Yaro]. [Both men] were presented with bicycles by the church."[31] Alhamdu's wages, however, were small; he earned thirty-one pounds per year—even with his Christian elementary and Bible school training, nearly six pounds less than guards at the mission compound, who tended to be local Muslims.[32]

RADICALIZATION

Riots erupted in Kano on May 16, 1953. According to the British authorities and Ahmadu Bello, then Sardauna of Sokoto, this episode made them fear for Nigeria's future.[33] The cause of the unrest was apparently a disagreement between politicians at the constitutional negotiations over regional autonomy in Lagos. Chief Obafemi Awolowo, the leader of the Action Group Party, made a disparaging remark about Ahmadu Bello's ancestor, Usman 'dan Fodio, the jihadist founder of the Sokoto Caliphate of the nineteenth century. Further, the Hausa were insulted as slaves of the whites because representatives of the largely Hausa political party, the Northern People's Congress (NPC), pressed for a gradual process of decolonization.[34] Ahmadu Bello and other Northern chiefs later reflected that they were easy targets because of their traditional robes; everyone else wore Western-style suits.[35]

The government report on the riots described the events leading to the violence with the following details. Following the stalled negotiations in Lagos, Awolowo's Action Group planned a "rally" in Kano, which the British government later concluded was "ill-advised" and "politically inept."[36] The Sardauna, Bello, visited Kano, and the local branch of the NPC planned a demonstration against the Action Group "rally." The Kano Native Administration also asked its Northern employees to strike to show their solidarity with the NPC; a senior official, Malam Wada, made an "inflammatory" speech to Public Works Department employees. Meanwhile, in the Sabon Gari neighborhood, the Igbo Union asked the Senior District Officer of Kano for protection.[37] The Leventis department store, run by Lebanese, sold 172 machetes, the "favored weapon" of the Southerners, the day of the demonstration.

Violence broke out during the afternoon of May 16 between what looked to be rival gangs. The Yoruba, the largest ethnic group after the Hausa in

Sabon Gari at the time,[38] mostly steered clear of Fagge, the "suburb" north of the walled old city, and Sabon Gari, where the violence was concentrated. The fighting was mainly between Hausa and Igbo. Of the 46 dead and 205 reported medical treatments and hospital admissions, 60 percent were recorded as Northerners and 40 percent as Southerners. Reliable statistics were hard to come by, according to the government, because of the shortage of official medical services for Southerners as compared to Northerners.[39] The SIM Eye Hospital treated several injured, and the Kano City Hospital also admitted many victims of violence, including many Southerners who lived outside the Old City. Northerners mostly wielded cudgels, spears, and bows and arrows—while the Southerners used machetes and Dane guns.

Confusion reigned. In one instance, a gang of Igbos tried to kill another Igbo.[40] At Ya da Kunya, the SIM leprosarium located eleven miles outside the city, the missionary Dr. Dreisbach heard reports that Hausas were being killed in Sabon Gari and buried in Igbo compounds, that Igbos were being killed in Fagge, and that Igbos were killing Hausa children.

The episode was seen as a political problem, not a religious one. The evidence largely supports this conclusion, as the cultural differences—religious and even ethnic—seemed to be secondary to the fundamental cause of conflict—the regional leaders' disagreements over the pathway to independence and their fomenting violence against each other's supporters. The British Resident in Kano later found no reason to alter policy with respect to the SIM, CMS, and other missions, even though the CMS location itself was at the center of the riots.[41] The postmortem on the riots exposed no religious problems but gross inadequacies of policing. The ability of the police to effectively respond was diminished by the dispersion of rioters over a wide distance from Fagge to Sabon Gari.[42]

The only person named as the leader of a gang in any report was Haruna 'dan Daura, a Christian Hausa policeman, who was arrested for leading a group of "hooligans."[43] 'Dan Daura's history in Kano—adopted and raised as a Christian by his uncle, a barber and World War I soldier accused of sorcery—was well known to the authorities. He attended the Cottons' school, but, unlike John Garba, who went from Kano to Zaria to finish school, 'dan Daura stayed in Kano and then left his studies.[44] He became a policeman in 1943. His arrest as a "gang leader" in Sabon Gari in 1953 was not well publicized.

After the riots, anxiety grew about Christians' presence among Muslims. Outside Kano Township, in Dutse District, a native evangelist was expelled from his lodging in town and forced to live in a nearby village.[45] In 1955, when African ECWA evangelists visited the District Head of Tofa, in rural southwestern Kano, he reportedly told them that "they have no right to preach to Muslims and that . . . it is so written in all rules of the mission allowing them to be in the north. They [the African evangelists] told him that was for white missionaries but he insisted that it was for 'mission' and they were 'mission.'"[46] The SIM legal department advised the white missionary at Tofa, Mike Glerum, and all other SIM missionaries in Kano "that the Africans concerned are indigenous Christians and not merely 'Mission men.' The whole crux of our dispute at the present time is that fact that the authorities will not recognise that there is an indigenous church and that the people concerned are not merely Mission 'hangers-on.'"[47]

The British authorities were, in general, unsure how to handle the question of minorities in the North, for fear of radicalizing them or Muslims. In 1954, the Yoruba leaders of the Western Region lobbied to remove the southernmost provinces of Northern Nigeria, including Ilorin, the southernmost emirate of the Sokoto Caliphate, and merge them into the Western Region. In addition to this Southern "push," the British were worried that the so-called "Middle Belt" movement for political recognition of the peoples in Ilorin, Adamawa, Benue, Kabba, Niger, Plateau, and Zaria, would weaken the far northern Muslim provinces, which could not stand to lose such a large portion of their voting base, regardless of religious affiliation.[48] Residents were ordered to not even acknowledge the Middle Belt and instead call these areas "Riverain Provinces." The Governor of Nigeria in 1956 wrote to the Secretary of State for the Colonies in London: "In the most Northerly Provinces less interest is shown [in the Middle Belt League], and it is mainly confined to a small section of the 'intelligentsia' who see possible economic advantage to their area and, more clearly, immediate personal political advantage to themselves in separation from the North. These groups have largely been influenced by the less reputable of the Missions, members of which have always felt that a unitary North circumscribes their opportunities for proselytisation."[49] The Resident in Kano had every reason to disregard any sign that Muslims and Christians could not live together. Blaming missions for their evangelical zeal, at this notably late juncture on the eve of independence, and Northern Christians like 'dan Daura for political conflicts provided the British authorities a convenient cover of religious differences to explain problems that they had not anticipated.

Apprehension grew in Northern cities where Emirs sought to reinforce their commitment to shari'a to reassure Muslims that their traditions would be protected. The Resident of Kano wrote in 1954 to the Civil Secretary for the Northern Region: "The problem is not, however, so much a question of a criminal law for different tribes as for persons of different religions and this is particularly so in Kano where there is a strong desire by the Emir and his Council to take action in accordance with every provision of the Moslem Law which is still permissible. It is, therefore, likely that cases of adultery which would not be an offense in a Magistrate's Court may be brought in the case of christians [sic] in Sabon Gari and be dealt with in accordance with Moslem Law."[50] By 1955, the British authorities removed the power of the *alkali* (Muslim judge) court of Waje (areas outside Kano Old City) over Sabon Gari, leaving only Fagge and Ungogo under its jurisdiction.[51] Christians in Sabon Gari thenceforward took their cases to the magistrate court. The truth was, however, that Christians had before rarely taken their cases to any formal court.

Northern Nigerian Christians had a strong incentive to separate their identities from the missions, but they continued to be dependent on foreign funding, particularly in relation to the medical work. In 1955, representatives of the African staff of the eye hospital sent a letter to the SIM management about their contract for 1956. The SIM did not want to make the reforms recommended by the British colonial administration in its efforts to Nigerianize key industries; the Gorsuch Commission in 1954 recommended a 20 percent raise to all Nigerian Civil Service workers and some nongovernmental workers.[52] The SIM Eye Hospital workers' letter responded to news that SIM management refused their offer to take just 10 percent in arrears. The African workers, who were all Christians, agreed to the smaller increase because they knew the hospital was a charitable institution, but they asked for other conditions in return. Among their demands was an earlier effective date for the arrears, more travel money for those on leave to return to their places of origin, and the SIM's agreement to repatriate staff who had lost employment in Kano.

The leaders of the staff clearly tried to connect their struggle to the secular national labor movement, but their efforts appear to have failed, because their contract for 1956 included no raises.[53] In fact, no workers' strikes occurred at the eye hospital until 1992, following the dismissal of fifteen employees for unionization.[54]

The SIM missionaries sought to avoid entanglements. They celebrated church history in the final years of colonial rule when Nigerian Christian representatives to the Northern Regional Delegation, Dauda Haruna and Pastor David Lot, visited England in 1954. The SIM office in London organized visits for them to Blantyre in Scotland, the birthplace of David Livingstone.[55] Yet the missionaries refused to assist the British authorities with political matters. In 1955, when the Civil Secretary for the Northern Region asked the missions to supply information on native Christians' religious classes, Canon Forster, who spoke for the missions belonging to the Christian Council of Nigeria (CCN) replied: "Mission schools and plots were used for political meetings all over Nigeria. . . . It was not the business of missionaries to interfere in politics either by encouraging or forbidding it."[56] The SIM, the largest mission in the Northern Region, was not a member of the CCN but agreed with the council. They urged the political authorities to consider Christians as a minority in need of protection per the UN Declaration on Human Rights, Article 19, but they certainly did not want to abet any political movement that would ruin their good standing. Though this strategy appealed to the missionaries as a form of neutrality, it did not lead to any Nigerian-based recognitions of a Northern Nigerian religious minority.

Harold Johnston, the Resident of Kano, celebrated progress toward independence in 1955:

> A country moving towards self-government reaches a point where the current of events takes control and begins to hurry it towards its destination. . . . During the past year the tug of this current has been perceptible in Kano and the roar of the approaching rapids has sometimes been clearly heard. With this sound in their ears, the great majority of the servants of Government and the Native Authorities have worked at their tasks with their old industry and with a new and growing sense of urgency. Africans and Europeans alike have devoted themselves manfully to their duties, have helped one another in their difficulties, and without regard for colour or creed have done all in their power to prepare the Province for the ordeals which undoubtedly lie ahead.[57]

On the ground, fights broke out in Katsina town when African ECWA members disseminated pamphlets. "Opposition crystallized into verbal abuse, physical assault, and bombardment with rocks, broken pottery, decaying fruit and vegetables, and gutter filth," wrote one SIM missionary. Opposition radicalized the Christians. "The effect of such persecution on the group of Christians involved was most heartening—no retaliation but an enthusiastic and vitalized witness."[58] Lay Christian evangelism, based on the travails and persecution Christians in Muslim Northern Nigeria endured, signaling their autonomy both from the missions and from Muslims.

The Kano authorities appointed Haruna 'dan Daura in 1958 to head the mixed court of Sabon Gari. The Resident justified his appointment by citing his police and religious credentials: "Mallam Haruna 'Dan Daura is at present serving as an Inspector in the Nigeria Police. He has an excellent Police record and, from his Police duties, a very good knowledge of law. He is a Northerner and a Christian and both I and the Native Authority consider that he will be a very suitable choice for this extremely difficult position."[59] Of course, no one commented on the fact that he was cited as a gang leader in the 1953 riot. The lines between neighborhood policing and vigilante militias were hard to draw in any event in places like Kano ever since the days of the "dual administration" that Morel described in the *Times of London* in 1911. Of course, by the late 1950s, there were many inconsistencies in the ways Christian Northern Nigerians were seen, sometimes as so unexceptional as to be harmless and, at others, as dangerous dissenters who threatened stability in Muslim areas.

INDEPENDENCE

Two years before independence, the British appointed a commission, named after Henry Willink, the Cambridge professor who headed it, to look into "minority affairs."[60] For the North, it noted that the dominant Northern People's Congress (NPC) controlled the majority of votes but did not represent minorities as the opposition Northern Elements Progressive Union (NEPU) did. Non-Muslim minorities feared that future foreign policy decisions by the NPC would lead to alliances with the Muslim Middle Eastern countries. Christians, who numbered about 550,000, as against more than 11 million Muslims and nearly 4.5 million "animists" or pagans, did not want separation, only constitutional protection for religious freedom. Protection of conversion, of course, had the double sense of referring to a change in religious identity and evangelism to convert others. The Willink Commission report read conversion precisely in this evangelical sense: "Islam is a dogmatic and proselytising religion—but not the only one. There are intolerant people on both sides of this controversy and there will always be instances of intolerant behavior. This is a matter that only legislation can point the way."[61]

Political party affiliation at the grassroots level was at times rancorous. The story of Yepwi, a Christian whom evangelist Inusa Samuila talked back into the fold after backsliding in the 1920s, is an example. Yepwi was known to the SIM as the first convert from among the "pagan" Gbagyi ethnic group. He was approximately seventy years old in 1960. He looked to

Inusa, the Christian convert from Islam, as a much more influential figure in his religious life than white missionaries. Yepwi became an important pastor and took the traditional Muslim title of Galadima. In the late 1950s, he began using the pulpit to promote the NPC political party, a rather bold act for an ethnic minority Christian living in one of the so-called Riverain Provinces.[62] Though ECWA was in charge at Karu, the area where Yepwi was pastor, the SIM missionaries were still influential and had a hand in forcing him out of his position.[63]

In 1959, Yepwi's son Thomas wrote to the white missionaries threatening to take his father's case to the high court. Thomas wrote, "My father has been ejected from liberty to enjoy the fundamental human rights, freedom of speech, movements and freedom of joining any political party by the SIM of the Northern Region."[64] The case never reached the courts. The SIM sidestepped Thomas's claims by stating that Yepwi's problem was with fellow African Christians, not with the missionaries. Like the situation with the eye hospital employees, the efforts to keep problems with Northern Nigerian Christians "internal" was to deny them a public identity in legal or political institutions. Few attempts seem to have been made to "legislate intolerance," as the Willink Commission report recommended.

Ahmadu Bello, the Sardauna of Sokoto and the first Northern premier, launched a broad Islamic evangelism campaign targeting the Riverain Provinces in 1963. He "accepted an invitation" to oversee a mass conversion to Islam of pagans in Kuta, Niger Province.[65] Kuta had been heavily evangelized by the SIM since 1909,[66] and Inusa Samuila himself made visits to Kuta, though it is not clear if the locals viewed him as a Christian or as a Muslim. Kuta was also a scene of evangelism by the Sufi Tijaniyya order, which competed with Ahmadu Bello's Qadiriyya order.[67] Bello's entourage presented 100 copies of the Qur'an, 1,000 rosaries, and 1,000 copies of a booklet titled *Worship and Law*. This public ceremony began his many conversion tours, including in Adamawa Province in 1964,[68] popularly regarded to have converted thousands of "pagans" and perhaps Christians to Islam.

Christian observers were alarmed. In 1967, Claude Molla, the general director of a Christian literature center in Cameroon, published an essay on Islam's competitive advances in sub-Saharan Africa in the Edinburgh-based publication *International Review of Mission*. He claimed that Ahmadu Bello announced that between December 1963 and April 1965, he gained almost 177,000 new converts to Islam.[69]

Oral history suggests an earlier start to the Sardauna's evangelical activities, before his political future was certain. In 1940, when he was a junior traditional titleholder in the Sokoto Native Administration, Ahmadu Bello shopped for paper and pens at the SIM bookstore in Gusau. He met a young man named Ahmadu John Abarshi, who was, as a child, given by his father to be educated, first by the Sudan Interior Mission at Wushishi, then by the Church Missionary Society in Wusasa. Abarshi went to Gusau to work because he was a Fulani by ethnicity and felt comfortable among Muslims. Abarshi said, "SIM opened the bookshop at Gusau, 137 miles from Sokoto. So they wanted a suitable somebody to place in that bookshop [someone who knew Hausa and knew Muslims]. I volunteered."[70] Abarshi sought to escape from his job at the leprosarium at Amanawa in Sokoto. "To give lepers injections you have to wear gloves," he told me, suggesting that the fear of contagion made working as a nurse or auxiliary very stressful. The bookstore was different. Everyone wanted to visit the place. He recounted:

> I met our late premier Ahmadu Bello there. He was chief scribe in the District Officer's office, Gusau. My first contact with him was when he came to buy carbon papers, typing materials. When I had to debit his account (I was directed by the manager to open his account), he laughed at my writing. He said, "You write beautifully. Where did you school?" I said, "SIM." He said, 'A'a, you look like a Fulani." I said I am. He said, "Like me." I said, "I have been hearing of you." He said, "Are you a Christian?" I said yes. He wanted to draw me, he wanted to *draw* me. I said no. I said if I leave, I'll join the [British] Government. He was in the Native Authority.[71]

Ahmadu Bello, who two years earlier had made an unsuccessful bid to become the Sultan of Sokoto and had instead received the traditional title of Sardauna, was a regular customer. This great man, Abarshi jokes, though eleven years and many social ranks his senior, showed interest in a simple store clerk, a Christian.[72] It no doubt felt good for Abarshi to be able to rebuff the Sardauna's offer. Not long after his meetings with Ahmadu Bello, the young man moved to Kaduna to join the police force, an institution within which he rose to the level of chief inspector.[73] Abarshi served in the police escorts for high-level delegations of the Sardauna in later years, and he served as support for the Nigerian troops during the Civil War. The work was extremely dangerous, and a collision with a car when he was on bicycle patrol was the beginning of the end of his career.

Northern Christians reminisce about watching Ahmadu Bello's rise to power. As a government servant, he formed a special board facilitating trips to Mecca and established the Society for the Victory of Islam in 1962. On the side, he continued to take evangelism tours, and Maguzawa remember these events by the ornate robes he passed out.[74] According to one Sokoto elite, Ahmadu Bello accepted Northerners as Christians or Muslims. "Pagans were naked," however, "and he was embarrassed. He wanted to 'put clothes on them.' The Sardauna and the *waziri* [another political leader] had books printed up to aid in this process."[75] This language of clothes, nakedness, and *kunya* (shame) and *wayo*—cleverness that children gained as they matured—is still used today in Hausa religious parlance, shared by both Muslims and Christians, perhaps with origins in this episode.

White missionaries, too, referred to clothing to distinguish people in the 1960s. It signaled what kind of education and status a man possessed. At the same time, it could provide effective "cover," even the loss of identity should one want that. Chuck Hershelman, the headmaster of the SIM primary school (unofficially opened in Kano Township in 1957), described the ease with which Muslim students blended into the SIM school. He said, "Muslim students would come in, change their names to Christian ones, but as soon as they graduated would revert back to Islam and take Muslim names because they could get employment more easily. They put on the cloak of Christianity because they knew that they'd get a better education." Hershelman referred to nonelites and made clear that "the Muslims [leaders] said they did not care, then sent their children to England for education. Muslim leaders got the best for themselves."[76] Many missionaries—white and black—claimed, without any evidence, these youngsters were "secret believers," allowing Muslims to exploit the Christian schools.

Schools were sorely lacking in the immediate postcolonial era. Abubakar Tafawa 'Balewa, the Nigerian prime minister, pressed the British authorities on this before they left: "Among the needs of the northern provinces are mass literacy, and for the education of our boys and girls to go side by side. We have only one secondary school—we ask for five more and two for girls."[77] The British had not prioritized schools and had blocked missions in their efforts to expand them. In the early 1960s, rural people attempted to take local ownership of the former SIM classes scattered throughout the countryside. Pastor Moses Ariye of ECWA told an audience in Toronto that Christian and Muslim villagers approached the church to take proprietorship of schools and to petition the government.[78] Religious affiliation became a means for villagers to increase access to education as communities responded, together, to seek political and social development.

The connection between schools and religious affiliation was important because villages converted en masse to Islam and Christianity in the early 1960s. Mass conversions had occurred in earlier decades, for instance when Inusa evangelized in Gbagyiland, but the pace and scale of mass conversion accelerated. Following the Sardauna's mass conversion campaigns in Kuta and in Adamawa Province, Christian evangelists began to hold their "feasts of repentance" among Maguzawa. As reported to missionary Titus Payne, the 1970s were a turning point. ECWA leaders claimed that Maguzawa were coming in the thousands. A white missionary remarked: "I am told that a public ceremony is held in which those changing their religion step forward into a central area. They cast their idols and fetishes and charms into a fire. They publicly state they repent of their paganism and all its evil ways. They choose Christianity and make a public profession of faith in Christ."[79] The Emir of Kano, Ado Bayero, called seventy Maguzawa to confirm the conversions, and he reportedly became very angry and demanded they "return to their paganism and forbade church-building." They answered that he gave permission to build hotels where prostitution, gambling, drinking, and the like were going on, so why should he forbid building a house of worship. For those Maguzawa who did not want to become Christians, Payne wrote, they had to move farther and farther into the rural areas to find a pagan village. He did not, of course, mention the possibility of Islam. Yet most Nigerians understood that there were two choices—Christianity or Islam—if one wanted to stay in closer proximity to urban areas.

Missionaries, 850 of whom were serving in Northern Nigeria in the late 1950s, remained after independence. Their days of trekking and market evangelism were long gone; now they ran printing presses, oversaw hospitals and clinics, and helped indigenous church bodies negotiate the terms of their leases with local governments so that former mission stations would become churches, schools, and clinic sites. In general, negotiations were carried out between SIM and ECWA District Council members, a process that even as early as 1961 led to disagreements and the feeling that the SIM was holding back the indigenous church.[80] White Christian missionaries still had the upper hand in negotiations with government, which was by now constitutionally secular but still Muslim in much of the North, but the Northern government wanted to see the SIM, CMS, and others continue to provide services during this critical period of social development.

FRACTURED LOYALTIES

In 1966, in the coup d'état led by a cadre of mostly Igbo soldiers, Prime Minister Abubakar Tafawa 'Balewa, the Sardauna Ahmadu Bello, and several other leaders were assassinated. The coup leader, Major General Johnson Aguiyi-Ironsi, was killed in a countercoup that brought into power General Yakubu Gowon, a Wusasa Christian, as the head of the Nigerian state. Despite attempts at political reform to address disagreements over the integration of the regions, including Gowon's attempt to create twelve states, tensions grew. According to Michael Gould, "One of the effects of the second coup were the uncontrolled racial attacks on the Igbo people, which created paranoid fear, leading to a determination that the East's destiny was secession from the federation."[81]

The killing of Igbos began in the Northern towns, and SIM missionaries who were there tried to help. Cris Oswold, a missionary in Jega, Sokoto, remembered that after the slaughter of Igbos in town, the police disappeared to allow mayhem to escalate. Christian women came to her after their husbands were murdered, and she gave them head scarves and directed them to the bike paths missionaries had in previous years followed to trek into the villages. The gangs would test people by asking them to speak Hausa. They even tested her.[82]

Oswold reported that many Christians, entire villages, lived in Sokoto Province in those days. The Sardauna had come to Jega on his conversion tours, but many who were Muslim said they converted to get gowns; so the counts are questionable, she says. When Muslims came with jeeps and megaphones and said they would burn villages down if residents did not convert, entire communities fled south and resettled. Such villages relocated to Kwoi, a town that suffered religious riots in the late 1980s.[83] Not all Muslims liked the Sardauna, Oswold said, remembering a Hausa businessman in Jega, who, when his worker told him that the Sardauna had been killed, pulled out a one-hundred-pound note and gave it to him. Oswold claimed that the pogroms were undertaken not by ordinary Muslims but by thugs who were "cleaned up" by politicians. The reference to thugs echoes the reports of the 1953 Kano riots and the Sardauna's own recollections that the killers in Kano were hired guns, upstarts, and wanderers from unruly neighborhoods like Fagge.[84] Oswold also believed that Saudi money was used to pay off moderate Muslims, a rumor that cannot be confirmed but shows the perceived or feared geopolitical alignments in Nigerian politics in the early independence era.

Northern Nigerian Christians were divided in their views of the Sardauna and the direction of the North in the 1960s. Ladi Joe, an Anglican Wusasa girl, was teaching at the Katsina Women's Training Center. From the school's opening in 1937, white women had served as teachers because of difficulties recruiting Muslim girls to train as teachers.[85] When Ahmadu

Bello visited the center in the 1960s, Ladi Joe was one of only two black women teachers. She taught health education; the other African woman, a Southerner, taught Islamic education.

"He shook hands with everyone, except me," she remembered. "I had taught the wives of the Emir of Katsina himself. They like your service, but not you."[86] Ahmadu Bello symbolized, for Christian women like Ladi Joe, the continuing frustration for recognition of Northern Nigerian Christians, and in particular women, as a positive force of colonial-era social welfare. Instead, she felt regarded as a symbol of foreign values imposed on Muslim societies. She felt that Southern Nigerians were allies before Northern Nigerian Christians were in the minds of Muslim Northern Nigerians. Christian men, on the other hand, such as Haruna 'dan Daura and Yepwi, tended to see the Sardauna as an enlightened and benevolent Muslim leader who promoted Northern regional unity by cultivating religiosity, both Muslim and Christian.

Though the far North was generally spared the violence of the Civil War between 1967 and 1970, the ethnic clashes in 1966 left a lasting imprint. As Henry and Reta Guenter, SIM missionaries in Bauchi, wrote: "There is much uncertainty and the tension is not all gone. Many lost all their properties by fire and looting, and many have lost husbands and fathers especially. Rioting always leaves much injustice in its wake and, as some would say, unsettled scores."[87] The itinerant ECWA evangelical activities, which included preaching tours of evangelists and the passing out of pamphlets under the banner of New Life for All, virtually came to a halt.

When the war was declared over in 1970, a Christian Northern soldier from Wusasa, General Yakubu Gowon, took over the federal government. In 1972, per the policy of indigenization, most of the SIM hospitals and clinics were brought into the state governments of Kano, Katsina, Bauchi, and Sokoto. Farther south, the wealth of ECWA allowed them to purchase or take over certificates of occupancy for SIM institutions and manage them. The leprosariums were folded into the government infectious diseases programs and became segregation areas for tuberculosis victims supported mainly by UNICEF and other programs.

The mission era largely came to an end, but indigenization did not dismantle Christian evangelical networks. A continuing but covert operation in the 1970s illustrates this. On February 12, 1975, a Chadian named Ayuba Agades was surrounded by men in his village in southern Chad. They arrived at night to round up men to perform *yondo* (a Sara male initiation rite). For two years, yondo initiation had inspired terror all over Chad. The rite was associated with the Sara, a southern ethnic group from which the president, Ngarta Tombalbaye, hailed. Following independence from France in 1960, he used it as part of his national "authenticity campaign" modeled after the authenticité movement of Mobutu of Zaire.[88] Tombalbaye gave up his name François to become Ngarta; Fort Lamy became N'Djamena. Mobutu described authenticité as "being oneself and not how others would like one to be . . . the motor of the construction of the nation . . . and cement to stop the mental alienation brought by the colonial experience."[89]

Knowing the initiators would come, Ayuba had given his pregnant wife, Damaris, some money and told her to wait, sell all of their property, and find him in Nigeria. He stole out of the village, crossing four days later into Cameroon. From there, he hitched a ride on a lorry to Maiduguri. White missionaries of the Sudan United Mission (SUM) and the indigenous church that grew out of it, EKAS (Eklisiyar Krista a Sudan), sheltered him before he went deeper into Nigeria.[90]

While the mood for self-expression and national consciousness flowered in independent Africa, Ayuba's story suggests that cultural identities were produced in fear and flight. Being a refugee made him more fully Christian. When he recounted his saga to the American missionary Charles Rhine in 1975, Ayuba claimed that he had been a Christian since 1960, even before he had married Damaris, but that his conversion was bitterly opposed by his father and uncle, both "pagans."[91] His in-laws also fought against him and Damaris. When she sold all her possessions to pay for her flight to follow her husband across the border to Nigeria, her father stole all her money. Both Ayuba and Damaris entered Northern Nigeria with little but the clothes on their backs and the profession of Christianity, which connected them to an underground network, a large informal relief operation that had formed in northeastern Nigeria. Christian communities in Adamawa and Jos and other cities gave cover to Chadians coming into their midst.[92] Northern Nigeria offered the possibility of escape and a new life because of its autonomous and underground Christian evangelical networks that allowed for the remaking of kinship, economic life, and social status.

Conclusion

CHRISTIANITY GAVE FORM to an array of negotiations between "tradition" and "modernity," not simply between the old and the new in Hausa communities.[1] It furnished a source of new identity and a new language for migration, a long-important social practice in this region of Sudanic Africa. While mission culture first enabled currents of historicism, it later drew migrants who were less focused on remembering than on forgetting as a way of being reborn.

Foreign missions, indigenous church-building, and evangelism created opportunities for collaboration with Muslim rulers that revealed to them the growing power of Christianity. Ahmadu Bello and Tafawa 'Balewa saw this potential through their personal experiences of the Sudan Interior Mission (SIM) missionaries and converts in Gusau and Bauchi. While Muslim conversion campaigns may have sought to erase or reduce Northern Nigerian Christianity, Christians undertook their own evangelical crusades. Christian Northern Nigerians long struggled to establish their religious authority and authenticity, independent of white missionaries and Southern Nigerians. Their activities forged a new brand of religious politics in the era of decolonization.

Christian revivalism in campaigns such as New Life for All, begun in 1966 in the Jos Plateau area, was a combined effort of several Northern Nigerian churches including the Evangelical Churches of West Africa (ECWA) and others. Scholars have tended to emphasize the charismatic and Pentecostal features of African Christian movements of this period, mainly drawing on research from Southern Nigeria, Ghana, and other "already" Christian places,[2] but the evidence from Northern Nigeria suggests that competition with Islam was at least equally important.[3] Christian renewal was especially important during the changing political situation for Christians in Northern Nigeria after the deaths of the more benevolent paternalist Muslim leaders and the takeover of the leprosariums by state governments with the Indigenization Decree of 1972. At the same time that rural ECWA members became entangled in struggles with local governments to transfer colonial-era certificates of occupancy from the SIM, they pushed evangelistic missions more deeply into rural areas of Kano, Bauchi, Sokoto, and beyond. Their reports of meeting Isawa and Maguzawa are reminiscent of white missionary and indigenous African accounts from the 1910s, except their eagerness to report on the persistence of heterodox religious identities as such may imply, to the irritation of Muslims, a critique of the Sardauna's mass conversion campaigns of the 1960s as superficial and fleeting.

An episode from 1977 reflects the local religious repertoire from the days of Inusa. Yakubu Yako, a worker with the ECWA missionary society, reported that he met a pilgrim from Sokoto who was traveling one thousand kilometers to Bima Hill in Gombe.[4] He was going to the final resting place of the Mahdists who, believing that the End was near in the early 1900s (as the British army advanced on them) began *hijra* (flight) to reach Mecca. Among those martyrs was Attahiru, the Sultan of Sokoto, who led refugees to Bima following the fall of Kano to the British.[5] The man who retraced the sultan's steps told the Christian evangelist that he had seen three signs of the nearing apocalypse: children disobeying parents, poor relations between husbands and wives, and famine and war in the world.[6] The themes of Pentecostal and charismatic Christian renewal provide less utility for understanding this episode, which unfolded in the context of the massive Sahelian drought of the 1970s, than local eschatological urgency, made more intense by the historical dynamics of Christian preaching among Muslims.[7]

Christian Northern Nigerians, despite their internal divisions, constituted a community once acknowledged as genuinely Northern Nigerian. Yet important internal distinctions exist among those who identify as Northern Nigerian Christians. Anglican Christians, particularly the older generations, were generally wealthier and better employed than their contemporaries among ECWA or nondenominational church members. The Anglicans formed a smaller and more exclusive community comprising many more Hausa and Fulani Christians than any of the other churches.

Although this ethnic exclusivity was cultivated somewhat by Dr. Walter Miller, the Wusasa Christians often elevated their ethnic and class identities over their religious ones. For example, a largely unspoken division arose for marriage practices, by which ECWA, EKAS, and members of other churches (who tend to be Hausa-speaking but not Hausa by ethnic origin), could intermarry, while Anglicans tended to marry within their own church. Some ethnic fluidity existed, but hard lines, particularly for converts of Hausa and Fulani ancestry, were also drawn.

Younger generations adhered less to such restrictions, identifying first as Northern Nigerian Christians before ethnic or denominational identities. The so-called Middle Belt movement in the 1950s was a Christian movement. Yet it was not solely a "Middle Belt" phenomenon outside the Muslim "North" because there were "politics of the middle" within Northern cities like Kano and Katsina and on Christian mission sites, where Christians struggled to create a political language for expressing their identities and aspirations. They borrowed the language of class from the labor movement and otherwise sought regional identification with the NPC of the Sardauna and Tafawa 'Balewa rather than identifying with Southerners. As John Peel observes of the SIM in Yorubaland, it did not garner many converts until the 1950s, during the era of political party-making.[8] A greater sense of African Christian unity operated in relation to the ECWA's formation and growth, perhaps as an alternative to "secular" nationalist politics. The historical language within religious groups about such movements—revivals, awakening, harvest—does not conform, often intentionally, to the political chronology or geography of Nigeria.

The practices and politics of historicism have been central to the creation of Christian identities. Inusa, John Garba, and the Dass preachers all hailed from very different origins, but they identified as religious and political dissenters from the nineteenth-century jihad. Christianity unified these histories of dissent from the margins of the caliphate and helped to prioritize religious rebirth over ethnic origins.

Northern Nigerian Christians formed networks through the practices of itinerant evangelism.[9] The Word has spread without missions, and Christian communities have grown in spite of many restrictions. The British authorities complained about "Christian propaganda," particularly after the 1920s, following Ethel Miller's vociferous attacks on Muhammad. Yet the emirate authorities rarely sought to restrict the content of Christian missionary preaching (*yin wa'azi*, literally "exhortation"). Neither the British nor the emirate authorities seemed to take Christians seriously as political subjects in the 1950s, but by the 1960s, the Sardauna's conversion tours suggest that he appreciated the appeal of Christianity and that it could potentially change, if not divide, the North. He used the language of rebirth in the context of opening opportunities for conversion to Islam, attempting to diminish historical territorial and cultural boundaries. Such discourses had been unique to Christianity in Northern Nigeria in the 1900s, but by the 1960s, they were deployed by Christian and Muslim Africans alike.

The late historian Dr. Yusufu Bala Usman wrote in the 1980s that the "political manipulation of religion" in Nigeria began during General Yakubu Gowon's regime (1966–1975).[10] Gowon, a son of evangelists who migrated from Pankshin, in the Plateau region of the "Middle Belt," to Wusasa, Zaria, attended Christian schools and 'Barewa (formerly Katsina) College, where he developed close relationships with many elite Muslims. When he became the military head of state in 1966, his Christian and Middle Belt identities were useful, seen as antidote to resentments among members of ethnic minorities who were heavily represented in the military. At the same time, he was an ally of the Hausa and Fulani elite.

Antimissionary sentiment intensified in Nigeria during the Civil War, according to Usman, because of "very powerful pro-secessionist [pro-Biafra] propaganda from Western Europe, America, and parts of Africa."[11] Gowon, the head of the Nigerian Federation throughout the war and one-time "'Barewa old boy" and a "good Northerner," became instead derided as the "Christian missionary's boy."[12] The image of the missionary was revived in national political discourse to discredit the legitimacy of those seen as the successors to the missionaries, such as Gowon's family, who were essentially accused of being loyal to foreign interests.

The perceived corruption of the Gowon regime and the excesses of Nigeria's oil boom gave fuel to the reformism of Alhaji Abubakar Gummi, the former Grand Qadi of the Northern Region and adviser to the late Sardauna. Gowon's Christianity became identified with political corruption, and suspicion that he was involved in the assassination of the coup leader who deposed him, General Murtala Muhammad, further polarized politics according to religious affiliation. For many Christians, suspicion of Gowon's hypocrisy and his history of close fraternity with Muslims led to distrust of any would-be political player with Muslim alliances and who was not wholly within the fold of Christianity.

As Northern Nigerian Christians faced new pressures in this increasingly polarized environment and actual physical danger as Nigeria's political situation deteriorated, they further embraced their victimization as a basis for communal identity. In favor of communal interests, Christians have sought again to mute their divisions. The tension between Northern and Southern Christians has long been apparent in historical sources that speak of the "immorality" of Sabon Gari, where many missionaries and Northern Nigerian Christians resisted settling. This tension among Christians has lessened or at least become less important in light of rising Muslim-Christian violence in the last two or three decades.

Another arena in which tensions have been transformed is at the intersection of religious and gender identities. While Christian men often maintained affiliations and alliances within Muslim society, this has been nearly impossible for most Christian women. Historically, women's Christianization is identified with the ending of slavery and with rejection of Muslim respectability. Indeed, any Christian woman is assumed to be of "pagan" ancestry because a Muslim woman, it is assumed, would of course never have voluntarily chosen the more marginal religion. While Christian women have found mobility in employment in secular development organizations, very few Christian communities have invested in the development of women as religious leaders, in contrast to the possibilities for elite Muslim women to be scholars.[13]

Indeed, the implementation of shari'a has led to a resurgence of Muslim adult women's enrollment in Islamic schools (*Islamiyya*), many seeking to learn about their legal rights. Among them, a revival of sorts is at work. Both Muslim men and women reveal their surprise at learning what is actually prescribed in the Qur'an and what are instead fads taken up as a result of outside influences. Men, for instance, decried the separation of men and women at prayer as an Arab import contrary to Muslim Nigerian precedent, as with the increasing use of the full burqa, which many criticize as unnecessary and potentially exploited by criminals seeking to steal in the market or carry weapons. Christian women tend to speak of Muslim women as victims, even elite Muslim women, on account of the imminent possibility that their husbands may take new wives and because of the much higher rates of divorce among Muslims. As John Garba pointed out several decades ago, Christians know much less about Muslims than Muslims know about Christians.[14]

Younger generations of Christians perceive that the fluidity or uncertain history of religious identity known to earlier generations has hurt Christian families and handicapped them economically. Watching older Christian men recant, take up Islam, and marry younger wives and have more children, they experienced loss and forfeiture in both financial and spiritual matters. Christians cannot inherit property from deceased Muslim relatives. Resolving Christian disputes legally is a challenge in Muslim areas, and neither churches nor organizations like the Christian Association of

Nigeria (CAN), founded in 1976, have the time or resources to establish formal bodies to handle domestic disagreements.

Even with recantations and marital estrangement, for Hausa and Fulani Christians, rooting themselves in specific ethnic and sometimes Islamic origin stories is a source of prestige in itself. They have long maintained their own organization, Masihiyawa.[15] However, the interests of other Christians to assimilate into a panethnic non-Muslim Hausa-speaking community has, in recent years, led to further revisionism. Many Hausa-speaking descendants of Chadians would rather forget the past. In one instance, I traveled to interview a known Chadian descendant who told me his father was instead from rural Kano. Others, especially women, are more open to speaking about their forefathers' forgotten roots across the border. Indeed, with the more thoroughgoing implementation of shari'a since 2000, some Christians claim descent from converts from paganism, even if their ancestors had been Muslim; ancestors are not immune to the label of apostate. The present generational, domestic, and legal consequences of past conversions have led some Christians to revise their personal histories.

Murray Last writes of the insecurity Muslims feel about the growth of Christianity within their midst, from the new parts of Kano City to rural communities throughout Hausaland.[16] Northern Nigerian Christians feel their own insecurity, on many accounts, but especially of being "made visible" by violence perpetrated by Islamists in newer heterogeneous settlements. These settlements are home not only to Christians but also to Muslim migrants from outside the area and to Kano or Bauchi people who relocated to new areas for larger houses or better provision of water, electricity, and other essential services. Christian Northern Nigerians have sought to blend in among recent Muslim migrants, rather than settle among "old migrants" in Sabon Gari, which has outgrown itself in any case.

Christian and Muslim women of more economically stable families are able to school and work together as teachers and health professionals. The Catholic Saint Louis Girls' School in Kano has a mixed religious student body and an official policy of "disallowing" conversion between religions. This prohibition is related to fears of school and university cults throughout Nigeria, but it also serves the purpose of assuring families that their daughters will have enlightening but "safe" exposure to the "other" religion. The girls must learn about each other's beliefs and must conduct their "own" prayers on campus.[17]

Overt but peaceful Muslim-Christian interaction has come to represent a privilege in today's Kano. The movement to separate religious classes for children in public schools—into CRK (Christian religious knowledge) and IRK (Islamic religious knowledge)—has ensured that teachers of these subjects are very different (Southern Nigerians seem to predominate in government schools as CRK teachers) and that students are often segregated.[18] The groups remain quite uneducated about each other's religion, but Christians, especially younger ones, often know little about Islam, as mentioned earlier.

Potentially productive religious interaction is a luxury that occurs at elite levels of society, although Muslim- and Christian-educated professional women tend to share charitable work in relation to poorer Muslim women and girls. Their cooperation has, since the 1960s, represented an acceptable form of social and economic intercourse, not unlike the elite paternalism of missionary and Muslim men a few decades earlier. These women have moved from education into the field of "development," which is an important economic niche, largely supported by international aid organizations.

Murray Last remarks on some emerging public initiatives to promote religious interactions as alternatives to the clashing civilizations model. The Interfaith Mediation Center based in Kaduna and begun by Imam Muhammad Ashafa Nuruddin and Pastor James Wuye has achieved international prominence. These men have taken their experience in communal mediation in Nigeria to settings in Kenya, and they regularly speak abroad.[19] In another type of religious dialogue, UNICEF has brought religious leaders together to promote the polio immunization campaign that has been met with resistance and fraught with controversy.[20] The local reception to these public health campaigns (informed by a meningitis epidemic in Kano in the 1990s during which Pfizer conducted a trial of an experimental meningitis drug that led to the deaths of eleven children in 1996 and the disability of dozens more) is traceable to the history of medical missions, which is often ignored in contemporary studies about resistance to polio immunization.[21] While medical missions were an example of Muslim-Christian cooperation, they also gave shape and space to forms of resistance to foreign medical philanthropy and biomedical measures, which at an important moment included attempts to separate children from their mothers, and to the expression of fears of dependency on external aid as early as the 1950s.

The potential avenues between Christianity and Islam have grown fewer and become more dangerous and thus covert. Near the 'dan Agundi gate in Kano City, where in earlier decades a crypto-Christian community lived, a seedy rooming house serving mostly transient young men became the temporary home of a man, his wife, and their five children in April 2001.[22] They appeared to be Muslims in their new lodging within the *birni*, as the walled Old City of Kano is known. Not long before, however, they were Christians. The man, a teacher at a bush school deep in the Kano hinterland, had struggled to feed his family. He made contact with a prominent Muslim evangelist—a retired judge. Perhaps conversion to Islam could get the teacher a better-paying job. He decided to leave behind Christianity, the religion to which his parents converted through the evangelism of foreign missionaries.

Once the family moved to the city, the retired judge encouraged the man to learn the *salat*, Muslim daily prayers, so that he could pray with his new neighbors. In their rented room, the convert's wife chafed. She felt her husband's opportunity came at the cost of her freedom, which she measured in terms of going to the village market and working in the fields. The man worried that his wife did not share his interest in Islam. It was Easter, and he feared that their absence from church would lead relatives to come to the city to search for them.

Whereas Ethel Miller observed African women seeking urban domesticity in the 1920s and 1930s, this rural woman in 2001 did not want to be an urban Muslim woman. At the same time, urban life and, with it, Islam, could potentially bring the family economic security. For the judge, crossing into non-Muslim spheres, even with all his authority and privileges, could have been dangerous. Immediately after the declaration of shar'ia, other Muslims may have suspected that he wanted to drink alcohol or pursue other business prohibited within Muslim areas. There would have also been the risk of reprisals from Christians for his evangelical activities.

While Christian missionaries' market preaching and temperance crusades of the 1920s as well as the Sardauna's conversion campaigns of the 1960s were public spectacle, more contemporary religious evangelism like the retired judge's is secretive. While increasingly dangerous, "conversion" remains a means of mobility at the margins.

The history of Muslim-Christian interaction in Northern Nigeria has yielded a rich and enduring popular memory and imagination traceable across vast distances, the reigns of particular sultans and republican leaders, and generational divides. The elements of this history are frequently deployed in the service of partisan agendas by self-appointed prophets. Murray Last discusses how the politicization of religion "builds upon a complex structure of ancient rhetoric and long-past histories, of memories of slights and oppression by forebears. There is a whole discourse that can be drawn upon by those who want to stir up animosities. This can constitute the evidence politicians want in order to make their 'clash of civilizations' seem not only respectable or reasonable, but inevitable."[23] Similarly,

Adam Higazi, in his study of recent vigilantism in Plateau State, notes that "history is interpreted and manipulated by all sides—particularly in the selective use of colonial sources—to fit current political agendas."[24]

The ease and efficacy of the use of "history" to exploit the panic over religious politics in Northern Nigeria depends in part on the limited nature of the available sources and the conditions of their creation, and the absence of others, to support or refute competing presentist versions of the past. This book and other studies, particularly current projects on Christian missions to Muslims being undertaken by African scholars,[25] offer new and different sources and histories of the colonial-era Muslim-Christian interaction in Northern Nigeria, which complicate facile narratives and show Northern Nigeria as a place of religious collaboration, experimentation, puzzlement, and sympathy.

Notes

INTRODUCTION

1. John Garba, *The Time Has Come . . . : Reminiscences and Reflections of a Nigerian Pioneer Diplomat* (Ibadan: Spectrum Books, 1989), 385, 387.
2. Ibid., 388.
3. For the most recent treatment of "onomastics" in Hausaland, see Murray Last, "Ancient Labels and Categories: Exploring the 'Onomastics' of Kano," in *Being and Becoming Hausa: Interdisciplinary Perspectives*, ed. Anne Haour and Benedetta Rossi (Leiden: Brill, 2010), esp. 61–62. Last argues that the names referring to the Magians, for instance, were part of the "legalising practice" of immigrant traders who settled in particular urban spaces. This essay develops points he has made in earlier articles. Marjorie Helen Stewart, "The Kisra Legend as Oral History," *International Journal of African Historical Studies* 13, no. 1 (1980): 51–70. I do not include here sects centered on Isa (Jesus, called Isawa in Hausa), whose history is embedded with Christian missionaries but quite possibly do predate them. I explore Isawa history in chapter 1.
4. Andrew F. Walls, "Africa as the Theatre of Christian Engagement with Islam in the Nineteenth Century," *Journal of Religion in Africa* 29, no. 2 (May 1999): 161.
5. Chimamanda Adichie, "Things Left Unsaid," *London Review of Books* 34, no. 19 (11 October 2012): 32–33. Adichie also mentions Lugard's wife, Flora Shaw, who coined the word *Nigeria*.
6. Paul Newman, *The Etymology of Hausa boko* (Mega-Chad Research Network, 2013), 1–13, http://www.megatchad.net/publications/Newman-2013-Etymology-of-Hausa-boko.pdf.
7. Human Rights Watch, *Spiraling Violence: Boko Haram Attacks and Security Force Abuses in Nigeria* (New York: Human Rights Watch, 2012). New research on Boko Haram is being generated quickly, but I draw attention to this report because it situates the group's politics and terrorism in the context of its relationship with the Nigerian state forces, which have exacted terrible atrocities on civilians.
8. An example other than boko can be found in Nikolai Dobronravine, "Hausa Ajami Literature and Script: Colonial Innovations and Post-Colonial Myths in Northern Nigeria," *Sudanic Africa* 15 (2004): 85–110. Dobronravine makes a very intriguing argument that *ajami* as Arabic text for the writing of non-Arabic languages was based on a missionary error. *Ajami* had meant "foreign," referring to non-Arabic languages, but did not mean Arabic script.
9. Jonathan Reynolds discusses the very different ways in which the two main political parties among Muslims in Northern Nigeria, the Northern People's Congress

(NPC) and the Northern Elements Progressive Union (NEPU), interpreted jihadist and caliphate history from the late colonial era through independence. Niels Kastfelt has introduced a new dimension by exploring how Christian Northern Nigerians refer to precolonial history that I build upon in this book. Reynolds, "The Politics of History: The Legacy of the Sokoto Caliphate in Nigeria," *Journal of Asian and African Studies* 32, nos. 1–2 (1997): 50–65; Kastfelt, "The Politics of History in Northern Nigeria" (occasional paper, Centre of African Studies, University of Copenhagen, September 2007).

10. Frieder Ludwig, "Christian-Muslim Relations in Northern Nigeria since the Introduction of Shari'ah in 1999," *Journal of the American Academy of Religion* 76, no. 3 (September 2008): 615–16.

11. I have chosen to protect the identity of this interviewee because of his public visibility. I have used Abdullah Yusuf Ali's *An English Interpretation of the Holy Qur'an*, 1st ed. (Bensenville, IL: Lushena Books, 1934), 278, because this version is the one that many colonial-era Northern Nigerians themselves used.

12. Wale Adebanwi examines the case of Tarok-Fulani tensions in Yelwa, in Plateau State, which is in general where many of the indigeneity claims of Christians have been the most vocal since the adoption of the new Nigerian Constitution with the transition to civilian rule in 1999. In long-Muslim Hausa areas, by contrast, indigeneity is less important than Muslim identity because Islam was a pathway by which non-Hausa people became Hausa. In the course of this research, I encountered the developing discourses of indigeneity among Christian Hausa who were converts from Maguzawa or non-Muslim Hausa areas. Adebanwi, "Terror, Territoriality, and the Struggle for Indigeneity and Citizenship in Northern Nigeria," *Citizenship Studies* 13, no. 4 (2009): 349–63. On religious incorporation, see the excellent introduction to Haour and Rossi, *Being and Becoming Hausa*, 24. This volume reengages the seminal literature in various disciplines to shift attention away from colonial-era historiography focused on Hausa traditionalism and onto the presentist overemphasis on Islam's monolithic influence in Northern Nigeria.

13. Murray Last, "Muslims and Christians in Nigeria: An Economy of Political Panic," *Round Table* 96, no. 332 (2007): 605–16; Last, "The Search for Security in Muslim Northern Nigeria," *Africa* 78, no. 1 (2008): 41–63.

14. Nathan Nunn, "The Importance of History for Economic Development," *Annual Review of Economics* 1 (2009): 65–92; see also Nunn's article "Religious Conversion in Colonial Africa," *American Economic Review: Papers and Proceedings* 100, no. 2 (May 2010): 147–52; Robert D. Woodberry, "The Missionary Roots of Liberal Democracy," *American Political Science Review* 106, no. 2 (May 2012): 244–74. Nunn is more cautious in extrapolating too much from religious factors, but his research is noteworthy for attempting to quantify the effects of religious and other cultural identities across generations.

15. Jan Vansina, "The Politics of History and the Crisis in the Great Lakes," *Africa Today* 45, no. 1 (January–March 1998): 37–44; Alison Des Forges, "The Ideology of Genocide," *Issue: A Journal of Opinion* 23, no. 2 (1995): 44–47; Catharine Newbury, "Ethnicity and the Politics of History in Rwanda," *Africa Today* 45, no. 1 (January–March 1998): 7–24.

16. Timothy Longman, *Christianity and the Genocide in Rwanda* (New York: Cambridge University Press, 2009).

17. A notable exception is the research of James Quirin that historicizes the "ancient" Ethiopia Jewry and "pagan-Hebraic" Kemant. He explores the caste, ethnic, and

political dynamics out of which these distinct identities emerged, noting the particular importance of the centralizing tendencies of the Christian Amharic monarchy. Quirin, "The Process of Caste Formation in Ethiopia: A Study of the Beta Israel (Felasha), 1270–1868," *International Journal of African Historical Studies* 12, no. 2 (1979): 235–58; Quirin, "Caste and Class in Historical North-West Ethiopia: The Beta Israel (Falasha) and Kemant, 1300–1900," *Journal of African History* 39, no. 2 (1998): 195–220.

18. Heather J. Sharkey, *American Evangelicals in Egypt: Missionary Encounters in an Age of Empire* (Princeton, NJ: Princeton University Press, 2008); Barbara Cooper, *Evangelicals in the Muslim Sahel* (Bloomington: Indiana University Press, 2006); Benjamin F. Soares, ed., *Muslim-Christian Encounters in Africa* (Leiden: Brill, 2006); Marie Miran and El Hadj Akan Charif Vissoh, "(Auto) Biographie d'une conversion à l'islam: Regards croisés sur une histoire de changement religieux dans le Bénin contemporain," *Cahiers d'etudes africaines* 195, no. 3 (2009): 655–704; Silvia Bruzzi, "Saints' Bodies, Islamic and Colonial Medicine in Eritrea (1887–1940)," in *Themes in Modern African History and Culture*, ed. Lars Berge and Irma Taddia (Padova: Biblioteca Universitaria, 2013), 69–83; Sean Hanretta, "'Kaffir' Renner's Conversion: Being Muslim in Public in Colonial Ghana," *Past and Present* 210, no. 1 (2011): 187–220.

19. Derek R. Peterson and Giacomo Macola, eds., *Recasting the Past: History Writing and Political Work in Modern Africa* (Athens: Ohio University Press, 2009), 8; Kastfelt, "Politics of History."

20. Last, "Muslims and Christians," 606, 607.

21. Hermann K. W. Kumm, *Khont-Hon-Nofer: The Lands of Ethiopia* (Westport, CT: Negro Universities Press, 1970), 11.

22. Last, "Muslims and Christians," 609–11.

23. Virginia A. Salamone and Frank A. Salamone, *The Lucy Memorial Freed Slaves' Home: The Sudan United Mission and the British Colonial Government in Partnership* (Lanham, MD: University Press of America, 2008).

24. Murray Last, "From Dissent to Dissidence: The Genesis and Development of Reformist Islamic Groups in Northern Nigeria" (working paper no. 5, Nigeria Research Network, University of Oxford, 2013).

25. Andrew E. Barnes, "'Evangelization Where It Is not Wanted': Colonial Administrators and Christian Missionaries in Northern Nigeria during the First Third of the Twentieth Century," *Journal of Religion in Africa* 25, no. 4 (November 1995): 412–41; Lamont King, "From Caliphate to Protectorate: Ethnicity and the Colonial Sabon Gari System in Northern Nigeria," *Journal of Colonialism and Colonial History* 4, no. 2 (Fall 2003).

26. Laurent Fourchard, "Dealing with 'Strangers': Allocating Urban Space to Migrants in Nigeria and French West Africa, End of the Nineteenth Century to 1960," in *African Cities: Competing Claims on Urban Spaces*, ed. Francesca Locatelli and Paul Nugent (Leiden: Brill, 2009), 187–218.

27. Andrew E. Barnes, *Making Headway: The Introduction of Western Civilization in Colonial Northern Nigeria* (Rochester, NY: University of Rochester Press, 2009), 177–98.

28. C. N. Ubah, "Christian Missionary Penetration of the Nigerian Emirates, with Special Reference to the Medical Missions Approach," *Muslim World* 77, no. 1 (1987): 16–27; Shobana Shankar, "Medical Missionaries and Modernizing Emirs in Colonial Hausaland: Leprosy Control and Native Authority in the 1930s," *Journal of African History* 48, no. 1 (March 2007): 45–68; Robert Stock, "Environmental Sanitation in

Nigeria: Colonial and Contemporary," *Review of African Political Economy* 15, no. 42 (1988): 19–31.

29. Murray Last, "The Nature of Knowledge in Muslim Northern Nigeria, 1457–2007," in *The Trans-Saharan Book Trade: Manuscript Culture, Arabic Literacy and Intellectual History in Muslim Africa*, ed. Graziano Krätli and Ghislaine Lydon (Leiden: Brill, 2011), 174–211; I. H. Abdalla, *Islam, Medicine, and Practitioners in Northern Nigeria* (Lewiston, NY: Edwin Mellen Press, 1997).

30. Donal B. Cruise O'Brien and Christian Coulon, eds., *Charisma and Brotherhood in African Islam* (New York: Oxford University Press, 1989).

31. The linkage between evangelism and labor can be complex, as Luise White has shown in describing Northern Zambians' perceptions of missions' use of African workers in the early 1900s. The materiality of the association between work, missions, and people involved not just wages, but food, colors, and blood. Africans were speaking about circulation in the Christian mission context, more specifically about why Africans worked there, often for little or no wages. Thus, the missionaries had little power over local constructions of ideas and images that were exchanged. L. White, "Vampire Priests of Central Africa: African Debates about Labor and Religion in Colonial Northern Zambia," *Comparative Studies in Society and History* 35, no. 4 (1993): 771.

32. Garba, *Time Has Come*, 387.

33. To the north, in Nigerién Hausaland, Barbara Cooper observes that males were in such a majority among Christian converts that the price of marriage was quite high. Outside Muslim Africa, in East Africa, Derek Peterson notes that the independence of women led Christian revivalists to worry about the future of their ethnic groups and to work against secular nationalists. Cooper, *Evangelicals*, 398; Peterson, *Ethnic Patriotism and the East African Revival: A History of Dissent, c.1935–1972* (New York: Cambridge University Press, 2012), chap. 7 and 10.

34. Bruzzi, "Saints' Bodies."

35. Barnes, *Making Headway*, 255–68; Isa Alkali Abba, "Sir Ahmadu Bello: The Sardauna of Sokoto's Conversion Campaign, 1964–1965, in Adamawa Division and Northern Sardauna Province," *Kano Studies* 2, no. 2 (1981): 53–60.

36. Murray Last, "Some Economic Aspects of Conversion in Hausaland (Nigeria)," in Levtzion, *Conversion to Islam*, 236–46.

37. Robin Horton, "African Conversion," *Africa* 41, no. 2 (April 1971): 105.

38. Robin Horton, "On the Rationality of Conversion Part II," *Africa* 45, no. 4 (1975): 394.

39. Benjamin F. Soares, *Islam and the Prayer Economy: History and Authority in a Malian Town* (Ann Arbor: University of Michigan Press, 2005).

40. Nehemia Levtzion, ed., *Conversion to Islam* (New York: Holmes and Meier, 1979), 17.

41. Scholarly thinking about diaspora has much to offer Africanists interested in identity-construction of migrants, especially for those who had no possibility of return but perhaps a new imagination of it. Studies of the Atlantic and Indian Ocean diasporas have developed the historical approach to identity formation as occurring in the ritual and spiritual imagination as much as in language, education, and occupation. Abner Cohen, *Custom and Politics in Urban Africa: A Study of Hausa Migrants in Yoruba Towns* (London: Routledge, 1969); Engseng Ho, "Empire through Diasporic Eyes: A View from the Other Boat," *Comparative Studies in Society and History* 46,

no. 2 (2004): 210–46; see also Eve M. Troutt Powell's discussion of studies of African identity-formation in the Atlantic as a useful interpretive lens for Sudanese slaves within Sudanic Africa and beyond. Powell, *Tell This in My Memory: Stories of Enslavement from Egypt, Sudan and the Ottoman Empire* (Stanford, CA: Stanford University Press, 2012).

42. James S. Coleman, *Nigeria: Background to Nationalism* (Berkeley: University of California Press, 1965), 32–40. Barnes discusses the Middle Belt movement as an "episodic push by groups of Northern Christians across the 1950s" in *Making Headway*, 242. I develop this point, showing in chapter 6 that the language of autonomy and belonging was diverse, not always conforming to secular politics nor even to a geographical "Middle Belt." Rather, in cities like Kano and in rural Hausa areas, new and sometimes very local movements for autonomy were asserted.

43. Moses E. Ochonu, *Colonialism by Proxy: Hausa Imperial Agents and Middle Belt Consciousness in Nigeria* (Bloomington: Indiana University Press, 2014), 161–78.

44. Mudimbe offers an interesting discussion of African theologians' interpretations of indigenous African religions mediated through the heavy influences of Christian missionaries as anthropologists. Perhaps more useful than his discursive treatment is Mario Aguilar's case of Oromo conversion from Islam to indigenous religions in independence-era Kenya, a process showing how local cultural encounters during political transitions in Kenya shaped new popular histories as modes of public narrative. V. Y. Mudimbe, *The Invention of Africa: Gnosis, Philosophy, and the Order of Knowledge* (Bloomington: Indiana University Press, 1988), 66, 81; Mario I. Aguilar, "African Conversion from a World Religion: Religious Diversification by the Waso Boorana in Kenya," *Africa* 65, no. 4 (October 1995): 525–44.

45. Peterson discusses how revivalist autobiographies in Central Kenya "laid out roles into which other people could cast themselves." The sharing of this idiom of civilizing converts among Muslims and Christians suggests how a religious script emerged with the rewriting of political history of precolonial history in light of colonial and postcolonial changes. Peterson, *Ethnic Patriotism*, 216.

46. Justice 'dan Daura allowed me to make photocopies of these letters. I have withheld the names of the authors.

47. Toyin Falola, *Violence in Nigeria: The Crisis of Religious Politics and Secular Ideologies* (Rochester, NY: University of Rochester Press, 1998). Perhaps the most famous cases are of Christians accused of desecrating the Qur'an by using its pages as toilet paper.

48. Karin Barber, ed., *Africa's Hidden Histories: Everyday Literacy and Making the Self* (Bloomington: Indiana University Press, 2006), 5.

49. Powell, in *Tell This in My Memory* (chap. 3), discusses the pressures on Sudanese freed slaves who wrote their histories navigating between the cultural imperatives of Christian missionaries and Muslims. Both of these strong forces, in which literacy was important, brought incredible pressure on Africans to identify in public in specific ways.

50. Sharkey, *American Evangelicals in Egypt*; Sharkey, "Muslim Apostasy, Christian Conversion, and Religious Freedom in Egypt," in *Proselytization Revisited: Rights Talk, Free Markets and Culture Wars*, ed. Rosalind I. J. Hackett (Durham, NC: Acumen, 2008), 139–57.

51. Derek Peterson offers a nuanced reading of the politics of autobiography and conversion narratives as revivalists confronted church leaders. His collection is particularly unique for including women's writings, which have not yet been found in

Northern Nigeria, a region where scholarly Muslim women's writings are much celebrated. Peterson, *Ethnic Patriotism*, chap. 9.

52. Last, "Muslims and Christians," 611.

CHAPTER 1: "A PLACE TO LAY OUR HEAD"

1. Henry G. Guinness, "The Soudan," *Faithful Witness* (7 December 1889): 356.

2. "A New Missionary Paper," *Faithful Witness* (7 December 1889): 365.

3. Emmanuel A. Ayandele, *The Missionary Impact on Modern Nigeria, 1842–1914* (New York: Humanities Press, 1967); Yusufu Turaki, *Theory and Practice of Christian Missions in Africa: A Century of SIM/ECWA History and Legacy in Nigeria, 1893–1993*, vol. 1 (Nairobi: International Bible Society Africa, 1999).

4. Barbara Cooper, *Evangelicals in the Muslim Sahel* (Bloomington: Indiana University Press, 2001), 7, 91–114.

5. Guinness, "Soudan." He made no mention of the African missionaries of the Church Missionary Society who had evangelized on the Niger River in earlier decades and were driven out by white missionaries. J. D. Y. Peel, *Religious Encounter and the Making of the Yoruba* (Bloomington: Indiana University Press, 2000); Andrew F. Walls, "Africa as the Theatre of Christian Engagement with Islam in the Nineteenth Century," *Journal of Religion in Africa* 29, no. 2 (1999): 155–74. Similar to tensions among the Yoruba Christian evangelists in Muslim areas highlighted in the work of Peel and Walls, Douglas H. Johnson has written about the Eastern Sudan, where Salim Wilson, a Dinka Christian, had wanted to return to preach to his own people, who were not Muslims, but Brooke, the zealous English layman who accompanied Wilson, was intent on evangelization among the Muslims. The two parted ways rather mysteriously, Brooke to join the Reverend John Robinson's mission to set up a station at Lokoja in Northern Nigeria. When Robinson died, Brooke was invalided home, returning to West Africa later. He died in Nigeria in 1892. Johnson, "Salim Wilson: The Black Evangelist of the North," *Journal of Religion in Africa* 21, no. 1 (February 1991): 33.

6. Henry G. Guinness, "Soudan Mission," *Faithful Witness* (14 June 1890): 173.

7. Andrew E. Barnes, "Aryanizing Projects: African Collaborators and Colonial Transcripts," *Comparative Studies of South Asia, Africa and the Middle East* 17, no. 2 (Fall 1997): 46–61; B. Cooper, *Evangelicals*, 85–86.

8. Karl Meinhof, "A Plea for Missionary Work among the Moslems of Central Africa," *Muslim World* 1, no. 2 (1911): 158. Later, of course, this discourse found itself into European claims that African Islam was not truly Islam for its local characteristics. B. Cooper, *Evangelicals*; Mahir Saul, "Islam and West African Anthropology," *Africa Today* 53, no. 1 (2006): 3–33.

9. Meinhof, "Plea for Missionary Work," 159.

10. Donald L. Donham, *Marxist Modern: An Ethnographic History of the Ethiopian Revolution* (Berkeley: University of California Press, 1999), 87.

11. Andrew Porter, "The Hausa Association: Sir George Goldie, the Bishop of Dover, and the Niger in the 1890s," *Journal of Imperial and Commonwealth History* 7, no. 2 (January 1979): 149–79.

12. Karl Pearson, *The Life, Letters and Labours of Francis Galton* (London: Cambridge University Press, 1914–1930), 207.

13. John E. Flint, *Sir George Goldie and the Making of Nigeria* (London: Oxford University Press, 1960), 95.

14. T. J. Tonkin, "A Missionary Martyr in West Africa," *Wide World Magazine* (April 1900): 670–76; Tonkin, "Muhammedanism in the Western Sudan," *Journal of the Royal African Society* 3, no. 10 (January 1904): 123–41.

15. Charles H. Robinson, "The Hausa Territories: Hausaland," *Geographical Journal* 8, no. 3 (September 1896): 207. See also Robinson's book, *Hausaland, or Fifteen Hundred Miles through the Central Soudan* (London: Sampson, Low, Marston, 1897).

16. Robinson, "Hausa Territories," 207.

17. "Open Doors: Be not Overcome of Evil, but Overcome Evil with Good," *Faithful Witness* (27 March 1900): 167–68.

18. Scholars have debated the extent to which the British changed Muslim governance. Historians of Christian missions tend to favor the view that the British merely superimposed bureaucratic structures without changing Islamic practice, while political historians have pointed out British interventions in the criminal justice system, taxation police, and the appointment of emirate officials. For the former, see Andrew E. Barnes, *Making Headway: The Introduction of Western Civilization in Colonial Northern Nigeria* (Rochester, NY: University of Rochester Press, 2009). For a view from the latter perspective, see, for instance, P. K. Tibenderana, "The Role of the British Administration in the Appointment of the Emirs of Northern Nigeria, 1903–1931: The Case of Sokoto Province," *Journal of African History* 28, no. 2 (July 1987): 231–57.

19. "Mohammedanism and Christianity Face to Face in North Africa," *Missionary Witness* (17 January 1905): 41.

20. Central Soudan Mission Newsletter, June 1896, Sudan Interior Mission International Archives, Fort Mill, South Carolina (hereafter cited as SIMIA), file "Central Soudan Mission, Thomas Holt, 1891–96, BM-1, Bio Material: 5 (pre-1900) Pioneers."

21. Hermann G. Harris, *Hausa Stories and Riddles, with Notes on the Language, Etc., and a Concise Hausa Dictionary* (London: Mendip Press, 1908). Harris's translation of the "Kano Chronicle," undertaken for British colonial officers, was also of interest for missionaries. The unpublished English translation is housed at the SIMIA and appears to be an early version containing phrases that were changed with subsequent translation efforts. Harris's translation, for Frederick Lugard, of key political proclamations upon formal British colonization, including the pledge of noninterference with Islam, incited rage among missionaries. They denounced Harris as an Islamophile when, at a Christian conference in England, "he stalked about in Arab costume like a showman." Walter Gowans to Rowland Bingham, 18 August 1893, SIMIA, file "Early Letters written by Gowans, Kent, Bingham," BM-1, Bio Materials.

22. *Audu: A Hausa Boy*, pamphlet by Walter Miller, ca. 1904, University of Birmingham Library Special Collections (hereafter cited as BIRM), CMS/ACC237 F1: 1.

23. Ladi Sani, interview by author, unrecorded, Kano, Nigeria, 29 May 2001; Halima and Binta Yusuf, interview by author, recorded, Wusasa, Nigeria, 5 August 2001. These women were grandchildren of Audu.

24. Extracts from letters from WRS Miller, 5 January 1902, BSC, CMS/ACC237 F3. African pilgrims sometimes encountered abuses and exploitation in Mecca or en route, as Hausa in Chad recalled. John A. Works, *Pilgrims in a Strange Land: Hausa Communities in Chad* (New York: Columbia University Press, 1976).

25. Miller to friends, 20 December 1901, BSC, CMS/ACC237 F1: 2.
26. Tonkin, "Muhammedanism," 140.
27. Miller to friends, 8 February 1902, BSC, CMS/ACC237 F1: 2.
28. Ibid.
29. Herbert Richmond Palmer, who served as Resident of Kano and Borno in the 1910s, classified Miller and the CMS bishop Tugwell as one camp that opposed the British Northern Nigerian administration. Palmer to Secretary of Northern Provinces, 2 July 1920, Rhodes House Library, Oxford (hereafter cited as RHL), MSS.Brit.Emp.s.276 Box 15, file 3, Gordon Lethem, "jangali," correspondence 1923–1924.
30. Miller, *Audu*, 15.
31. "Outstretched Hands from Ethiopia," *Missionary Witness* (25 September 1906): 132–33.
32. "Secretary's Notes: Missionary Martyrs: Or, Pioneer Work in the Central Soudan," *Faithful Witness* (21 November 1899): np.
33. "Outstretched Hands," 132–33.
34. "A Missionary Martyr," *Faithful Witness* (August 1896): 303.
35. Jean-Paul Rothiot, "Une chefferie précoloniale au Niger face auz représentants coloniaux: Naissance et essor d'une dynastie," *Cahiers d'histoire* 85 (2001): 63–87.
36. Ibid. Inusa Samuila, "To God Be the Glory," written in Hausa and translated by Rev. Albert Diamond, SIMIA, Evangelical Churches of West Africa (hereafter cited as ECWA) Biographical Sketches L-S, Fort Mill, South Carolina, 19. This life history is based on his unpublished handwritten diary I collected in Nigeria, but the two differ significantly. I have analyzed these differences in Shankar, "A Fifty-Year Muslim Conversion to Christianity: Religious Ambiguities and Colonial Boundaries in Northern Nigeria, c. 1910–1963," in *Muslim-Christian Encounters in Africa*, ed. Benjamin Soares (Leiden: Brill, 2006), 89–114. All portions of his story in this chapter are taken from these two texts unless otherwise cited.
37. Paul E. Lovejoy and Jan S. Hogendorn, "Revolutionary Mahdism and Resistance to Colonial Rule in the Sokoto Caliphate, 1905–6," *Journal of African History* 31, no. 2 (1990): 217–44; David Robinson, *Muslim Societies in African History* (New York: Cambridge University Press, 2004), 173–76.
38. Paul E. Lovejoy and Jan S. Hogendorn, *Slow Death for Slavery: The Course of Abolition in Northern Nigeria, 1897–1936* (Cambridge: Cambridge University Press, 1993), 56.
39. Lovejoy and Hogendorn, "Revolutionary Mahdism," 225.
40. Ibid.
41. Samuila, "To God," 3.
42. Lovejoy and Hogendorn, *Slow Death for Slavery*, 60; Mohammed B. Salau, "The Role of Slave Labor in Groundnut Production in Early Colonial Kano," *Journal of African History* 51, no. 2 (2010): 147–65.
43. Ayandele, *Missionary Impact*; E. P. T. Crampton, *Christianity in Northern Nigeria* (Zaria: Gaskiya, 1976).
44. Lovejoy and Hogendorn, *Slow Death for Slavery*, 84, 96.
45. From Karl Kumm, General Secretary, SUM, to Secretary of State for Colonies, 22 November 1906, National Archives, Kaduna (hereafter cited as NAK), SNP 751/1908, Freed Slaves Homes Proposed by Soudan United Mission to Takeover.
46. Hermann K. W. Kumm, *Khont-Hon-Nofer: The Lands of Ethiopia* (Westport, CT: Negro Universities Press, 1970), 120–21.

47. Ibid., 120.
48. Ibid., 11.
49. William Wallace, Acting High Commissioner, to Secretary of State for the Colonies, 8 April 1908, NAK, SNP 751/1908.
50. Quoted in Paul E. Lovejoy, "Concubinage and the Status of Women Slaves in Early Colonial Northern Nigeria," *Journal of African History* 29, no. 2 (1988): 249.
51. Ibid., 253, 249.
52. Typescript "Fillani Rulers and their [illegible]," by Walter R. Miller, 1904, RHL, MSS.Lugard 53/6.
53. Lugard to Walter Miller, 11 September 1907, RHL, MSS Brit.Emp.s.62.
54. Edward Lugard to Frederick Lugard, 7 October 1908, RHL, MSS Brit.Emp. s.62: 3.
55. Professor Philip Shea, personal communication with author, Bayero University, Kano, 5 January 2001.
56. A. Helser to C. Gordon Beacham, 3 December 1927, SIMIA, Helser, AD 1937 CH-3/A.
57. Miller to friends in England, 20 December 1901, BIRM, CMS/ACC237 F1.; Memorandum from WR Miller [draft?], c.1930, BSC, CMS/ACC237 F6: 2.
58. His description is remarkably similar to scenes from *Jaguar*, the ethnographic film about Zarma migrants to Gold Coast made by Jean Rouch in 1954 and released in 1967.
59. Samuila, "To God," 5.
60. Yarima Inusa Samuila, unpublished Hausa diary, 1910: 1.
61. Samuila, "To God," 6.
62. Miller to friends, 3 May 1915, BSC, CMS/ACC237 F1: 2; "A Remarkable Movement among Moslems in Nigeria," *Evangelical Christian* (August 1913): 16, 250.
63. Typescript titled "Ningi History," culled from notes of J. F. J. Fitzpatrick report of 15 August 1914, NAK; SIMIA, People Groups, Isawa: 1–2.
64. Miller to friends, 3 May 1915, 2.
65. Pictures of missionaries wearing indigenous clothing studying with Muslim scholars are common in missionary periodicals of this period. This is ironic considering the insult heaped by the more evangelical missionaries on any Westerner considered an "Arabophile." Barbara Cooper offers a nuanced discussion of the cultural politics of Hausa language translation and the contentious issue of Islamic influence on Hausa Bible translation. B. Cooper, *Evangelicals*, 122–31.
66. Louis Brenner, *Controlling Knowledge: Religion, Power, and Schooling in a West African Muslim Society* (Bloomington: Indiana University Press, 2001), 103–7. Brenner discusses the various reformation and countermovements that occurred in Muslim schooling in colonial Bamako. On a much smaller and more obscured scale, a similar process occurred with the intermingling of Muslim, Christian, and Maguzawa elements in the rural evangelism of African Christians.
67. See Brian Larkin's discussion of this wonder in the first chapter of his book *Signal and Noise: Media, Infrastructure, and Urban Culture in Nigeria* (Durham, NC: Duke University Press, 2008).
68. Paul Krusius, "Die Maguzawa," *Archiv für anthropologie* 42 (1915): 288–315.
69. Captain A. J. N. Tremearne, in his collection of folktales and other oral culture in Hausa, cites one example of a Bamaguje accused of marrying his own daughter. His defense of his incest? To blame the *malam* for telling him that this was acceptable.

Tremearne, *Hausa Superstitions and Customs: An Introduction to the Folklore and the Folk* (London: John Bale, Sons and Danielsson, 1913), 26.

70. The old woman Baba remembered that Maguzawa were known for their expertise in curing madness, an ailment that was more common in the dry season. She told the story of the chief of Zarewa, who went mad, wandered off into the bush, and turned up in Kano "muttering mad words." A Bamaguje came to treat him in his compound, but, even then, his madness returned at harvesttime. Others, too, during the harmattan, were afflicted with madness of muttering or of violence (e.g., smashing pots). Baba of Karo and Mary F. Smith, *Baba of Karo: A Woman of the Moslem Hausa* (New Haven, CT: Yale University Press, 1981), 154–55.

71. Alex Ireland to Chris Ferrier, 1 February 1974, SIMIA, Malumfashi Misc. files, 1946–1974.

72. Samuila, "Glory Be to God," 12.

73. Note signed HR Palmer, 11 October 1916, Arewa House Archives (hereafter cited as AHA), 15225 1/25/183.

74. L. N. M. Gepp to Resident Kano, 15 March 1915, AHA file 15225 1/25/183.

75. Miller to friends, 2 December 1912, BSC CMS/ACC237 F1: 2.

76. Ibid.

77. Acting Cantonment Magistrate HC Hall from Zungeru to Secretary of the Administration, 22 March 1908, NAK, SNP 751/1908, Freed Slaves Homes Proposed by Soudan United Mission to Takeover.

78. Maxwell, 26 June 1911, RHL, MS.AFr.S.1112, vol. 5.

79. Maxwell, 3 June 1911.

80. Maxwell, 8 September, 1911, 92. He uses *dattibai*, which is the same as *dattijo*.

81. J. Lowry Maxwell diaries, 18 April 1911, RHL, MS.AFr.S.1112, vol. 5.

82. Karen Tranberg Hansen, ed., *African Encounters with Domesticity* (New Brunswick, NJ: Rutgers University Press, 1992); Elizabeth E. Prevost, *The Communion of Women: Missions and Gender in Colonial Africa and the British Metropole* (New York: Oxford University Press, 2010).

83. Marriage Certificates of both white and black couples, 1915–1935, SIMIA, Minna Marriage Certificate Book.

84. Benani, A Freed Slave from Ed Rice files (typed), n.d., SIMIA, ECWA (box) Biographical Sketches, A–F.

85. Extracts from letter of Ethel Miller, 26 November 1907, BSC, CMS/ACC237 F10, Papers, etc., of WRS Miller.

86. Minutes of Missionary Conference, Lokoja, 1910, International Missionary Council/Conference of British Missionary Societies Joint Archives, UCLA (hereafter cited as IMC/CBMS), fiche 100.

87. Hannatu Samande, interview by author, recorded, 24 May 2001, Jos, Nigeria.

88. Samuila, "Glory Be to God," 18–19.

89. N. A. Dyce-Sharp, "Epidemic Disease in West Africa: The Menace of the Future," *Transactions of the Royal Society of Tropical Medicine and Hygiene* 19, no. 4 (1925–1926): 257. This doctor, who worked with the West African Medical Service investigating the outbreak of relapsing fever, reported on his conversation about the Zarmawa with the Emir of Gwandu. See chapter 4 in this book for more information on his research.

90. Samuila, "Glory Be to God," 18–19.

91. Tremearne, *Hausa Superstitions*, 5.

92. Finn Fuglestad, *A History of Niger, 1850–1960* (New York: Cambridge University Press, 1986), 90–93.

93. Speech by His Excellency the Governor-General to the Reps of Mohammedans in Lagos, 1914, RHL, MSS Brit.Emp.s.62, Lugard correspondence: 3.

94. Eugenie St. Germain to Mr. Percy, 7 August 1954, SIMIA, ECWA (box) Biographical Sketches, L–S.

95. Panya Baba, "Nigeria's Isawas [sic]: Muslims Who Follow Jesus," *Africa Now* (June–August 1979): 6–7. This article written by a Nigerian church leader emphasizes the importance of purity among the Isawa, symbolized by white clothes and strict endogamy and isolation from others. While white missionary sources were much more concerned with the Isawa political history of disagreement with the Muslim authorities, the historian Ian Linden noted some of these same austere characteristics in his research in Zaria in the 1970s. Linden, "The Isawa Mallams c.1850–1919: Some Problems in the Religious History of Northern Nigeria" (paper presented at the Ahmadu Bello Social Sciences Seminar, 1974); Linden, "Between Two Religions of the Book: The Children of the Israelites (c. 1846–c. 1920)," in *Varieties of Christian Experience in Nigeria*, ed. Elizabeth Isichei (New York: Macmillan, 1982), 79–98.

96. Adeline Masquelier, *Prayer Has Spoiled Everything: Possession, Power, and Identity in an Islamic Town of Niger* (Durham, NC: Duke University Press, 2001).

97. Samuila, "Glory Be to God," 34.

98. Waibinte E. Wariboko, "I Really Cannot Make Africa My Home: West Indian Missionaries as 'Outsiders' in the Church Missionary Society Civilizing Mission to Southern Nigeria, 1898–1925," *Journal of African History* 45, no. 2 (2004): 221–36.

99. First, the cane was cut, a difficult task since the stalk was quite tough. Once the cane was brought from the field, small boys scraped each stick to prepare it for pressing. The cane was placed into the presser, which was turned in circles manually; by the 1930s, horses were tethered to the machines, but it was unlikely that the first Gimi residents had horses. Workers then boiled and stirred the juice for hours. Once cooled, the sugar was formed into cones and transported quickly for sale. In Miller's words, this self-supporting Christian village within a Muslim emirate was a missionary experiment. Mallam P. O. Ishaku, "The Making of Brown Sugar in Northern Nigeria," *Nigeria* 12 (1937): 8–9; Walter R. Miller, *Reflections of a Pioneer* (London: Church Missionary Society, 1936), chap. 10.

100. Miller, *Reflections*, chap. 10.

101. Audu family: Zainabu, Halima, Christiana Donli (née Audu), Martha Maiwada (née Audu), Janet Sadauki, Philippa Thompson, Mrs. Victoria Audu Audu (née Joe), interview by author, recorded, Wusasa, Nigeria, 5 August 2001.

102. Walter Miller, "Twenty-Five Years of Missionary Work in Northern Nigeria," unpublished draft paper, 1939, BSC, CMS/ACC237 F6, papers of WRS Miller: 5.

CHAPTER 2: A NEW "MIDDLE" CLASS IN THE MUSLIM CITY, 1918–1925

1. Edmund D. Morel, "Northern Nigeria and Its Problems," *Times of London*, 15 August 1911. The series ran in seventeen installments from 15 August to 18 October.

2. Edmund D. Morel, "A Visit to the Emir of Kano," *Times*, 5 September 1911, 3.

3. Ibid.

4. Mahmudu 'Ko'ki, *Alhaji Mahmudu 'Ko'ki: Kano Malam*, trans. and ed. Neil Skinner (Zaria: Ahmadu Bello University Press, 1977), 59.

5. Karim al-Maghili, the North African visitor to Kano and other Sudanese Islamic centers, is an example who comes immediately to mind. His visit to Kano during the reign of Kano *sarki* (chief) Muhammadu Rumfa is considered the turning point in full Islamization of the Kano state. This official status inaugurated Kano's and Katsina's international reputations as Islamic centers in which Muslims would settle, opening the way for changes in the structures of these cities. See Alan Frishman, "The Impact of Islam on the Urban Structure and Economy of Kano, Nigeria," *Journal of the Institute of Muslim Minority Affairs* 7, no. 2 (1986): 464–75; Murray Last, "Historical Metaphors in the Kano Chronicle," *History in Africa* 7 (1980): 161–78.

6. Charles Good provides a useful discussion describing medical missions as a multifaceted enterprise that did not ignore theology but covered a range of cultural and material practices in south-central Africa. Good, *The Steamer Parish: The Rise and Fall of Missionary Medicine on an African Frontier* (Chicago: University of Chicago Press, 2004).

7. Kano Province Report No. 45 For the Year Ending 31 December 1911, by Acting Res. E. J. Arnett, Kano History and Culture Bureau (hereafter cited as KHCB), File no. SNP/7/13 (114), item 113.

8. Mohammed B. Salau has written recently about the expansion of slavery in Abbas's push to expand groundnut production. Though he makes no explicit connection between this economic innovation and new farming techniques, it is worth considering that Abbas's interest in Christian farming techniques stemmed from this initiative. Salau, "The Role of Slave Labor in Groundnut Production in Early Colonial Kano," *Journal of African History* 51, no. 2 (2010): 147–65.

9. Ibid.

10. Andrew E. Barnes, in his brief history of the Catholic mission in Jos, does not mention Abbas's emissaries in Shendam in the 1910s but does note that a priest "spent some time in Kano" in 1928 for a government-sponsored first-aid course. Though the Catholic mission had established a post in Kano Sabon Gari by this time, this inclusion is significant in light of the longer-term relationship that began informally and the precursor of Muslim-Christian cooperation in medical work to come in the 1930s. Barnes, "Catholic Evangelizing in One Colonial Mission: The Institutional Evolution of Jos Prefecture, Nigeria, 1907–1954," *Catholic Historical Review* 84, no. 2 (April 1998): 244.

11. Notes of interview between Sir Hesketh Bell and Rev. F. Baylis, Secretary. CMS, 27 June 1911, Arewa House Archives (hereafter cited as AHA) File 15227.

12. Letter from Acting Resident Kano to Chief Secretary Zungeru, 5 October 1912, AHA File 1522.

13. Morel, "Northern Nigeria," *Times*, 8 September 1911.

14. William Neville M. Geary, "Land Tenure and Legislation in British West Africa," *Journal of the Royal African Society* 12, no. 47 (April 1913): 243–44.

15. Family of Joseph Sani, interview by author, unrecorded, Kano, Nigeria, 29 May 2001.

16. W. F. Gowers to Acting Governor, Northern Nigeria, 8 January 1913, AHA File 15227.

17. Ibid.

18. Sean Stilwell, "Constructing Colonial Power: Tradition, Legitimacy and Government in Kano, 1903–1963," *Journal of Imperial and Commonwealth History* 39, no. 2 (2011): 202, 205.

19. A. P. Stirrett, "Threefold Appeal for Special Work in Nigeria," *Missionary Witness* (August 1911): 203.

20. Morel, "Northern Nigeria," 8 September 1911.

21. 'Ko'ki, *Alhaji Mahmudu' Ko'ki*, 18–19.

22. Alan Christelow, "Slavery in Kano, 1913–1914: Evidence from the Judicial Records," *African Economic History* 14 (1985): 69.

23. Kano Province Report for year ending 30 June 1915, KHCB 382P/1915: 15.

24. Kano Province Annual Report, No. 49, for 31.12.14, by Ag. Resident ACG Hastings, 31 December 1914, Kano Province Annual Report 1914, KHCB, SNP/10/1914 (139P/1914): 3–4; various letters from Emirs of Northern Nigeria to Lugard, Rhodes House Library, Oxford (hereafter cited as RHL), MSS Brit.Emp.s.77; Gazetteer, Muri Division, to 1919, by Fremantle: 72.

25. "In 1916 a pagan at Nukko, a self-styled 'Mahdi,' who went by the name of 'Mairigan Karifi' or the 'invulnerable one,' raided the surrounding villages and eventually went to attack Donga town itself. He was wounded when quite close to it and retired. The Resident, Mr. Fremantle, with 20 police, followed him up and surprised him at Nukko hill. He was convicted on a charge of murder and executed in Nukko in 1917. But for his timely arrest it appeared that the rising would have spread and assumed serious proportions." *Muri Gazetteer*, 72.

26. "Segregation of Europeans," Minute by His Excellency the Governor, 9 November 1919, AHA 44006, Segregation of Europeans.

27. Ibid., 9.

28. "Letter to Mr. Bingham from E. F. Rice, Kano," *Evangelical Christian and Missionary Witness* (April 1922): 135; Abdul Rahman Nayyar to E. J. Arnett, August to October 1922, RHL, Papers of E. J. Arnett, correspondence, etc., MSS. Afr.s.952, 1902–1940, Box 2, folder 2.

29. Notes on Ahmadiyya, 30 December 1929, Public Records Office, Kew (hereafter cited as PRO), CO/40256/22 Nig.

30. James F. Cotton, "Trials and Triumphs in Nigeria," *Missionary Witness* (September 1914): 279.

31. Ibid., 280.

32. Kano Province Annual Report 1924, KHCB, SNP 9/12, 8.

33. Mohammedan Propaganda, 30 July 1926, AHA, 1/1/3. K.2392.

34. 'Ko'ki, *Alhaji Mahmudu 'Ko'ki*, 77, 95.

35. Huddleston, Acting Secretary, Northern Provinces, to Resident Kano, 6 April 1926, KHCB R. 910.

36. Between May and October 1926, the Resident of Kano collected information contained in the file R.910, KHCB.

37. John Carrow, District Officer, Kano Division, to Resident Kano, 19 December 1926, KHCB, R. 910: 1.

38. "An African Missionary: Mr. Dugald Campbell in Glasgow," *Glasgow Herald* (13 December 1930): 2.

39. Resident Kano Division to Resident Kano Province, 10 June 1926, KHCB R.910: 2.

40. Resident Kano to Secretary of the Northern Provinces, 7 May 1926, KHCB, R. 910: 2.

41. Heather J. Sharkey, *American Evangelicals in Egypt: Missionary Encounters in an Age of Empire* (Princeton, NJ: Princeton University Press, 2008), 63–71. Sharkey's description of the Christian missionaries' disappointment with the British failure to protect Muslim converts, as well as the Muslim authorities' avoidance of the death penalty or other harsh legal punishment for apostasy, is very similar to what happened in Northern Nigeria. It is also quite striking that the idea of secret believers became a recognition of the "disjuncture between private belief and public religion" (71).

42. Emir's note forwarded by the Resident Kano to the Secretary for the Northern Provinces, 13 October 1926, Confidential no. 47/21, KHCB, R.910: 3.

43. Beminster to Resident, Kano Province, Confidential No. 4/1926/3, KHCB, R.910.

44. Ibid.

45. District Officer, Kano Division, to Resident of Kano Province, 19 December 1926, KHCB R.910: 2.

46. John Carrow forwarding Emir's letter to Resident Kano, 2 October 1926, R.910: 2.

47. CW Alexander, "Christian Missionaries in Mohammedan Emirates," 2 October 1926, KHCB, R.910: 2.

48. Daga Sarkin Kano Abdullahi Bayero, 7 January 1927, KHCB, R.910: 5.

49. John Garba provides a lengthy account of the trick his grandfather played to hold his grandson back from making the trip. In Hausa custom, by which the family worked, grandparents and grandchildren were much closer than parents and children. The resistance of Garba's grandfather to his own son, to the extent of theft, is quite important. Garba, *The Time Has Come . . . : Reminiscences and Reflections of a Nigerian Pioneer Diplomat* (Ibadan: Spectrum Books, 1989), 20–23.

50. Garba, *Time Has Come*, 29.

51. Ibid., 20.

52. Ibid., 7.

53. Haruna 'dan Daura, interview by author, recorded, 2 August 1001, Jos, Nigeria.

54. District Officer to Kano Resident, 19 December 1926, KHCB R.910: 3.

55. Garba, *Time Has Come*, 31.

56. District Officer, Kano, to Resident, 19 December 1926: 2–3.

57. Garba, *Time Has Come*, 28.

58. Enid Schildkrout, "Age and Gender in Hausa Society: Socio-Economic Roles of Children in Urban Kano," *Childhood* 9, no. 3 (2002): 342–68.

59. Garba, *Time Has Come*, 33.

60. Ibid., 43.

61. Moma Akawu (John Garba), personal papers, "The Nigerian Exercise Book," 13 June 1929.

62. Joseph Mohammed Sani, "An Essay on My Education," unpublished account, n.d.

63. Sani, "Essay," 8.

64. Garba, *Time Has Come*, 53.

65. Sani, "Essay," 9.

66. Garba, *Time Has Come*, 54, 63.

67. Ibid., 67. As a point of comparison, James Coleman wrote about the fact that supply of schooling in Northern Nigeria never reached demand: "There has been no large class of unemployed 'Standard VI Boys,' who played such an important role in the nationalist movement in the south." Coleman, *Nigeria: Background to Nationalism* (Berkeley: University of California Press, 1965), 355.

68. Garba, *Time Has Come*, 54–55.

69. Observing many such women in Northern Nigeria today, the problem has to do with their high level of achievement and the scarcity of men who can match them in terms of family connections, education, and ethnic background.

70. In his description of the Muslim prayer economy in Nioro, Mali, Benjamin F. Soares discusses the gifts given to Muslim leaders and their accumulation through transactions to give blessings, conduct prayers, and perform other services. Here, however, 'dan Daura's work seems more akin to the makers of talismans or herbalists. Soares, "The Prayer Economy in a Malian Town," *Cahiers d'etudes africaines* 36, no. 144 (1996): 739–53; Robert E. Handloff, "Prayers, Amulets, and Charms: Health and Social Control," *African Studies Review* 25, nos. 2–3 (June–September 1982): 185–94; Michael M. Horowitz, "Barbers and Bearers: Ecology and Ethnicity in an Islamic Society," *Africa* 44, no. 4 (October 1974): 371–82.

CHAPTER 3: A CHRISTIAN FEMINIST FREELANCE

1. Nancy Rose Hunt, *A Colonial Lexicon: Of Birth Ritual, Medicalization, and Mobility in the Congo* (Durham, NC: Duke University Press, 1999); Lata Mani, *Contentious Traditions: The Debate on Sati in Colonial India* (Berkeley: University of California Press, 1998); Lynn M. Thomas, *Politics of the Womb: Women, Reproduction, and the State in Kenya* (Berkeley: University of California Press, 2003).

2. Ethel Miller came with Dr. Frances "Daisy" Wakefield and a Miss E. Fox in 1907 as the first Anglican women missionaries to Northern Nigeria. Ethel Miller, "Beginnings Chapter I," unpublished draft of book manuscript, University of Birmingham Library Special Collections (hereafter cited as BIRM), CMS/ACC237 Z2, papers, etc. of W. R. S. Miller: 36.

3. "The Late Miss Clothier," *Missionary Witness* (4 October 1910): n.p.

4. Percy Girouard to Frederick Lugard, 25 January 1908, Rhodes House Library, Oxford (hereafter cited as RHL), MSS.Brit.emp.s.63, Lugard correspondence: 34–35.

5. Lugard to Girouard, 12 April 1908, RHL, MSs.Brit.emp.s.63.

6. Maxwell diaries, 8 September 1911, 93–94.

7. Maxwell diaries, 15 May 1911, 23.

8. Barbara Cooper, "Reflections on Slavery, Seclusion and Female Labor in the Maradi Region of Niger in the Nineteenth and Twentieth Centuries," *Journal of African History* 35, no. 1 (1994): 61–78; Paul E. Lovejoy, "Concubinage and the Status of Women Slaves in Early Colonial Northern Nigeria," *Journal of African History* 29, no. 2 (1988): 245–66.

9. Ethel P. Miller, "Things as They Are: The Problem in Nigeria," *Muslim World* 2, no. 4 (1912): 436–42.

10. Ethel P. Miller, *Change Here for Kano: Reminiscences of Fifty Years in Nigeria* (Zaria: Gaskiya, 1959), 24.

11. Yusufu Turaki, *Theory and Practice of Missions in Africa: A Century of SIM/ECWA History and Legacy in Nigeria, 1893–1993*, vol. 1 (Nairobi: International Bible Society Africa, 1999), 214.

12. Missionary Conference at Lokoja, 1910, International Missionary Council/Conference of British Missionary Societies Joint Archives, UCLA (hereafter cited as IMC/CBMS), fiche 100.

13. Turaki, *Theory and Practice*, 214–15. These conferences continued, but the constituent bodies' constitutions changed when African-led churches formally took over from missions in leadership and evangelical activities in the early 1950s.

14. Wusasa women elders, group interview by author, Wusasa, Nigeria, 5 August 2001.

15. Extracts from diary of Walter Miller, 4 August (no year), BSC, CMS/ACC237 F1; extracts from Ethel Miller, 1907, BCS, CMS/ACC237 F3.

16. "Benani, A Freed Slave from Ed Rice files," undated typescript, Sudan Interior Mission International Archives, Fort Mill, South Carolina (hereafter cited as SIMIA), Evangelical Churches of West Africa (hereafter cited as ECWA), ECWA (box) Biographical Sketches, A–F. Barbara Cooper discusses the gendered participation in preaching among Euro-Americans and among Africans to note that women were important, even as African women seemed invisible and the Euro-American women's numbers grew, albeit under male leadership of the mission. B. Cooper, *Evangelicals in the Muslim Sahel* (Bloomington: Indiana University Press, 2006), 109–10, 172–77.

17. Alvarez to Baylis, 27 June 1911, CMS Group IV, African Missions, Part 11, Yale Divinity School Library reel 220.

18. See B. Cooper, *Evangelicals*, 110, citing Dana L. Robert, "'The Crisis of Missions': Premillennial Mission Theory and the Origins of Independent Evangelical Missions," in *Earthen Vessels: American Evangelicals and Foreign Missions, 1880–1980*, ed. Joel A. Carpenter and Wilbert R. Shenk (Grand Rapids, MI: Eerdmans, 2012), 29–46; Judith Rowbotham, "'Soldiers of Christ'? Images of Female Missionaries in Late Nineteenth-Century Britain: Issues of Heroism and Martyrdom," *Gender and History* 12, no. 1 (April 2000): 82–106. Several essays in the following volume take up this issue: Sue Morgan, ed., *Women, Religion and Feminism in Britain, 1750–1900* (New York: Palgrave Macmillan, 2002).

19. Emmeline Stuart, "The Ministry of Healing," in *Daylight in the Harem: A New Era for Moslem Women*, ed. Annie Van Sommer and Samuel M. Zwemer (Edinburgh: Oliphant, Anderson, and Ferrier, 1911), 133–48.

20. Wakefield to the Continuation Committee of the International Board of Missions, 23 April 1916, IMC/CBMS fiche 104.

21. Official Vatican Network, news.va., http://www.vatican.va/holy_father/benedict_xvi/speeches/2005/november/documents/hf_ben_xvi_spe_20051113_beatifications_en.html.

22. Information for New Missionaries pamphlet, c. 1916, SIMIA, Field Director and International Liaison Officer Eras, Handbooks, Immigration, etc. 1893–1990, Administration handbook for missionaries, 1916–1990.

23. Ethel Miller, "Beginnings," 23. Her use of the word *maffick*, a British word for public rejoicing or celebration, is noteworthy for its colonial origin. It was coined around 1900 from the place Mafeking in South Africa, where the British garrison was under Boer attacks for many months during the Anglo-Boer War.

24. Deputy Governor of Northern Nigeria A. T. Weatherhead, foreword to E. Miller, *Change Here for Kano*, i.

25. Extracts from letter of Ethel Miller, 26 November 1907, BCS, CMS/ACC237 F10.

26. E. Miller, *Change Here*, 6.

27. Group of Mariri residents, including liman, interview by author, Mariri, Kano, Nigeria, 22 Jul. 2001.

28. Resident Kano Province to Secretary of Northern Provinces, 5 December 1929, Arewa House Archives (hereafter cited as AHA), Files 4268, vol. I: 2–3.

29. Ibid.; B. Cooper, *Evangelicals*, 261–62.

30. Resident Kano to Secretary of Northern Provinces, 5 December 1929: 2.

31. The biography of Marshal Feng that Ethel Miller translated had been previously published by the China Inland Mission. On this publication, she simply wrote her initials. *Marshal Feng: Nagarin 'dan Yako Mai-Bin Isa Almasihu*, trans. E. P. M. (Minna: Niger Press), 1925. Notice her use of the phrase "one who followed" (*mai-bin*), which does not appear in other texts of this period.

32. Ethel P. Miller, *Hausa Heroines* (Minna: Niger Press, 1923).

33. Ibid., 33.

34. Miller, *Hausa Heroines*, cover; Patricia Jalland, *Women, Marriage, and Politics, 1860–1914* (New York: Oxford University Press, 1986), 238; Julia Bush, *Edwardian Ladies and Imperial Power* (Leicester: Leicester University Press, 2000); Deborah Gaitskell, "The Imperial Tie: Obstacle or Asset for South Africa's Women Suffragists before 1930?" *South African Historical Journal* 47, no. 1 (2002): 1–23.

35. Phyllis Lassner, *Colonial Strangers: Women Writing at the End of the British Empire* (New Brunswick, NJ: Rutgers University Press, 2004).

36. Ethel P. Miller, *The Truth about Muhammad: An Appeal to Englishmen in Nigeria* (Minna: Niger Press, n.d.).

37. Ibid.

38. Ethel Miller, *Women Count*. Details of publication are not available from the copy I obtained in the Arewa House Archives, File no. 4268, vol. 1, "Ethel Miller."

39. Notes on Interview of Resident Kano with Lieutenant Governor, 2 January 1927, Kano History and Culture Bureau (hereafter cited as KHCB), R.910: 2.

40. Stanhope White, *'Dan Bana: The Memoirs of a Nigerian Official* (London: Cassell, 1966), 204. Crampton notes that the SIM denied they had been involved with Yahaya's decision not to convert. SIM sources suggest that the SIM did not know him until the 1930s. E. P. T. Crampton, *Christianity in Northern Nigeria* (Zaria: Gaskiya, 1975), 160.

41. A. P. Stirrett to Major Fremantle, Resident Niger, 9 September 1926, SIM, Nigerian Box 14, Early Administrative Era Niger, Sokoto, and Zaria Provinces, 1913–1959.

42. Melville Jones to Chief Secretary of the Colony, 25 January 1930, AHA, File 4268 vol. 1.

43. G. Lethem, Secretary, to Chief Secretary of the Colony, 25 January 1930, AHA, File 4268 vol. 1: 3.

44. Resident Kano to Secretary of Northern Provinces, 6 August 1937, AHA File 4268 vol. 1.

45. Ethel Miller, "Defence Mechanism or Protection?" *Nigerian Daily Times*, 18 August 1934.

46. Resident Kano to Secretary of Northern Provinces, 23 August 1934, AHA File 4268, vol. 1.

47. Peter K. Tibenderana, "The Beginnings of Girls' Education in the Native Administration Schools in Northern Nigeria, 1930–1945," *Journal of African History* 26, no. 1 (1985): 93–94.

48. J. H. Oldham, "Northern Nigeria," *International Review of Mission* 7 (1917): 43–44.

49. Oldham et al. to Thomson, 23 June 1927, AHA file K5533, "Religious Tolerance."

50. Andrew E. Barnes, "'Some Fire Behind the Smoke': The Fraser Report and Its Aftermath in Colonial Northern Nigeria," *Canadian Journal of African Studies* 31, no. 2 (1997): 209. Female education was a tangential interest to Fraser, who felt that educated men should have educated wives (220).

51. The phrase "education in religious tolerance" or "religious toleration" was one used frequently in Oldham's correspondence with the British authorities on behalf of the missions. British officers also used it among themselves as they weighed allowing Christian societies into Muslim lands. A file in Arewa House containing this correspondence bears the name "Religious Toleration," K.5533 vol. 1.

52. In the Anglo-Egyptian Sudan, the British acknowledged their preference for containing Islam in the North, and, with it, practices of female circumcision, but they also viewed Muslim "Arab" Africans as superior. They were caught in the apparently contradictory British and Islamic "civilizing missions" in this case of female circumcision, but, in the end, opted for reforming rather than abolishing the practice altogether. Janice Boddy, *Civilizing Women: British Crusades in Colonial Sudan* (Princeton, NJ: Princeton University Press, 2007). The second half of the book is particularly pertinent to this discussion.

53. Report on Women's Education, Ilorin Province, 30 April 1929, RHL, MSS. Afr.s.1520, Sylvia Leith-Ross papers.

54. Tibendarana, "Beginnings of Girls' Education," 99.

55. Kano Province Annual report 1938 I, KHCB, Kano Province Annual Report 1938 I, File no. 30847.

56. Tibendarana, "Beginning of Girls' Education," 93.

57. AP Stirrett to Major Fremantle, Resident Niger, 28 September 1926, SIMIA, Nigeria Box 4, Early Admin Era.

58. "She Spent Her Life Teaching Abroad," *Saint Petersburg Times*, 6 August 1973, 8.

59. Faye Moyer to Gordon Beacham, n.d., SIMIA, Wushishi Misc., 1904–1945, SR-32/A.

60. Margery Perham, notes on Kano for West African Passage, 1932-2, RHL, MSS. Perham, box 46, file 6, 7.

61. Perham notes, 59, 61.

62. Perham notes on Kano, 43.

63. Ibid., 62.

64. Ibid.

65. From Cecil Northcott, 1955, BSC, CMS/ACC237 Z2.

66. Andrew E. Barnes, "'Religious Insults': Christian Critiques of Islam and the Government in Colonial Northern Nigeria," *Journal of Religion in Africa* 34, nos. 1–2 (2004): 62–81.

67. Guli Francis-Deqhani, "Medical Missions and the History of Feminism: Emmeline Stuart of the CMS Persia Mission," in Morgan, *Women, Religion and Feminism in Britain*, 208.
68. E. Miller, "Beginnings," 36.

CHAPTER 4: CHRISTIAN MEDICAL MISSIONS
AS MUSLIM CHARITY

1. Emmeline Stuart, "The Ministry of Healing," in *Daylight in the Harem: A New Era for Moslem Women*, ed. Annie Van Sommer and Samuel M. Zwemer (Edinburgh: Oliphant, Anderson, and Ferrier, 1911), 133–48.
2. Michael Worboys, "Colonial and Imperial Medicine," in *Medicine Transformed: Health, Disease and Society in Europe, 1800–1930*, ed. Deborah Brunton (Oxford: Manchester University Press, 2004), 211–38; Christophe Bonneuil, "Development as Experiment: Science and State Building in Late Colonial and Postcolonial Africa, 1930–1970," *Osiris*, 2nd ser., 15 (2000): 258–81.
3. N. A. Dyce-Sharp, "Epidemic Disease in West Africa: The Menace of the Future," *Transactions of the Royal Society of Tropical Medicine and Hygiene* 19, no. 4 (1925): 256–64; Ralph Schramm, *A History of the Nigerian Health Services* (Ibadan: Ibadan University Press, 1971), 188.
4. Megan Vaughan, *Curing Their Ills: Colonial Power and African Illness* (Stanford, CA: Stanford University Press, 1991).
5. Dyce-Sharp, "Epidemic Disease," 261.
6. Ibid., 258.
7. Ibid.
8. E. Muir, *Leprosy in Nigeria: A Report on Anti-Leprosy Work in Nigeria with Suggestions for Its Development* (Lagos: Government Printer, 1936), 3.
9. Paul E. M. Fine, "Leprosy: The Epidemiology of a Slow Bacterium," *Epidemiologic Reviews* 4, no. 1 (1982): 161–88.
10. Muir, *Leprosy in Nigeria*, 9.
11. Kathleen Vongsathorn, "Gnawing Pains, Festering Ulcers and Nightmare Suffering: Selling Leprosy as a Humanitarian Cause in the British Empire, c. 1890–1960," *Journal of Imperial and Commonwealth History* 40, no. 5 (2012): 863–78; Michael Worboys, "The Colonial World as Mission and Mandate: Leprosy and Empire, 1900–1940," *Osiris*, 2nd ser., vol. 15 (2000): 207–18.
12. John Manton, "Leprosy in Eastern Nigeria and the Social History of Colonial Skin," *Leprosy Review* 82 (2011): 125.
13. Laszlo Kato, "The Centenary of the Discovery of the Leprosy Bacillus," *Canadian Medical Association Journal* 109, no. 7 (October 1973): 629.
14. Shubhada S. Pandya, "The First International Leprosy Conference, Berlin, 1897: The Politics of Segregation," *Historia, Ciencas, Saude-Manguinhos* 10, supp. 1 (2003): 162–63, 170.
15. Ibid.
16. Pandya, "First International Leprosy Conference," 168–69.
17. Vincent J. Marsala, "U.S. Senator Joseph E. Ransdell, Catholic Statesman: A Reappraisal," *Louisiana History* 35, no. 1 (Winter 1994): 35–49.

18. Sanjiv Kakar, "Leprosy in British India, 1860–1940: Colonial Politics and Missionary Medicine," *Medical History* 40, no. 2 (1996): 228.

19. J. M. Dalziel, "Some Notes on Leprosy in Sokoto Province, The Northern Nigeria Medical Report 1910," *Northern Nigeria Gazette supplement*, 31 May 1911, Public Records Office, Kew (hereafter cited as PRO), Government Gazettes 1910–1911, CO/586/3: 153.

20. Supplement to the *Official Gazette* 11, no. 2, PRO, Government Gazettes 1910–1911 CO/586/3: 265.

21. Dalziel, "Some Notes," 154.

22. Leprosy Proclamation, no. 8, 1911, PRO, Government Gazettes 1910–1911, CO/586/3.

23. Shobana Shankar, "Medical Missionaries and Modernizing Emirs in Colonial Hausaland: Leprosy Control and Native Authority in the 1930s," *Journal of African History* 48, no. 1 (March 2007): 45–68.

24. Manton, "Leprosy in Eastern Nigeria," 127.

25. The *Muslim World* magazine had many articles about how best to reach Muslims specifically; an additional set of essays, *Daylight in the Harem*, also contained an essay specifically about "The Ministry of Healing." The SIM's founder had a complete change of heart about medical missions after the death of his cotravelers Walter Gowans and Thomas Kent. Bingham disavowed the idea that prayer healing was the only method evangelical missionaries should use. Van Sommer and Zwemer, *Daylight in the Harem*; Rowland V. Bingham, *The Bible and the Body: Healing in the Scriptures* (Toronto: Evangelical Publishers, 1952).

26. Extracts from WRS Miller, July–August 1903, BSC, CMS/ACC237 F3.

27. A. P. Stirrett, *Cerebro-Spinal Meningitis and Relapsing Fever*, Sudan Interior Mission International Archives, Fort Mill, South Carolina (hereafter cited as SIMIA), Diaries AP Stirrett, 1913, 1924, 1930.

28. Paul S. Landau, "Explaining Surgical Evangelism in Colonial Southern Africa: Teeth, Pain and Faith," *Journal of African History* 37, no. 2 (1996): 261–81; David Hardiman, ed., *Healing Bodies, Saving Souls: Medical Missions in Asia and Africa* (Amsterdam: Rodopi, 2006).

29. A major catalyst for experiments with esters appears to have been Prohibition in the United States. Distillers turned to pharmaceuticals. The chair of the American Mission to Lepers, a Protestant organization that would increasingly compete with BELRA, was William Jay Schieffelin, a New York philanthropist and heir to a distillery that had, under Prohibition beginning in 1920, moved into drug production. http://www.fundinguniverse.com/company-histories/Schieffelin-amp;-Somerset-Co-Company-History.html. See also John Parascandola, "Chaulmoogra oil and the Treatment of Leprosy," *Pharmacy in History* 45, no. 2 (2003): 47–57.

30. E. A. O Travers, "The Treatment of Leprosy at Kuala Lumpur, Federated Malay States," *Journal of the Royal Society of Medicine* 19 (1926): 1–9.

31. Ibid., 2.

32. Individual letters from 1922 to 1928, in file, Leprosy Plants, ECB 1/1, Kew Gardens Special Collections.

33. Graeme Thomson to LCMS Amery, 30 December 1927, PRO, CO 583/156/2: 1.

34. Ibid.

35. P. Morris to Acheson, 2 February 1928, PRO, CO 583/156/2.

36. Notes in Colonial Office on proposed Government/mission cooperation in medical work, 3 March 1928, PRO, CO 583/156/2.

37. Ibid.

38. Graeme Thomson to Lord Passfield, Secretary of State for the Colonies, 16 September 1929, PRO, CO 583/167/3.

39. Adamawa Province Annual Report 1931 by Resident WOP Rosedale, comments of Lieutenant-Governor Lethem, Rhodes House Library, Oxford (hereafter cited as RHL), MSS.Brit.Emp.s.276 Box 5/1 (file 1), 96–102.

40. Graeme Thomson to Joseph Oldham, 14 December 1930, PRO, CO 583/176/15; Graeme Thomson to Lord Passfield, S of S, 16 September 1929, PRO CO 583/167/3.

41. Interview at Kaduna between Cameron, mission society reps (Playfair, Farrant, Bullen) and Carrow, Acting Principal Asst. Scty, Lethem, Scty NP, CW Alexander, Lieut-Gov NP, 6 August 1931, PRO, CO 583/181/5: 4.

42. Ibid., 3, 7.

43. Yusufu Turaki, *Theory and Practice of Christian Missions in Africa: A Century of SIM/ECWA History and Legacy in Nigeria, 1893–1993*, vol. 1 (Nairobi: International Bible Society Africa, 1999).

44. Kano Province Annual Reports 1930, 1932, Kano History and Culture Bureau (hereafter cited as KHCB), Kano PROF; SNP 17/2/, vol.1: 9.

45. Northern Division Quarterly Report 1930, KHCB, ND 41/1930/1.

46. Assistant Director of Medical Service to Assistant Dir. Of Medical and Health Services, Northern Provinces, 15 June 1931, Arewa House Archives (hereafter cited as AHA), Hospital Fees, K.6658 1/9/44; Resident Kano to Secretary of Northern Provinces, 27 July 1931, AHA Hospital Fees: 1–2.

47. Letter from Mrs. C. Gordon Beacham (Marjorie) to Chris Ferrier, 20 August 1983, SIMIA, Kano Miscellaneous 1934–1945.

48. Resident Kano to Reverend C. G. Beacham, 29 January 1934, KHCB R.910.

49. See Toc H, http://www.toch-uk.org.uk/History.html.

50. Lambert, "My Life with Lepers," University of Birmingham Library Special Collections (hereafter cited as BIRM), ACC 118 F1, chap. 1; Lambert, "A Leper Colony in Nigeria," *Journal of the Royal African Society* 36, no. 143 (April 1937): 213–16.

51. Lambert, "Leper Colony," 214.

52. Lambert, "My Life," 12.

53. Lambert, "Leper Colony," 214.

54. Miller to Dr. Muir, 17 March 1936, BSC, CMS/ACC237 F2: 2.

55. Beacham to Hooper, 7 July 1932, International Missionary Council/Conference of British Missionary Societies Joint Archives, UCLA (hereafter cited as IMC/CBMS), Fiche 105.

56. Memorandum from WR Miller [draft?], c. 1930?, BSC, CMS/ACC237 F6: 2.

57. See the above footnote 29, discussing William Jay Schieffelin. Also Fleming Revell, the Christian publisher, was a member of the American Mission to Lepers board, and his firm published many of the books written by SIM workers.

58. Helser to Bingham, 17 July 1936, SIMIA, Correspondence Dr. Albert Helser 1936–1956 CH-2, CH-3/A.

59. Ibid. The Brethren began writing letters to Helser to ask how he could join such a mission, which Helser explained to highlight the tension between modernists and fundamentalists in the Brethren fold. Helser was an avowed antimodernist.

60. K. Weiler, "Mabel Carney at Teachers College: From Home Missionary to White Ally," *Teachers College Record* (2005): tcrecord.org,; Richard Glotzer, "The Career of Mabel Carney: The Study of Race and Rural Development in the United States and South Africa," *International Journal of African Historical Studies* 29, no. 2 (1992): 309–36.

61. Albert D. Helser, *African Stories* (New York: Revell, 1930); Helser, *Education of Primitive People: A Presentation of the Folklore of the Bura Animists, with a Meaningful Experience Curriculum* (New York: Revell, 1934).

62. Joseph M. Hodge, *Triumph of the Expert: Agrarian Doctrines of Development and the Legacies of British Colonialism* (Athens: Ohio University Press, 2007); Edward H. Berman, "American Influence on African Education: The Role of the Phelps-Stokes Funds Education Commissions," *Comparative Education Review* 15, no. 2 (1971): 132–45.

63. E. R. J. Hussey, "An American's Educational Philosophy for Africa," *Journal of the Royal African Society* 39, no. 157 (1940): 365.

64. RL Findlay for Secretary Northern Provinces to Chief Secretary to Government, Lagos, AHA 1/44/356, or 26516/S.4, vol. 1: 2.

65. Thomas A. Lambie, *A Doctor without a Country* (New York: Revell, 1939).

66. "Peaceful Invasion of the Northern Emirates of Nigeria," *Sudan Witness* (January–February 1938).

67. Edwin A. Harris, *Munganga: Memoirs of a Country Doctor* (published by the author with Richard B. Harris Sr., June 1987), SIMIA, 133–34.

68. Ibid., 135.

69. Humphrey J. Fisher, "Prayer and Military Activity in the History of Muslim Africa South of the Sahara," *Journal of African History* 12, no. 3 (1971): 391–406; Hezekiel Mafu, "The Impact of the Bible on Traditional Rain-Making Institutions in Western Zimbabwe," in *The Bible in Africa: Transactions, Trajectories and Trends*, ed. Gerald O. West and Musa W. Dube (Leiden: Brill, 2000), 400–14.

70. Lambert, "My Life," 18.

71. Harris, *Munganga*, 133.

72. Ibid.

73. Heather Sharkey, *American Evangelicals in Egypt: Missionary Encounters in an Age of Empire* (Princeton, NJ: Princeton University Press, 2008), 70–71. She explains that the American missionaries in Egypt used this idea of secret believers for women, especially, who could not practice a public Christian life.

74. Kano Leprosy Settlement 2nd Quarterly Report, 30 June 1938, SIMIA, Kano Lep Resumes 1937–1945.

75. Harris, *Munganga*, 138, 142.

76. Kano Leper Settlement Reports, 1937, 1939, SIMIA Kano Lep. Misc. Reports and Info, 1937–1945.

77. Helser to Playfair, 3 June 1937, SIMIA, Helser, AD: 1.

78. Superintendent SIM Lep Sett to Dir. Medical Services, Lagos, 7 January 1939, SIMIA, Kano Province Correspondence 1926–1939, Nigeria Box 011 Early Administrative Era.

79. Report by Miss Hooge, 13 March 1939, SIMIA, Katsina Leprosarium Misc. 1937–1942 SR-20/A. This report listed 12 male native dressers as compared to 3 female for a patient population of 370. Hannatu Samande, interview by author, recorded,

Jos, Nigeria, 24 May 2001. Ahmadu John Abarshi, interview by author, unrecorded, Kaduna, Nigeria, 1 June 2001.

80. *Sudan Witness*, Annual Report for 1938, 2.

81. Ruth Paul, interview by author, Kaduna, Nigeria, 2 June 2001.

82. Harris, *Munganga*.

83. From Dr. Entner's Letter, 9 September 1938, SIMIA, Katsina Lep Settlement Misc 1937–1942, 2.

84. *Sudan Witness*, Annual Report for 1938, 3.

85. Albert D. Helser, *Leper Settlements in Northern Nigeria* (Jos: Niger Press, 1939), 41.

86. Ibid., 43.

87. Ibid., 24.

88. Shobana Shankar, "The Social Dimensions of Christian Leprosy Work among Muslims: American Missionaries and Young Patients in Colonial Northern Nigeria, 1920–40," in Hardiman, *Healing Bodies*, 291.

89. N. Pauline Guyer, "A Missionary on Trek," *Sudan Witness* 16, no. 5 (September–October 1940), 14.

90. Handwritten note by Mrs. Vander Schie, 8 May 1939, Katsina, Katsina Station Reports, Katsina Misc. 1939 No. SR-20/A.

91. Ibid.

92. Martha Wall, "Life or Death," *Sudan Witness* 16, no. 6 (November–December 1940): 2–3.

93. Ibid.

94. Harold Saul, Kano settlement 3rd Quarter resume, 1941, SIMIA, Kano Lep. Resumes 1937–1945.

95. Jega report, 15 August, 1938, SIMIA, Jega Misc 1936–1945.

96. Malumfashi 2nd Quarterly Report 1939, SIMIA, Malumfashi Resumes 1937–1945: 1.

97. Vander Schie letter, 1939.

98. Malumfashi 2nd Quarter Report 1939: 2.

99. Chief Commissioner, Northern Provinces, to Chief Secretary to the Government, Lagos, 22 June 1939, AHA, Provincial Leprosy Settlements 1/44/356.

100. Ibid.

101. Daga Sarkin Musulmi Abubakar Sokoto zuwa ga Resident na Lardin Kasar Sokoto Mr. Ross, AHA, Provincial Leprosy Settlements 1/44/356.

102. Correspondence between Adams, emirs, Lugard, and others between 1939 and 1941, AHA, Provincial Leprosy Settlements 1/44/356.

103. Crown Counsel to Secretary, Northern Provinces, 11 November 1939, AHA, Provincial Leprosy Settlements 1/44/356.

104. Adams, "Minute by the Chief Commissioner," Northern Provinces, 1941, AHA Provincial Leprosy Settlements 1/44/356; John W. Cell, "On the Eve of Decolonization: The Colonial Office's Plans for the Transfer of Power in Africa, 1947," *Journal of Imperial and Commonwealth History* 8, no. 3 (1980): 235–57.

105. Playfair to Helser, 26 April 1940, SIMIA, Helser correspondence: 2.

106. Adams, "Minute," 1941.

107. Ibid.

108. Letter to Holms in NY, from Kano, 8 November 1939, SIMIA, Playfair personal papers, etc.

109. Adams, "Minute," 1941.
110. Typed schedule, Davis, 1939, SIMIA, Roni Station Reports, Roni Resumes 1938–1945 SR-29/A.
111. Adams, "Minute," 1941.
112. "Minute by His Honour the Chief Commissioner, Northern Provinces, n.d., ca. 1940, AHA Provincial Leprosy Settlements 1/44/3568.
113. Resident Kano to SIM, 14 March 1942, SIMIA, Kano Province Correspondence Medical (Leprosy) 1941–1950, Nigeria Box 012 Early Administrative Era.
114. Memoir of Henry Guenter, written in 1990–1991, SIMIA: 46.
115. Malam Sale Tomas, interview by author, unrecorded, Kumbotso, Kano State, 12 August 2001; Malam Usman Karkarna, interview by author, Ya da Kunya, Kano State, 12 June 2001.
116. Paraphrase of telegram to Chief Sec from Chief Commissioner, 13 May 1940, AHA 1/44/356, or 26516/S.4 Vol. I.
117. Gordon Beacham, "Annual Field Report for Nigeria and French West Africa," *Sudan Witness* 17, no. 2 (April 1941): 6.

CHAPTER 5: JOINING IN THE MELEE

1. Annual Report 1941, Kano Leprosarium Reports 1938–1945, Sudan Interior Mission International Archives, Fort Mill, South Carolina (hereafter cited as SIMIA), Kano Station Reports; Notes on Kano Provincial Leprosarium Board Meeting, 1941, SIMIA, Kano Province Correspondence Medical (Leprosy) 1933–1940.
2. Notes on Kano Board Meeting 1941.
3. Katsina Leper Settlement, Resume for 4th Quarter 1939, SIMIA, Katsina Lep Resumes 1938 SR-2A.
4. John W. Cell, "On the Eve of Decolonization: The Colonial Office's Plans for the Transfer of Power in Africa, 1947," *Journal of Imperial and Commonwealth History* 8, no. 3 (1980): 235–57; Frederick Cooper, *Africa since 1940: The Past of the Present* (New York: Cambridge University Press, 2002), chap. 2 and 3; Aaron Windel, "British Colonial Education in Africa: Policy and Practice in the Era of Trusteeship," *History Compass* 7, no. 1 (2009): 1–21.
5. Message from His Excellency the Governor Bernard Bourdillon to Residents' Conference, Northern Provinces, 1943, PRO, CO 583/263, 30553.
6. Ibid., 2.
7. "The Problems of Northern Nigeria as the Natives See it, Account of an Interview with Lord Lugard," by Abubakar Imam, 1944, Rhodes House Library, Oxford (hereafter cited as RHL), MSS Perham Box 305/5: 14.
8. Bourdillon to Residents' Conference, 1943.
9. Leprosy Control Scheme (proposed), 15 September 1949, PRO, Leprosy CO 583/288/1.
10. Albert Helser, *The Glory of the Impossible: Demonstrations of Divine Power in the Sudan* (Toronto: Evangelical Publishers, 1940), 42.
11. Bete Gagare, interview by author, unrecorded, Dass, Nigeria, 8 May 2001.
12. James Audu, "The Establishment and Growth of SIM School for the Blind, Kano from 1930s to 1972" (BA thesis, ABU, Zaria, 1973), 20–25, SIMIA, Kano Station Reports, Kano Blind School 1939–1975.

13. Bete Gagare, interview by Ruth Cox, transcript at Evangelical Churches of West Africa (hereafter cited as ECWA) HQ Archives, Jos, Nigeria.

14. Samuel Aruwan, "Bitrus Gani Dies at 67," 22 February 2011, allafrica.com, accessed July 24, 2011, http://allafrica.com/stories/201102220265.html.

15. See EMS Mission News, August 2010, 10. Available online at http://www.emsofecwa.org/emsmissionnewsaugust2010.pdf. The publication claims that Musa Tsakani is 113 years old and began his ministry in 1929.

16. Bete Kano, n.d., SIMIA, ECWA (box) Biographical Sketches A–F.

17. Heinrich Barth, *Travels and Discoveries in North and Central Africa: Being a Journal of an Expedition Undertaken under the Auspices of H.B.M. Government* (New York: Harper, 1857–1859); Charles H. Robinson, *Hausaland, or Fifteen Hundred Miles through the Central Soudan* (London: Sampson, Low, Marston, 1897).

18. Bete Gagare, interview by author, unrecorded, Dass, Nigeria, 8 May 2001.

19. Anne Wooding and Dan Wooding, *Blind Faith* (Garden Grove, CA: ASSIST Books, 1996), 83.

20. Resume for Kano, 1st quarter, 1939, SIMIA, Kano Resumes 1935–1945 SR-18/A. Anne Wooding (née Blake) gets the start date of the war wrong and clearly authored the biography of Bete in the SIM archives, which contains verbatim phrases found in her published autobiography.

21. Bete Gagare, interview by author, unrecorded, Dass, Nigeria, 8 May 2001.

22. Playfair to Resident Kano, 1 April 1943, SIMIA, Kano Province Correspondence 1940–1946, Nigeria Box 011 Early Administrative Era.

23. Audu, "SIM Blind School," 25.

24. Dr. Marion Douglas Hursh, interview conducted by Galen Wilson, transcript 2, Billy Graham Center Archives, 1, 29 June 1982, Wheaton, Illinois. Transcript available at http://www2.wheaton.edu/bgc/archives/trans/186t02.htm.

25. Ibid.

26. M. Douglas Hursh report, n.d., SIMIA, Ministries-Kano Eye Hospital, 1943–1984, Nigeria Box 078 medical department; obituary, http://www.independent.co.uk/news/people/obituary-viscount-muirshiel-1541565.html.

27. Hursh report, n.d.

28. "Makarantar Makahi," *Labarin Ekklesiya* 81 (December 1955–January 1956): 23–26.

29. Mariri group interview by author, 22 July 2001, Kano, Nigeria. Included assistant liman. Qur'anic schoolteacher.

30. Ibid.

31. Hursh interview transcript 2, http://www2.wheaton.edu/bgc/archives/trans/186t02.htm.

32. Bete Gagare, interview by Ruth Cox, transcript at ECWA HQ Archives, Jos, Nigeria.

33. As a parallel to the inability of disabled Islamic teachers to become Imams, Bete never was ordained as a pastor or as a reverend, a curious fact since he was so enormously popular among Christian missionaries and African congregants alike. Phil Shea, personal communication, 15 May 2001.

34. Ruth Cox, "The Lord's Work: Perspectives of Early Leaders of the Evangelical Church of West Africa Regarding the Spread of Christianity" (PhD thesis, Trinity International University, 2000); EMS Mission News, August 2010, 10.

35. Hursh report to Medical Officer of Health Kano, 6 January 1944, SIMIA, Kano Eye Hospital 1943–1944, No. SR-18/A.

36. It is quite possible for conjunctivitis to reach epidemic proportions, as it did in the early 1970s. A form of the eye virus was discovered in Ghana and Nigeria and named Apollo for the recent space shuttle launch. It was believed to have a new virus strain that spread long distances through touching of equipment, shaking hands, and so on. W. F. Parrott, "An Epidemic Called Apollo: An Outbreak of Conjunctivitis in Nigeria," *Practitioner* 206, 232 (1971): 253–55.

37. M. Douglas Hursh report, n.d., SIMIA, Nigeria Box 078 medical department.

38. Resume for Kano, 2nd Quarter 1942, SIMIA, Kano Station Reports, Kano Resumes 1935–1945 SR-18/A: 2.

39. Ibid., see other Kano Station Reports 1941–1942, SIMIA, Kano Resumes 1935–1945 SR-18/A.

40. KO/850/1/3, 14 April 1940, Appendix A, Arewa House, Staging Posts.

41. HC Stockwell, Major Gen Commander WA Division, to Gen HQ, WA, Demobilization preliminary survey, Arewa House Archives (hereafter cited as AHA), 5/1/15, 33354A vol. 2, 15.

42. Report of Major James of the 82nd WA division in Burma, non div units in India and WA Pioneer groups in Mid East, 11 January 1946, 5/1/15, 33354A vol. 2, Resettlement of Ex soldiers in Civil Life after the War: 10.

43. HC Stockwell, Maj Gen Commander WA Division, to Gen HQ, WA, Demobilization preliminary survey, AHA, 5/1/15, 33354A vol. 2, 15.

44. Secretary Western Provinces to Secretary of Government Lagos, 15 October 1941, AHA, 5/1/14, 33354, Examination of Problems which may arise after the war.

45. Kano Province Annual Report 1946, Kano History and Culture Bureau (hereafter cited as KHCB), File no. 41986, 15.

46. Letter to Dr. Albert Helser, 2 July 1941, SIMIA, AD Helser 1941.

47. Report, January to June 1949, SIMIA, Kano Leprosarium Misc Reports and Info 1946–1951 SR-19/A.

48. Demobilization survey, 15.

49. Annual report, 1 October 1950–30 September 1951, SIMIA, Kano Leprosarium Reports 1946–1963 SR-19.

50. John E. Lesch, *The First Miracle Drugs: How the Sulfa Drugs Transformed Medicine* (Oxford: Oxford University Press, 2007), 283–84.

51. Rev. Ishaku Bello and wife Abu, interview by author, recorded, Kano, Nigeria, 26 April 2001.

52. See photo 5.2 of the first collection of "waifs" to Roni. Reverend Ishaku died two years after I interviewed him, so I could not show him this picture to see if he could recognize himself.

53. Rev. Ishaku Bello and wife Abu, interview by author, recorded, Kano, Nigeria, 26 April 2001.

54. Mario Azevedo, "Power and Slavery in Central Africa: Chad (1890–1925)," *Journal of Negro History* 67, no. 3 (1982): 198–211.

55. Lori Leonard, "'Looking for Children': The Search for Fertility among the Sara of Southern Chad," *Medical Anthropology* 21, no. 1 (2002): 79–112.

56. John Carrow, Resident Kano to Secretary of the Northern Provinces, 9 September 1944, AHA 38048, Stray Children.

57. Acting Resident McCabe to Secretary Northern Provinces, 7 November 1944, AHA 38038, Stray Children.

58. Ibid., marginalia by JH Carrow.

59. Pamphlet titled *The Kano Boys' School of the SIM*, SD-1, SIMIA, pamphlets.

60. Letter from M. Glerum to friends at home, 6 November 1946, SIMIA, Kano Miscellaneous 1964–1974 No. SR-18, Kano Station Reports.

61. Kano Province Report 1939 I, KHCB, Kano Province Report 1939 I, File no. 32098, 15.

62. Gazetteer of Kano, by WF Gowers, 1921, RHL, MSS.Brit.Emp.s.276 Box 19/5, Lethem Papers, 42–43.

63. "Behold the Lamb of God," *Sudan Witness*, January–February 1940, 11–12, SIMIA, Matazu Misc. 1939–1942 SR-25/A.

64. Haruna 'dan Ladi, interview by author, recorded, Roni, Nigeria, 13 May 2001.

65. Acting Resident Katsina Province to Playfair of the SIM, 26 October 1946, population figures of Maguzawa, SIMIA, Katsina Province Correspondence the Resident 1940–1952, Box 13, Early Administrative Era., Katsina/Niger Province 1911–1959.

66. Aondover Tarhule and Ming-Ko Woo, "Towards an Interpretation of Historical Droughts in Northern Nigeria," *Climatic Change* 37, no. 4 (1997): 605, 608.

67. Lydia Jantz and Jessie Whitmore to Playfair and Beacham, 5 September 1943, SIMIA, Malumfashi Misc. 1937–1943.

68. Tarhule and Wood citing Michael Watts, *Silent Violence: Food, Famine and Peasantry in Northern Nigeria* (Berkeley: University of California Press, 1983), "Towards an Interpretation," 608, 611.

69. Katsina LS Report, 1st Quarter 1944, SIMIA, Katsina Leprosarium Misc. 1937–1942 SR-20/A.

70. Malumfashi, Quarterly Resume, 1st quarter 1944, SIMIA, Malumfashi Resumes 1937–1945 SR-24/A.

71. Resume, 1st Quarter 1948, SIMIA, Malumfashi Resumes 1946–1965 SR-24.

72. Jantz and Whitmore, 5 September 1943.

73. Jessie Whitmore to Helser and Playfair, 19 August 1943, Malumfashi Misc 1937–1943, SIMIA.

74. Minutes of Meeting of Kano Provincial Lep Board, January 1943, SIMIA, Nigeria Box 012 Early Administrative Era, Kano Province Correspondence Medical (Leprosy) 1941–1950: 2.

75. Influence of soldiers 18/6/1944, AHA, 9/1/12, 37412, vol. 1.

76. Eugenie German, "The Family on Trek," 22 February–6 March 1946 or 1947, SIMIA Malumfashi Misc. 1946–1947.

77. Ibid., 2.

78. Report of the Feeding Test of Nestle's Condensed Milk, Milkmaid Brand, compare with an equal amount of Fulani [local herders' milk], SIMIA, Katsina Leprosy Settlement, misc. papers 1937–1942.

79. Kano Province Annual Report 1938 I, KHCB, File no. 30847: 29.

80. Hawa'u Lynne M. Aliyu, "The Contribution of the SIM on Women's Education in Kano State with Special Reference to Kabo Girls' School" (BA thesis, Bayero University Kano, 1975), 28.

81. The post–World War II appears to have witnessed this increase in other parts of Nigeria and colonial Africa generally. See Laurent Fourchard, "Lagos and the Invention of Juvenile Delinquency in Nigeria, 1920–60," *Journal of African History* 47, no. 1 (2006): 115–37; also Luise White discusses the first appearance of teenage girls as prostitutes in Nairobi in *Comforts of Home* (Chicago: University of Chicago Press, 1990), chap. 7 and 8.

82. Alhaji Garba Bako, interviews by author, unrecorded, Kano, Nigeria, 11 March 2001; 15 April 2001.

83. Ibid.

84. Ruth Heinrich, *Yarns on Africa Today: Builders Together* (London: Livingstone Press, 1940), 69–80, School of Oriental and African Studies Special Collections, Library Special Collections, London.

85. Ibid., 73, 76.

86. Obituary, *British Medical Journal*, 3 June 1933, 988–89.

87. Henrich, *Yarns*, 78.

88. Pamphlet, *Kano Boys' School*, 2.

89. Dr. and Mrs. J. A. Dreisbach, "A Boys' Brigade Camp for Boys with Leprosy," *Sudan Witness* 26, no. 4 (July 1950): 13–14.

90. Resume for Kano 1 October–31 December 1937, SIMIA, Kano Resumes 1935–1945 SR-18/A, Kano Station Reports.

91. Acting Prov. Supt. of Ed to SIM, 12 June 1936, SIMIA, Nigeria Box 012 Nigerian Administrative, Kano Province Correspondence Education 1935–1949.

92. Dreisbach, "Boys' Brigade Camp," 14.

93. Ibid., 12.

94. Ibid., 13.

95. Mai Kudi Kure, interview by Ruth Cox, Jos, Nigeria, 25 October 1996, transcript at ECWA Archives, Jos.

96. Garba Bako, interview by author, 15 April 2001.

97. Jessie Whitmore to Mrs. Playfair, 30 September 1942, SIMIA, Malumfashi Miscellaneous 1937–1943.

98. Ibid., 5.

99. Personal communication, Ladi Wayi, 12 December 2011.

100. Office of the Acting Governor to Secretary of State for the Colonies, 22 January 1948, PRO, Government/mission cooperation, Appendix 21.

101. Cheverton to Regional Deputy Director of Medical Services, Kaduna, "SIM and Leprosy Work in Kano Katsina, and Sokoto, 1948, AHA 31440/S.1: 4.

102. Acting Resident Kano Province to Secretary NP, 2 October 1948, "Application by the SIM for grants of occupancy," KHCB R.910.

103. Malam Ado and Hadiza, interview by author, Kagadama, Jigawa State, Nigeria, 22 April 2001.

104. A. E. Omoti, "Complications of Traditional Couching in a Nigerian Local Population," *West African Journal of Medicine* 24, no. 1 (January–March 2005): 7–9; M. Goyal and M. Hogeweg, "Couching and Cataract Extraction: A Clinic Based Study in Northern Nigeria," *Community Eye Health* 10 (1997): 6–7. The practice is done very secretively, according to one field study, so that successful couching operations are difficult to assess, as well as the fact that patients who have their cataracts successfully pushed out do not often show for any further care. Yet there is acknowledgment that couching can work and is undergone by many patients because it is cheap and sometimes successful. W. E. Schrader, "Traditional Cataract Treatment and the Healers Perspective: Dialogue with Western Science and Technology in Nigeria, West Africa," *Annals of African Medicine* 3, no. 3 (2004): 153–58.

105. Hursh interview, transcript 1.

106. Ibid.

107. Hursh interview, transcript 2.

108. John F. Wilson, "Blindness in Colonial Africa," *African Affairs* 52, no. 207 (1953): 141.
109. Ibid.
110. Wilson, "Blindness in Colonial Africa," 142.

CHAPTER 6: SECURITY AND SECRECY IN THE ERA OF INDEPENDENCE, 1950–1975

1. SIM, "Independence Year Report of the SIM," Sudan Interior Mission International Archives, Fort Mill, South Carolina (hereafter cited as SIMIA), Pamphlets Nigeria Box, 2.
2. Ibid.
3. James Coleman, *Nigeria: Background to Nationalism* (Berkeley: University of California Press).
4. Herman H. Gray and John A. Dreisbach, "Leprosy among Foreign Missionaries in Northern Nigeria," *International Journal of Leprosy* 29, no. 3 (July–September 1961): 279–90. Their review around 1960 estimates that about 850 Protestant missionaries were present in Northern Nigeria; Andrew Barnes appears to agree with a general estimate of the number of Catholic and Protestant Christian mission stations to be in the hundreds.
5. Patrick J. Furlong, "Azikiwe and the National Church of Nigeria and the Cameroons: A Case Study of the Political Use of Religion in African Nationalism," *African Affairs* 91, no. 362 (July 1992): 433–52.
6. Yusufu Turaki, *Theory and Practice of Christian Missions in Africa: A Century of SIM/ECWA History and Legacy in Nigeria, 1893–1993*, vol. 1 (Nairobi: International Bible Society Africa, 1999), 536.
7. *What Is ECWA?* Pamphlet printed by Salama Press, Jos, ECWA HQ, ca. late 1950s–1960s, SIMIA, ECWA History and Growth, 8.
8. Ibid.
9. Malumfashi, 1st Quarter 1951, SIMIA, Malumfashi Resumes 1946–1965 SR-24.
10. Malumfashi, 2nd Quarter resume, 1950, SIMIA, Malumfashi Resumes, 1946–1965 SR-24.
11. Dutse Resume, July–September 1953, SIMIA, Dutse Resumes 1948–1967 SR-9.
12. TerMeer to DO, Kano Division, 2 July 1951, Kano History and Culture Bureau (hereafter cited as KHCB), SIM, R.935.
13. AD Helser to DO Kano Division, 20 May 1952, SIMIA, Kabo Misc 1947–1974.
14. E. Hillier, Social Welfare Officer, Northern Region, to Senior Crown Counsel, 11 July 1952, Arewa House Archives (hereafter cited as AHA), file 53021.
15. Ibid., 2.
16. Mrs. Ladi Sani, interview by author, Kano, Nigeria, 29 May 2001, Kano, Nigeria. She was the daughter of P. O. Ishaku, classmate and former friend of Tafida.
17. Hillier to Crown Counsel, 2.
18. See Sir Sydney Phillipson's reports on education and leprosy in 1948, Public Records Office, Kew (hereafter cited as PRO), CO 583/298/5.
19. Katsina Leprosarium 2nd Quarter resume, 1953, SIMIA, Katsina Leprosarium Resumes 1946–1968, SR-20.
20. Dutse resume, June–July 1950, SIMIA, Dutse Resumes 1948–1967 SR-9; also through 1960.

21. Regional Deputy Director of Medical Services, to Secretary of the Northern Provinces, 16 May 1951, AHA, File 50081.

22. Secretary of State for the Colonies to Reverend Forster, 29 September 1950, KHCB: 2.

23. Civil Secretary of the Northern Region to all Residents, 28 January 1953, KHCB, R.910.

24. Governor of Nigeria to Secretary of State for the Colonies, 23 June 1953, PRO, CO 583/302/9.

25. Letter from CHC Edwards to DO i/c Jos Division, 16 December 1953, SIMIA, Miscellaneous Mission Info, Mainly Early.

26. Malumfashi resume, 4th Quarter, 1950, SIMIA, Malumfashi resumes, 1946–1965; Kano Province Annual Report 1953, KHCB, Kano Province Annual Report 1953, File 8323.

27. Ibid. Another example of grassroots media from Fika Emirate, in Borno, was brought to my attention by my former Hausa teacher, Alhaji Maina Gimba. His grandfather was a chief of Potiskum and started his own newspaper, thereby tying his traditional title to his literary efforts.

28. Dutse resumes, 1952, SIMIA, Dutse Resumes.

29. Saint Louis Secondary School Golden Jubilee, 1951–2001, unpublished booklet; Halima A. B., Gloria U., Linda A., and Maimuna S., Christian and Muslim prefects, interview by author, unrecorded, 24 July 2001. On account of their ages having been under fifteen, I have not used their full names.

30. Resume for Kano, April–June 1946, SIMIA, Kano Resumes 1946–1966 No. Sr-18.

31. Resume for Kano, October–December 1951, SIMIA, Kano Resumes 1946–1966 No. Sr-18.

32. Annual Report for Kano Station, 1953–1954, SIMIA, Kano Reports 1946–1969.

33. Ahmadu Bello, *My Life* (Cambridge: Cambridge University Press, 1962), 136–37.

34. It would be interesting to know how far back in time this association of the Hausa with the British colonialists developed, since, as Kristin Mann points out, Hausa were brought to Lagos from 1862 to serve in the Hausa Regiment, the police force established by John Hawley Glover, the second colonial governor of Lagos after the British bombardment in 1851. Mann, *Slavery and the Birth of an African City: Lagos, 1760–1900* (Bloomington: Indiana University Press, 2007), 110.

35. Bello, *My Life*, 128.

36. Sir J. MacPherson to Mr. Lyttleton, 21 May 1953, CO 554/428, no. 24, in Martin Lynn, ed., *British Documents on the End of Empire*, series A (London: Commonwealth Institute, 2001), 581.

37. Report on the Kano Disturbances, 16–19 May 1953, AHA, RP/A53, 20.

38. Ibid., 2.

39. Ibid., 20.

40. Ibid., 11.

41. Weatherhead, Kano Resident, to Civil Secretary, Northern Region, 28 August 1952, KHCB, R.910, 2.

42. MacPherson to Lyttleton, 583.

43. Report on Kano, 19.

44. Haruna 'dan Daura, interview by author, recorded, Jos, Nigeria, 1 August 2001.

45. Dutse Resume, 2nd Quarter 1954, SIMIA, Dutse Resumes, Dutse Station Reports (box).

46. Letter from Harold Wolfe to Mike Glerum, from Tofa, 12 February 1955, SIMIA, Miscellaneous Mission Info, Mainly Early.

47. From CHC Edwards [SIM legal dept.] to Mike Glerum, 23 February 1955, SIMIA, Miscellaneous Mission Info, Mainly Early.

48. Secret Letter No. 53019/152, from the Civil Secretary's Office, Northern Region, Kaduna, to Zaria Resident, January 1954, KHCB, File no. R.216.

49. Secret and Personal Savingram No. 15 from the Governor, Secretary of State for the Colonies, London, 10 March 1956, KHCB, File no. R.216.

50. Letter Confidential No. C.706/26 from AT Weatherhead, Resident Kano, to Civil Secretar., Northern Region, Letter Confidential No.C.706/26 from A. T. Weatherhead, Resident Kano, to Civil Scty., Northern Region, KHCB, File no. R.254.

51. Secret No. No.C.706/32, from Resident Kano to Civil Scty, 28 January 1955, File no. R.254.

52. Dafe Otobo, "Bureaucratic Elites and Public-Sector Wage Bargaining in Nigeria," *Journal of Modern African Studies* 24, no. 1 (1986): 101–26.

53. Letter from Rev. Victor Musa to Finance Division, Evangelical Churches of West Africa (hereafter cited as ECWA) English Section, 11/2/92, ECWA Eye Hospital, ECWA Kano DCC General File Miscellaneous, EEH/DCC/S.61.

54. *Triumph* article by Juliet Umahi, 3 September 1992, ECWA Eye Hospital, Publications Quantities, EEH/PQ/S.62.

55. Eric S. Horn, "African Convert Visits London," *Sudan Witness* 30, no. 1 (January 1954): 20.

56. Meeting at Kaduna, Wed., 20 April 1955, SIMIA, Miscellaneous Mission Info, Mainly Early.

57. Kano Province Annual Report 1955,KHCB, Kano Province Annual Report 1955: 13.

58. Katsina Resume, 2nd Quarter 1957, SIMIA, Katsina Station Reports.

59. Secret R.258/4 from B. Greatbatch, Resident Kano, to Permanent Secretary, Ministry for Local Government, Northern Region, 25 April 1958, KHCB, R.258.

60. Report of the Commission appointed to enquire into the fears of Minorities and the means of allaying them, July 1958, AHA, 1/2/A28, RP/A28. For a fuller discussion of the Willink Commission, see Niels Kastfelt, *Religion and Politics in Nigeria: A Study in Middle Belt Christianity* (New York: British Academic Press, 1994).

61. Ibid., 65.

62. Esther Anderson to missionaries, 11 November 1959, SIMIA, Karu Misc. 1947–1971.

63. Ibid.

64. Thomas Yepwi, son of Yepwi, to Director of SIM at Jos, 7 November 1959, SIMIA, Karu Misc. 1947–1971.

65. John N. Paden, *Ahmadu Bello, Sardauna of Sokoto: Values and Leadership in Nigeria* (London: Hodder and Stoughton, 1986), 566–69.

66. Turaki, *Theory and Practice*, 180.

67. Jonathon Reynolds discusses the problems associated with the Tijaniyya in Kuta, clearly a hotbed of evangelical activity, in the 1920s. Reynolds, "Good and Bad Muslims: Islam and Indirect Rule in Northern Nigeria," *International Journal*

of *African History Studies* 34, no. 3 (2001): 614; see also John N. Paden, *Religion and Political Culture in Kano* (Berkeley: University of California Press, 1973).

68. Isa Alkali Abba, "Sir Ahmadu Bello: The Sardauna of Sokoto's Conversion Campaign, 1964–1965, in Adamawa Division and Northern Sardauna Province," *Kano Studies* 2, no. 2 (1981): 53–60.

69. Claude F. Molla, "Some Aspects of Islam in Africa South of the Sahara," *International Review of Mission* 56, no. 224 (October 1967): 459.

70. Ahmadu John Abarshi, interview by author, unrecorded, Jos, Plateau State, Nigeria, 1 June 2001.

71. Ibid.

72. In reviewing John Paden's biography of Ahmadu Bello, John Peel points out that more information about the Sardauna self-making would have been very interesting, particularly considering that his mother was a "only a concubine, part of the annual tribute sent to Sokoto from Adamawa" and his placing Fulani tribalism aside for Hausaphone regional identity. Peel also rightly points out that Paden did not consider the perspectives of Southern Nigerians concerning the Sardauna, and the same could be said of his lack of attention to the views of Northern Nigerian Christians. J. D. Y. Peel, "Two Northerners Contrasted in Their Visions of Nigerian Unity," *Canadian Journal of African Studies* 22, no. 1 (1988): 144–48.

73. The Nigerian Police Force, and the military as well, became places of religious and ethnic mixing, and, as I found in my research, a respite from the religious segregation that existed in broader society. Philip T. Ahire, *Imperial Policing: The Emergence and Role of the Police in Colonial Nigeria, 1860–1960* (Bristol: Open University Press, 1991).

74. References were made to me at Christian stations in southern Kano and Katsina about the Sardauna's tours by younger pastors who could not remember the events but who had clearly heard stories from elders. They spoke about the regular evangelizing—Christian and Muslim—in their areas, and the political organization that made them decide on Christian conversion. As of 2005, communities in Karaye, Rogo, and other places had formed large blocs who had come into trouble with the Kano State authorities for their voting preferences that went against the main of rural Kano.

75. Paden, *Religion and Political Culture*, 569.

76. Chuck Hershelman, interview by author, 25 April 2003, SIMIA.

77. Quoted in Trevor Clark, *A Right Honourable Gentleman: Abubakar from the Black Rock* (London: Edward Arnold, 1991), 98.

78. Interview with Pastor Moses Ariye, 4 December 1963, SIMIA, ECWA box, folder ECWA History and Growth.

79. Handwritten manuscript by Titus Payne, n.d., about Maguzawas, nd, SIMIA, ECWA box, file EMS History and Relationship with SIM 1949–1987.

80. Henry Guenter to Field Director, SIM, 6 June 1961, ECWA, Jos, Ruth Cox papers.

81. Michael Gould, *The Struggle for Modern Nigeria: The Biafran War, 1967–1970* (New York: Tauris, 2012), 39.

82. Chris Oswold, interview by author, unrecorded, Sebring, Florida, SIM retirement home, 26 June 2002.

83. White paper on the report of the Committee to Investigate Causes of Riots and Disturbances in Kaduna State, 6–12 March 1987.

84. Bello, *My Life*, 136–37; Report on the Disturbances Kano, 1953, 17–18.

85. Peter K. Tibendarana, "The Beginnings of Girls' Education in the Native Administration Schools in Northern Nigeria, 1930–1945," *Journal of African History* 26, no. 1 (1985): 105.

86. Ladi Joe, interview by author, unrecorded, Sabon Gari, Kano, 7 June 2001.

87. Henry and Reta Guenter, Bauchi, 8 July 1966, ECWA HQ, Ruth Cox papers.

88. Kenneth Lee Adelman, "The Recourse to Authenticity and Negritude in Zaire," *Journal of Modern African Studies* 13, no. 1 (March 1975): 134–39.

89. Ibid., 134.

90. Story of Ayuba Agades of Kelo, Chad, told to Charles Rhine on 16 July 1975, SIMIA, Box 18 "ECWA: Biographical Sketches, A–F."

91. Ibid., 137.

92. Maud Gauquelin, "Les tchadiens evangeliques au Nigeria: Histoire missionaire de la Sudan United Mission, migration moundang et violence evangelique, " IFRA-Nigeria e-papers 5 (2 December 2010).

CONCLUSION

1. Great debates have raged over how much missions transformed African societies, and excellent scholarship on this topic is required reading in African history. I cite just one work because it employs Africanist scholarship as a body of theory effectively to explore China's mission history and thereby offer a wider, if not global, lens on the impact of missionary movements. Ryan Dunch, "Beyond Cultural Imperialism: Cultural Theory, Christian Missions, and Global Modernity," *History and Theory* 41, no. 3 (October 2002): 301–25.

2. Matthews A. Ojo, "The Contextual Significance of the Charismatic Movements in Independent Nigeria," *Africa* 58, no. 2 (1988): 175–92; Brian Larkin and Birgit Meyer, "Pentecostalism, Islam, and Culture: New Religious Movements in West Africa," in *Themes in West Africa's History*, ed. Emmanuel K. Akyeampong (Athens: Ohio University Press, 2006).

3. See, for example, the biography of Paul Gindiri, described as a "confrontational preacher" and a key founder of a local New Life for All chapter. The sketch of his life is written by Musa Gaiya, who illustrates well the interweaving of the "precolonial roots" of exclusion and the radical Christian activism of a born-again revivalist. http://www.dacb.org/stories/nigeria/gindiri_paul.html.

4. Newssheet titled "Bima Rock," April 1977, SIMA, Tribes-Maguzawa 1978–1986.

5. D. J. M. Muffett, *Concerning Brave Captains: Being a history of the British Occupation of Kano and Sokoto and of the Last Stand of the Fulani Forces* (London: Deutsch, 1964); Muhammad Khalid Masud, "The Obligation to Migrate: The Doctrine of *Hijra* in Islamic Law," in *Muslim Travellers: Pilgrimage, Migration, and the Religious Imagination*, ed. Dale F. Eickelman and James Piscatori (Berkeley: University of California Press), 29–49.

6. "Bima Rock."

7. Michael Watts, "Hazards and Crisis: A Political Economy of Drought and Famine in Northern Nigeria," *Antipode* 15, no. 1 (1983): 34; Aondover Tarhule and Ming-Ko Woo, "Towards an Interpretation of Historical Droughts in Northern Nigeria," *Climatic Change* 37, no. 4 (1997): 601–16.

8. J. D. Y. Peel, "Postsocialism, Postcolonialism, Pentecostalism," in *Conversion after Socialism: Disruptions, Modernisms and Technologies of Faith in the Former Soviet Union*, ed. Mathijs Pelkmans (New York: Berghahn Books, 2009), 183–200.

9. Peter Van der Veer has fruitfully explored the connection between pilgrimage and other forms of religious mobility and the lived practices shaping religious nationalism in India. The Christians in Northern Nigeria, led by very influential men including Fulani Christian Reverend Garba Dutse, have pushed for a government pilgrimage sponsorship akin to the hajj board run by Northern Nigerian state governments. Peter Van der Veer, *Hindus and Muslims in India* (Berkeley: University of California Press, 1994); M. A. Bidmos, "The Islamic Approach to Religious Dialogue: With Special Reference to Nigeria," *Journal of Muslim Minority Affairs* 8, no. 1 (1987): 22–27.

10. Yusufu Bala Usman, *The Manipulation of Religion in Nigeria, 1977–1987* (Kaduna: Vanguard, 1987), 82–85.

11. Ibid., 82.

12. Ibid., 82–85.

13. The name of Nana Asma'u, the prolific writer and activist who was the daughter of Shehu Usman dan Fodio, is still invoked by Muslims and some Christians, as a pioneer of non-Western feminism and as a model of women's pious scholarship. Alaine S. Hutson has written about women in the Tijaniyya, a rival order to 'dan Fodio's Qadiriyya. Hutson, "The Development of Women's Authority in the Kano Tijaniyya, 1894–1963," *Africa Today* 46, nos. 3–4 (1999): 43–64.

14. John M. Garba, *The Time Has Come . . . : Reminiscences and Reflections of a Nigerian Pioneer Diplomat* (Ibadan: Spectrum Books, 1989), 385.

15. Northern Nigeria scholars have done important research relating to the ethnic Christian organizations, as the acknowledgments and footnotes of Frieder Ludwig's article suggests. The issue of the Masihiyawa came up at the recent International Conference on SIM History in Africa, Addis Ababa, Ethiopia, 9–13 July 2013. Many non-Hausa scholars of Christianity point to this organization as evidence that some Hausa Muslims did accept Christianity. Muslims are quick to point to the lowly origins of these converts, a contention that Christian believers do not like. While we know Hausa and Fulani did accept Christianity, what is less spoken about and very intriguing is the historical construction of ethnicity through religions and religious encounters. Becoming Hausa is just as important as being Hausa, as is made clear in the essays in *Being and Becoming Hausa: Interdisciplinary Perspectives*, ed. Anne Haour and Benedetta Rossi (Leiden: Brill, 2010).

16. Murray Last, "The Search for Security in Muslim Northern Nigeria." *Africa* 78, no. 1 (2008): 41–63.

17. Although there is very little research on Christian-Muslim women's interactions in Northern Nigeria, the activities of early postcolonial elite women make clear their shared charitable impulses were important badges of respectability. Mary Solomon Lar, *Ambassador for Christ: Mary Lar's Reflections on Nigeria, Past and Present* (Bedford, England: British Church Growth Association, 1997), 36–37; Ladi S. Adamu, *Hafsatu Ahmadu Bello: The Unsung Heroine* (Kaduna: Adams Books, 1995), 55; Kathleen McGarvey, *Muslim and Christian Women in Dialogue: The Case of Northern Nigeria* (Bern: Peter Lang, 2009). On campus cults, see Misty L. Bastian, "Vulture Men, Campus Cultists and Teenaged Witches: Modern Magics in Nigerian Popular Media," in *Magical Interpretations, Material Realities: Modernity, Witchcraft and the Occult in Postcolonial Africa*, ed. Henrietta L. Moore and Todd Sanders (New York: Routledge,

2003); also Ebenezer Obadare, "White-Collar Fundamentalism: Interrogating Youth Religiosity on Nigerian University Campuses," *Journal of Modern African Studies* 45, no. 4 (2007): 517–37.

18. Rosalind I. J. Hackett gives a very useful background to the conflicts over religious education from the 1950s forward and to the creation of these subjects. Hackett, "Conflict in the Classroom: Educational Institutions as Sites of Religious Tolerance/ Intolerance in Nigeria," *Brigham Young University Law Review* 2 (1999): 537–60.

19. I was able to attend one of their lectures, personally discuss my research with them, and view their film, *An African Answer*, at the US Institute of Peace in October 2011.

20. UNICEF, *Partnering with Religious Communities for Children* (New York: UNICEF, 2012); Alhaji Dr. Suleiman Sani Wali, personal communication with author, Kano, 5 August 2001.

21. There are some general references to the mission medical work. Elisha P. Renne, *The Politics of Polio in Northern Nigeria* (Bloomington: Indiana University Press, 2010).

22. I first learned of this man from the Muslim judge and his relations in April 2001. The hotel where the man and his family were lodging was part of the building attached to my own house. I met the man twice during Easter Week but never asked his name, his village's exact location, or his specific Christian denomination because of his precarious situation. He also was somewhat confused about my relationship with the Muslim evangelist who was his benefactor and who had arranged the meeting. Thus, any identifying details about this incident have not been included.

23. Murray Last, "Muslims and Christians in Nigeria: An Economy of Political Panic," *Round Table* 96, no. 332 (2007): 609–10.

24. Adam Higazi, "Social Mobilization and Collective Violence: Vigilantes and Militias in the Lowlands of Plateau State, Central Nigeria," *Africa* 78, no. 1 (2008): 114.

25. See note 15 above. The recent conference sponsored by the SIM brought many Nigerian scholars to Ethiopia to collaborate with scholars working on the histories of African Christianity throughout the Sudanic region from west to east. Still active, the fundamentalist mission's relationship has changed considerably with the Nigerian church over the last two decades. SIM recognizes the importance of African history to supply examples of past pluralisms and recast debates about colonialism and its legacies, American interventions in Africa, and indigenous and local identity politics in Christian-Muslim relations.

Bibliography

PERSONAL PAPERS

Daura, Haruna 'dan
Garba, John M.
Samuila, Inusa
Sani, Joseph M.

ARCHIVAL SOURCES

Nigeria

Arewa House Archives, Kaduna (AHA)
Evangelical Churches of West Africa (formerly SIM) Archives, Jos (ECWA)
ECWA Eye Hospital files, Kano
Kano History and Culture Bureau, Kano (KHCB)
National Archives, Kaduna (NAK)

United Kingdom

Public Records Office, Kew (PRO)
Rhodes House Library, Oxford (RHL)
School of Oriental and African Studies Library, Special Collections, London
University of Birmingham Library, Special Collections, Birmingham (BIRM)

United States

International Missionary Council/Conference of British Missionary Societies Joint Archives, UCLA (IMC/CBMS)
Sudan Interior Mission International Archives, Fort Mill, South Carolina (SIMIA)
Yale Divinity School Special Collections

INTERVIEWS BY AUTHOR

Nigeria

Abarshi, Ahmadu John, 1 June 2001, Kaduna, Kaduna State
Abubakar, Mairo, 12 June 2001, Ya da Kunya, Kano State

Adamu, Mammani, 19 July 2001, Babbar Ruga, Katsina State
Ahmadu, Alhaji, 22 July 2001, Mariri, Kano State
Ahmadu, Malam Idi, 6 June 2001, Ya da Kunya, Kano State
Alhaji, 17 August 2001, Giginyu, Kano State
Alhamdu, Samuila, 26 April 2001, Ungogo, Kano State
Audu, Malam and Dije, 22 April 2001, Kagadama, Jigawa State
Audu family: Zainabu, Halima, Christiana Donli (née Audu), Martha Maiwada (née Audu), Janet Sad'auki, Philippa Thompson, Mrs. Victoria Audu (née Joe), 5 August 2001, Wusasa, Kaduna State
Baikie, Adamu, 2 June 2001, Zaria, Kaduna State
Bako, Alhaji Garba, 11 March 2001; 15 April 2001, Kano City, Kano State
Bello, Ishaku, and Abu (Zainabu), 26 April 2001, ECWA Kano, Kano State
Bete, Malam, 8 May 2001, Dass, Bauchi State
Cox, Ruth, 5 May 2001, ECWA Kano, Kano State
Datti, Malam Haruna, 9 March 2001, Roni, Jigawa State
Daura, Haruna 'dan, 1 August 2001, Jos, Plateau State
Dawa, Saminu Mai, 16 February 2001, Karaye, Kano State
Dije (Hadiza), 29 April 2001, Roni, Jigawa State
Dongora, Murtala Mati, 28 February 2001, ECWA Kano, Kano State
Dutse, Umaru Garba, 15 April 2001, Dutse, Jigawa State
Gagare, Bete, 8 May 2001, Dass, Bauchi State
Gambo, Hindatu Gani, 22 April 2001, Roni, Jigawa State
Gata, Iliya, 18 May 2001, Karaye, Kano State
Gobso, Malam Sale, 15 June 2001, Roni, Jigawa State
Hammack, Sue, 2 August 2001, ECWA Jos, Plateau State
Hassan, Yakubu, 18 May 2001, Karaye, Kano State
Ibrahim, Dorothy, 5 August 2001, Wusasa, Kaduna State
Ibrahim, Malam, 22 July 2001, Mariri, Kano State
Joe, Mrs. Ladi, 7 June 2001, Sabon Gari Kano, Kano State
Karkarna, Hadiza, 2 March 2001, Fago, Jigawa State
Karkarna, Malam Usman Audu, 6 June 2001, Ya da Kunya, Kano State
Karkarna, Usman, 12 June 2001, Ya da Kunya, Kano State
Kassim, Yahaya, 18 May 2001, Karaye State
Kirupananthan, Subramaniam, 21 April 2001, ECWA Kano, Kano State
Kukasheka, Mato Usman, 11 June 2001, Malumfashi, Katsina State
Ladi, Malam Umaru 'dan, 1 March 2001, Roni, Jigawa State
Lukshi, Sule Hanna Kuka, 8 May 2001, Dass, Bauchi State
Mai Dawa, Saminu, 11 February 2001, Karaye, Kano State
Maitankari-Abraham, Lami, 5 August 2001, Kaduna State
Mohammed family: Elizabeth M., Hauwa Umaru, Wusasa, 5 August 2001, Wusasa, Kaduna State
Mokelu, Uko, 26 January 2001, Sabon Gari, Kano State
Moore, James Daboh, 9 February 2001, Tofa, Kano State
Muhammadu, Hama, 17 August 2001, Giginyu, Kano State
Nagazau, Isti, 18 May 2001, Karaye, Kano State
Nakawari, Lawan, 27 May 2001, Kano City, Kano State
Ogwu, Ahmadu, 12 June 2001, Ya da Kunya, Kano State
Onamusi, Grace, 27 January 2001, Sabon Gari, Kano State

Paul, Ruth, 2 June 2001, Kaduna, Kaduna State
Saint Louis School prefects, 24 July 2001, Bompai, Kano State
Samande, Hannatu, 24 May 2001, Jos, Plateau State
Samande, Ishaya and Hannatu, 9 May 2001, Jos, Plateau State
Sani family: Mrs. Ladi, Binta, and Ahmed, 29 May 2001, Kano, Kano State
Sani, Musa, 13 February 2001, ECWA Kano, Kano State
Shiyambola, William, 5 February 2001, ECWA Kano, Kano State
Sule, Alhaji Yusufu Maitama, 22 July 2001, Nassarawa, Kano State
TerMeer, Paul, 23 April 2001, ECWA Kano, Kano State
Tomas, Malam Sale, 12 August 2001, Dawan Kaya, Jigawa State
Tsakani, Musa, 8 May 2001, Dass, Bauchi State
Umaru, Ado, 24 April 2001, ECWA Kano, Kano State
Umaru, Alhaji, 22 July 2001, Mariri, Kano State
Umaru, Audu, 17 August 2001, Giginyu, Kano State
Usman, Ayuba, 3 and 8 February 2001, Pan Shekara, Kano State
Usman, Inuwa, 5 June 2001, Ya da Kunya, Kano State
Usman, Malam Umaru (Baba Ladan), 6 June 2001, Ya da Kunya, Kano State
Waaldyk, Kaess, 19 July 2001, Babbar Ruga, Katsina State
Wayi, Anna, 27 May and 21 July 2001, Zoo Road, Kano State
Yahuza, Malam Dahiru, 26 April 2001, Tofa, Kano State
Yola, Hajiya Amina Datti, 24 July 2001, Bompai, Kano State
Yusuf, Binta, 5 August 2001, Wusasa, Kaduna State
Yusuf, Halima, 5 August 2001, Wusasa, Kaduna State
Zubairu, Malam Hamza, 22 April 2001, Roni, Jigawa State

Sebring, Florida; and Charlotte, North Carolina, United States*

Beacham, George, 25 June 2002
Beveridge, Anna, 24 June 2002
Braband, Wally and Violet, 25 June 2002
Cummins, Marge, 25 June 2002
Hay, Ian and June, 25 June 2002
Hershelman, Chuck, 25 April 2003
Miller, Harold and Boby, 24 June 2002
Oswold, Cris, 26 June 2002
Wickstrom, Lloyd and Marjorie, 25 June 2002

*The SIM archives were moved to Fort Mill, South Carolina, around 2005.

PRIMARY SOURCE PERIODICALS

Africa Now
British Medical Journal
Evangelical Christian and Missionary Witness
Faithful Witness
Leprosy Notes
Nigeria magazine

Northern Nigeria Gazette
Sudan Witness

WORKS CITED AND CONSULTED

Abba, Isa Alkali. "Sir Ahmadu Bello: The Sardauna of Sokoto's Conversion Campaign, 1964–1965, in Adamawa Division and Northern Sardauna Province." *Kano Studies* 2, no. 2 (1981): 53–60.

Abdalla, I. H. *Islam, Medicine, and Practitioners in Northern Nigeria*. Lewiston, NY: Edwin Mellen Press, 1997.

Adamu, Ladi S. *Hafsatu Ahmadu Bello: The Unsung Heroine*. Kaduna: Adams Books, 1995.

Adas, Michael. *Prophets of Rebellion: Millenarian Protest Movements against the European Colonial Order*. Chapel Hill: University of North Carolina Press, 1979.

Adebanwi, Wale. "Terror, Territoriality, and the Struggle for Indigeneity and Citizenship in Northern Nigeria." *Citizenship Studies* 13, no. 4 (2009): 349–63.

Adeleye, Raji A. *Power and Diplomacy in Northern Nigeria, 1804–1906: The Sokoto Caliphate and Its Enemies*. New York: Humanities Press, 1971.

Adelman, Kenneth Lee. "The Recourse to Authenticity and Négritude in Zaire." *Journal of Modern African Studies* 13, no. 1 (March 1975): 134–39.

Adesoji, Abimbola O. "Between Maitatsine and Boko Haram: Islamic Fundamentalism and the Response of the Nigerian State." *Africa Today* 57, no. 4 (2011): 99–119.

Adichie, Chimamanda. "Things Left Unsaid." *London Review of Books* 34, no. 19 (11 October 2012): 32–33.

Aguilar, Mario I. "African Conversion from a World Religion: Religious Diversification by the Waso Boorana in Kenya." *Africa* 65, no. 4 (October 1995): 525–44.

Ahire, Philip T. *Imperial Policing: The Emergence and Role of the Police in Colonial Nigeria, 1860–1960*. Bristol: Open University Press, 1991.

Ali, Abdullah Yusuf. *An English Interpretation of the Holy Qur'an*. 1st ed. Bensenville, IL: Lushena Books, 1934.

Aliyu, Hawa'u Lynne M. "The Contribution of the SIM on Women's Education in Kano State with Special Reference to Kabo Girls' School." BA thesis, Bayero University Kano, 1975.

Aliyu, Sani Abba. "Christian Missionaries and Hausa Literature in Nigeria, 1840–1890: A Critical Evaluation." *Kano Studies*, n.s. 1, no. 1 (2000): 93–118.

Aruwan, Samuel. "Bitrus Gani Dies at 67." 22 February 2011. allafrica.com, accessed July 24, 2011, http://allafrica.com/stories/201102220265.html.

Ayandele, Emmanuel A. *The Missionary Impact on Modern Nigeria, 1842–1914*. New York: Humanities Press, 1967.

Azevedo, Mario. "Power and Slavery in Central Africa: Chad (1890–1925)." *Journal of Negro History* 67, no. 3 (1982): 198–211.

Baba of Karo and Mary F. Smith. *Baba of Karo: A Woman of the Moslem Hausa*. New Haven, CT: Yale University Press, 1981.

Baba, Panya. "Nigeria's Isawas [sic]: Muslims Who Follow Jesus." *Africa Now* (June–August 1979): 6–7.

Barber, Karin, ed. *Africa's Hidden Histories: Everyday Literacy and Making the Self*. Bloomington: Indiana University Press, 2006.

Barnes, Andrew E. "Aryanizing Projects, African Collaborators and Colonial Transcripts." *Comparative Studies of South Asia, Africa and the Middle East* 17, no. 2 (Fall 1997): 46–61.
——. "Catholic Evangelizing in One Colonial Mission: The Institutional Evolution of Jos Prefecture, Nigeria, 1907–1954." *Catholic Historical Review* 84, no. 2 (April 1998): 240–62.
——. "'Evangelization Where It Is not Wanted': Colonial Administrators and Christian Missionaries in Northern Nigeria during the First Third of the Twentieth Century." *Journal of Religion in Africa* 25, no. 4 (November 1995): 412–41.
——. "'The Great Prohibition': The Expansion of Christianity in Colonial Northern Nigeria." *History Compass* 8, no. 6 (2010): 440–54.
——. *Making Headway: The Introduction of Western Civilization in Colonial Northern Nigeria*. Rochester, NY: University of Rochester Press, 2009.
——. "'Religious Insults': Christian Critiques of Islam and the Government in Colonial Northern Nigeria." *Journal of Religion in Africa* 34, nos. 1–2 (2004): 62–81.
——. "'Some Fire Behind the Smoke': The Fraser Report and Its Aftermath in Colonial Northern Nigeria." *Canadian Journal of African Studies* 31, no. 2 (1997): 197–228.
Barth, Heinrich. *Travels and Discoveries in North and Central Africa: Being a Journal of an Expedition Undertaken under the Auspices of H.B.M. Government*. New York: Harper, 1857–59.
Bastian, Misty L. "Vulture Men, Campus Cultists and Teenaged Witches: Modern Magics in Nigerian Popular Media." In *Magical Interpretations, Material Realities: Modernity, Witchcraft and the Occult in Postcolonial Africa*, edited by Henrietta L. Moore and Todd Sanders, 71–96. New York: Routledge, 2003.
Beacham, Gordon. "Annual Field Report for Nigeria and French West Africa." *Sudan Witness* 17, no. 2 (April 1941): 1–13.
Bello, Ahmadu. *My Life*. Cambridge: Cambridge University Press, 1962.
Berman, Edward H. "American Influence on African Education: The Role of the Phelps-Stokes Funds Education Commissions." *Comparative Education Review* 15, no. 2 (1971): 132–45.
Besancenot, J. P., M. Boko, and P. C. Oke. "Weather Conditions and Cerebrospinal Meningitis in Benin (Gulf of Guinea, West Africa)." *European Journal of Epidemiology* 13, no. 7 (1997): 807–15.
Bidmos, M. A. "The Islamic Approach to Religious Dialogue: With Special Reference to Nigeria." *Journal of Muslim Minority Affairs* 8, no. 1 (1987): 22–27.
Bingham, Rowland V. *The Bible and the Body: Healing in the Scriptures*. Toronto: Evangelical Publishers, 1952.
——. *Seven Sevens of Years and a Jubilee: The Story of the Sudan Interior Mission*. Grand Rapids, MI: Zondervan, 1943.
Bivins, Mary Wren. *Telling Stories, Making Histories: Women, Words, and Islamic Reform in a Nineteenth-Century Hausaland and the Sokoto Caliphate*. Portsmouth: Heinemann, 2007.
Blyden, Edward W. *Christianity, Islam and the Negro Race*. Edinburgh: Edinburgh University Press, 1967.
——. "West Africa before Europe." *Journal of the Royal African Society* 2, no. 8 (July 1903): 359–74.
Boddy, Janice. *Civilizing Women: British Crusades in Colonial Sudan*. Princeton, NJ: Princeton University Press, 2007.

Boer, Jan Harm. *Christianity and Islam under Colonialism in Northern Nigeria*. Jos: Christian Council of Nigeria, 1988.

Bonneuil, Christophe. "Development as Experiment: Science and State Building in Late Colonial and Postcolonial Africa, 1930–1970." *Osiris*, 2nd ser., 15 (2000): 258–81.

Brenner, Louis. *Controlling Knowledge: Religion, Power and Schooling in a West African Muslim Society*. Bloomington: Indiana University Press, 2001.

Brilliant, Girija E., and Lawrence B. Brilliant. "Using Social Epidemiology to Understand Who Stays Blind and Who Gets Operated for Cataract in a Rural Setting." *Social Science and Medicine* 21, no. 5 (1985): 553–58.

Bruzzi, Silvia. "Saints' Bodies, Islamic and Colonial Medicine in Eritrea (1887–1940)." In *Themes in Modern African History and Culture*, edited by Lars Berge and Irma Taddia, 69–83. Padova: Biblioteca Universitaria, 2013.

Bunza, Mukhtar U. *Christian Missions among Muslims: Sokoto Province, Nigeria, 1935–1990*. Trenton, NJ: Africa World Press, 2007.

Bush, Julia. *Edwardian Ladies and Imperial Power*. Leicester: Leicester University Press, 2000.

Carpenter, Joel A. "Fundamentalist Institutions and the Rise of Evangelical Protestantism, 1929–1942." *Church History* 49, no. 1 (March 1980): 62–75.

Cell, John W. "On the Eve of Decolonization: The Colonial Office's Plans for the Transfer of Power in Africa, 1947." *Journal of Imperial and Commonwealth History* 8, no. 3 (1980): 235–57.

Chernin, E. "The Early British and American Journals of Tropical Medicine and Hygiene: An Informal Survey." *Medical History* 36, no. 1 (1992): 70–83.

Christelow, Alan. "Slavery in Kano, 1913–1914: Evidence from the Judicial Records." *African Economic History* 14 (1985): 57–74.

Clark, Trevor. *A Right Honourable Gentleman: Abubakar from the Black Rock*. London: Edward Arnold, 1991.

Clements, Keith. *Faith on the Frontier: A Life of J. H. Oldham*. Edinburgh: Continuum, 1999.

Cohen, Abner. *Custom and Politics in Urban Africa: A Study of Hausa Migrants in Yoruba Towns*. London: Routledge, 1969.

Coleman, James S. *Nigeria: Background to Nationalism*. Berkeley: University of California Press.

Comaroff, John L., and Jean Comaroff. *A Companion to Gender History*. Edited by Teresa A. Meade and Merry E. Wiesner-Hanks. New York: Blackwell, 2004.

———. *Of Revelation and Revolution: The Dialectics of Modernity on a South African Frontier*. Vol. 2. Chicago: University of Chicago Press, 1992.

Cooper, Barbara M. *Evangelicals in the Muslim Sahel*. Bloomington: Indiana University Press, 2006.

———. "Reflections on Slavery, Seclusion and Female Labor in the Maradi Region of Niger in the Nineteenth and Twentieth Centuries." *Journal of African History* 35, no. 1 (1994): 61–78.

Cooper, Frederick. *Africa since 1940: The Past of the Present*. New York: Cambridge University Press, 2002.

Cotton, James F. "Trials and Triumphs in Nigeria." *Missionary Witness* (September 1914): 279–80.

Cox, Ruth. "The Lord's Work: Perspectives of Early Leaders of the Evangelical Church of West Africa Regarding the Spread of Christianity." PhD thesis, Trinity International University, 2000.
Crampton, E. P. T. *Christianity in Northern Nigeria*. Zaria: Gaskiya, 1976.
Des Forges, Alison. "The Ideology of Genocide." *Issue: A Journal of Opinion* 23, no. 2 (1995): 44–47.
Dobronravine, Nikolai. "Hausa Ajami Literature and Script: Colonial Innovations and Post-Colonial Myths in Northern Nigeria." *Sudanic Africa* 15 (2004): 85–110.
———. "Shurut kutub Injil bi-khtira li-Injil" of Ibn Maryam: A Sufi Reconstruction of the New Testament (Sudanic Africa, after 1727), unpublished paper, ca. 2006.
Donham, Donald L. *Marxist Modern: An Ethnographic History of the Ethiopian Revolution*. Berkeley: University of California Press, 1999.
Dreisbach, Dr. and Mrs. J. A. "A Boys' Brigade Camp for Boys with Leprosy." *Sudan Witness* 26, no. 4 (July 1950): 13–14.
Dunch, Ryan. "Beyond Cultural Imperialism: Cultural Theory, Christian Missions, and Global Modernity." *History and Theory* 41, no. 3 (October 2002): 301–25.
Dyce-Sharp, N. A. "Epidemic Disease in West Africa: The Menace of the Future." *Transactions of the Royal Society of Tropical Medicine and Hygiene* 19, no. 4 (1925): 256–64.
Ejembi, C. L., Elisha P. Renne, and H. A. Adamu. "The Politics of the 1996 Cerebrospinal Meningitis Epidemic in Nigeria." *Africa* 68, no. 1 (1998): 118–34.
Eshete, Tibebe. *The Evangelical Movement in Ethiopia: Resistance and Resilience*. Waco, TX: Baylor University Press, 2009.
———. "The Sudan Interior Mission (SIM) in Ethiopia (1928–1970)." *Northeast African Studies*, n.s., 6, no. 3 (1999): 27–57.
Falola, Toyin. *Violence in Nigeria: The Crisis of Religious Politics and Secular Ideologies*. Rochester, NY: University of Rochester Press, 1998.
Fiedler, Klaus. *The Story of Faith Missions*. Oxford: Regnum Books, 1984.
Fine, Paul E. M. "Leprosy: The Epidemiology of a Slow Bacterium." *Epidemiologic Reviews* 4, no. 1 (1982): 161–88.
Fisher, Humphrey J. "Prayer and Military Activity in the History of Muslim Africa South of the Sahara." *Journal of African History* 12, no. 3 (1971): 391–406.
Flint, John E., and E. Ann McDougall "Economic Change in West Africa in the Nineteenth Century." In *History of West Africa*, vol. 2, edited by J. F. Ade Ajayi and Michael Crowder, 379–402. London: Longman, 1974.
———. *Sir George Goldie and the Making of Nigeria*. London: Oxford University Press, 1960.
Fourchard, Laurent. "Dealing with 'Strangers': Allocating Urban Space to Migrants in Nigeria and French West Africa, End of the Nineteenth Century to 1960." In *African Cities: Competing Claims on Urban Spaces*, edited by Francesca Locatelli and Paul Nugent, 187–218. Leiden: Brill, 2009.
———. "Lagos and the Invention of Juvenile Delinquency in Nigeria, 1920–60." *Journal of African History* 47, no. 1 (2006): 115–37.
Francis-Deqhani, Guli. "Medical Missions and the History of Feminism: Emmeline Stuart of the CMS Persia Mission." In Morgan, *Women, Religion and Feminism*, 197–212.
Frank, Katherine. *A Voyager Out: The Life of Mary Kingsley*. Boston: Houghton Mifflin, 1986.

Frishman, Alan. "The Impact of Islam on the Urban Structure and Economy of Kano, Nigeria." *Journal of the Institute of Muslim Minority Affairs* 7, no. 2 (1986): 464–75.

Fuglestad, Finn. *A History of Niger, 1850–1960.* New York: Cambridge University Press, 1986.

Furlong, Patrick J. "Azikiwe and the National Church of Nigeria and the Cameroons: A Case Study of the Political Use of Religion in African Nationalism." *African Affairs* 91, no. 362 (July 1992): 433–52.

Furniss, Graham, and Philip J. Jaggar, eds. *Studies in Hausa Language and Linguistics: In Honour of F. W. Parsons.* London: Kegan Paul, 1988.

Gaitskell, Deborah. "The Imperial Tie: Obstacle or Asset for South Africa's Women Suffragists before 1930?" *South African Historical Journal* 47, no. 1 (2002): 1–23.

Gale, Thomas S. "Lord F. D. Lugard: An Assessment of His Contribution to Medical Policy in Nigeria." *International Journal of African Historical Studies* 9, no. 4 (1976): 631–40.

Garba, John M. *The Time Has Come . . . : Reminiscences and Reflections of a Nigerian Pioneer Diplomat.* Ibadan: Spectrum Books, 1989.

Gauquelin, Maud. "Les Tchadiens evangeliques au Nigeria: Histoire missionaire de la Sudan United Mission, migration moundang et violence évangélique." *IFRA-Nigeria e-papers* 5, 2 December 2010.

Geary, William Neville M. "Land Tenure and Legislation in British West Africa." *Journal of the Royal African Society* 12, no. 47 (April 1913): 236–48.

Gillespie, James A. "International Organizations and the Problem of Child Health, 1945–1960." *DYNAMIS* 23 (2003): 115–42.

Glotzer, Richard. "The Career of Mabel Carney: The Study of Race and Rural Development in the United States and South Africa." *International Journal of African Historical Studies* 29, no. 2 (1992): 309–36.

Good, Charles M. *The Steamer Parish: The Rise and Fall of Missionary Medicine on an African Frontier.* Chicago: University of Chicago Press, 2004.

Gould, Michael. *The Struggle for Modern Nigeria: The Biafran War, 1967–1970.* New York: Tauris, 2012.

Goyal, M., and M. Hogeweg. "Couching and Cataract Extraction: A Clinic Based Study in Northern Nigeria." *Community Eye Health* 10 (1997): 6–7.

Gray, Herman H., and John A. Dreisbach. "Leprosy among Foreign Missionaries in Northern Nigeria." *International Journal of Leprosy* 29, no. 3 (July–September 1961): 279–90.

Green, Nile. *Bombay Islam: The Religious Economy of the West Indian Ocean, 1840–1915.* New York: Cambridge University Press, 2011.

Greenberg, Joseph H. "Studies in African Linguistic Classification: IV. Hamito-Semitic." *Southwestern Journal of Anthropology* 6, no. 1 (Spring 1950): 47–63.

Greene, Sandra E. *Sacred Sites and the Colonial Encounter: A History of Meaning and Memory in Ghana.* Bloomington: Indiana University Press, 2002.

Guinness, Henry G. "The Soudan." *Faithful Witness* (7 December 1889): 356–57.

———. "Soudan Mission." *Faithful Witness* (14 June 1890): 173.

Guyer, Jane I. "Wealth in People and Self-Realization in Equatorial Africa." *Man*, n.s., 28, no. 2 (1993): 243–65.

Guyer, Jane I., and Samuel M. Eno Belinga. "Wealth in People as Wealth in Knowledge: Accumulation and Composition in Equatorial Africa." *Journal of African History* 36, no. 1 (1995): 91–120.

Guyer, N. Pauline. "A Missionary on Trek." *Sudan Witness* 16, no. 5 (September–October 1940): 13–15.

Hackett, Rosalind I. J. "Conflict in the Classroom: Educational Institutions as Sites of Religious Tolerance/Intolerance in Nigeria." *Brigham Young University Law Review* 2 (1999): 537–60.

Handloff, Robert E. "Prayers, Amulets, and Charms: Health and Social Control." *African Studies Review* 25, nos. 2–3 (June–September 1982): 185–94.

Hanretta, Sean. "'Kaffir' Renner's Conversion: Being Muslim in Public in Colonial Ghana." *Past and Present* 210, no. 1 (2011): 187–220.

Hansen, Karen Tranberg, ed. *African Encounters with Domesticity*. New Brunswick, NJ: Rutgers University Press, 1992.

Haour, Anne, and Benedetta Rossi, eds. *Being and Becoming Hausa: Interdisciplinary Perspectives*. Leiden: Brill, 2010.

Hardiman, David, ed. *Healing Bodies, Saving Souls: Medical Missions in Asia and Africa*. Amsterdam: Rodopi, 2006.

Harris, B. P. "Impressions of Medicine in Nigeria." *Canadian Medical Association Journal* 95, no. 2 (July 1966): 72–75.

Harris, Hermann G. *Hausa Stories and Riddles, with Notes on the Language, Etc., and a Concise Hausa Dictionary*. London: Mendip Press, 1908.

Heap, Simon. "'We Think Prohibition Is a Farce': Drinking in the Alcohol-Prohibited Zone of Colonial Northern Nigeria." *International Journal of African Historical Studies* 31, no. 1 (1998): 23–51.

Heinrich, Ruth. *Yarns on Africa Today: Builders Together*. London: Livingstone Press, 1940.

Helser, Albert D. *African Stories*. New York: Revell, 1930.

———. *Education of Primitive People: A Presentation of the Folklore of the Bura Animists, with a Meaningful Experience Curriculum*. New York: Revell, 1934.

———. *The Glory of the Impossible: Demonstrations of Divine Power in the Sudan*. Toronto: Evangelical Publishers, 1940.

———. *Leper Settlements in Northern Nigeria*. Jos: Niger Press, 1939.

Higazi, Adam. "Social Mobilization and Collective Violence: Vigilantes and Militias in the Lowlands of Plateau State, Central Nigeria." *Africa* 78, no. 1 (2008): 107–35.

Ho, Engseng. "Empire through Diasporic Eyes: A View from the Other Boat." *Comparative Studies in Society and History* 46, no. 2 (2004): 210–46.

Hodge, Joseph M. *Triumph of the Expert: Agrarian Doctrines of Development and the Legacies of British Colonialism*. Athens: Ohio University Press, 2007.

Hodgson, Dorothy L. *The Church of Women: Gendered Encounters between Maasai and Missionaries*. Bloomington: Indiana University Press, 2005.

Horn, Eric S. "African Convert Visits London." *Sudan Witness* 30, no. 1 (January 1954): 19–20.

Horowitz, Michael M. "Barbers and Bearers: Ecology and Ethnicity in an Islamic Society." *Africa* 44, no. 4 (October 1974): 371–82.

Horton, Robin. "African Conversion." *Africa* 41, no. 2 (April 1971): 85–108.

———. "On the Rationality of Conversion, Part II." *Africa* 45, no. 4 (1975): 373–99.

Human Rights Watch. *Spiraling Violence: Boko Haram Attacks and Security Force Abuses in Nigeria*. New York: Human Rights Watch, 2012.

Hunt, Nancy Rose. *A Colonial Lexicon: Of Birth Ritual, Medicalization, and Mobility in the Congo*. Durham, NC: Duke University Press, 1999.

Hussey, E. R. J. "An American's Educational Philosophy for Africa." *Journal of the Royal African Society* 39, no. 157 (1940): 361–66.
Hutson, Alaine S. "The Development of Women's Authority in the Kano Tijaniyya, 1894–1963." *Africa Today* 46, nos. 3–4 (1999): 43–64.
Ishaku, Mallam P. O. "The Making of Brown Sugar in Northern Nigeria." *Nigeria* 12 (1937): 8–9.
Jalland, Patricia. *Women, Marriage, and Politics, 1860–1914*. New York: Oxford University Press, 1986.
James, Wendy, and Douglas H. Johnson, eds. *Vernacular Christianity: Essays in the Social Anthropology of Religion*. New York: JASO/Lilian Barber Press, 1988.
Jamison, D. G. "Modern Trends in Leprosy." *Postgraduate Medical Journal* 45, no. 524 (June 1969): 408–14.
Janzen, John M. *The Quest for Therapy: Medical Pluralism in Lower Zaire*. Berkeley: University of California Press, 1978.
Johnson, Douglas H. "Salim Wilson: The Black Evangelist of the North." *Journal of Religion in Africa* 21, no. 1 (February 1991): 26–41.
Kakar, Sanjiv. "Leprosy in British India, 1860–1940: Colonial Politics and Missionary Medicine." *Medical History* 40, no. 2 (1996): 215–30.
Kalu, Ogbu U., ed. *African Christianity: An African Story*. Trenton, NJ: Africa World Press, 2007.
Kastfelt, Niels. "The Politics of History in Northern Nigeria." Occasional paper, Centre of African Studies, University of Copenhagen, September 2007.
———. *Religion and Politics in Nigeria: A Study in Middle Belt Christianity*. New York: British Academic Press, 1994.
Kato, Laszlo. "The Centenary of the Discovery of the Leprosy Bacillus." *Canadian Medical Association Journal* 109, no. 7 (October 1973): 627–29.
King, Lamont. "From Caliphate to Protectorate: Ethnicity and the Colonial Sabon Gari System in Northern Nigeria." *Journal of Colonialism and Colonial History* 4, no. 2 (Fall 2003).
Kirk-Greene, A. H. M., ed. *Barth's Travels in Nigeria: Extracts from the Journal of Heinrich Barth's Travels in Nigeria, 1850–1855*. London: Oxford University Press, 1962.
———. "The Peoples of Nigeria: The Cultural Background to the Crisis." *African Affairs* 66, no. 262 (January 1967): 3–11.
'Ko'ki, Mahmudu. *Alhaji Mahmudu 'Ko'ki: Kano Malam*. Translated and edited by Neil Skinner. Zaria: Ahmadu Bello University Press, 1977.
Krusius, Paul. "Die Maguzawa." *Archiv für Anthropologie* 42 (1915): 288–315.
Kumm, Hermann K. W. *Khont-Hon-Nofer: The Lands of Ethiopia*. Westport, CT: Negro Universities Press, 1970. First published Marshall Brothers, 1910.
Laitin, David D. "The Sharia Debate and the Origins of Nigeria's Second Republic." *Journal of Modern African Studies* 20, no. 3 (1982): 411–30.
Lambert, William A. "A Leper Colony in Nigeria." *Journal of the Royal African Society* 36, no. 143 (April 1937): 213–16.
Lambie, Thomas A. *A Doctor without a Country*. New York: Revell, 1939.
Landau, Paul S. "Explaining Surgical Evangelism in Colonial Southern Africa: Teeth, Pain and Faith." *Journal of African History* 37, no. 2 (1996): 261–81.
Lar, Mary Solomon. *Ambassador for Christ: Mary Lar's Reflections on Nigeria, Past and Present*. Bedford, England: British Church Growth Association, 1997.

Larkin, Brian. *Signal and Noise: Media, Infrastructure, and Urban Culture in Nigeria.* Durham, NC: Duke University Press, 2008.

Larkin, Brian, and Birgit Meyer. "Pentecostalism, Islam, and Culture: New Religious Movements in West Africa." In *Themes in West Africa's History*, edited by Emmanuel K. Akyeampong, 286–312. Athens: Ohio University Press, 2006.

Lassner, Phyllis. *Colonial Strangers: Women Writing the End of the British Empire.* New Brunswick, NJ: Rutgers University Press, 2004.

Last, Murray. "Ancient Labels and Categories: Exploring the 'Onomastics' of Kano." In Haour and Rossi, *Being and Becoming Hausa*, 59–84.

———. "Children and the Experience of Violence: Contrasting Cultures of Punishment in Northern Nigeria." *Africa* 70, no. 3 (2000): 359–93.

———. "From Dissent to Dissidence: The Genesis and Development of Reformist Islamic Groups in Northern Nigeria." Working paper no. 5, Nigeria Research Network, University of Oxford, 2013.

———."Hausa." In *Encyclopedia of Medical Anthropology: Health and Illness in the World's Cultures*, vol. 2, edited by Carol R. Ember and Melvin Ember, 718–29. New York: Kluwer Academic, 2004.

———. "Healing the Social Wounds of War." *Medicine, Conflict and Survival* 16, no. 4 (2000): 370–82.

———. "Historical Metaphors in the Kano Chronicle." *History in Africa* 7 (1980): 161–78.

———. "Muslims and Christians in Nigeria: An Economy of Political Panic." *Round Table* 96, no. 332 (2007): 605–16.

———. "The Nature of Knowledge in Muslim Northern Nigeria, 1457–2007." In *The Trans-Saharan Book Trade: Manuscript Culture, Arabic Literacy and Intellectual History in Muslim Africa*, edited by Graziano Krätli and Ghislaine Lydon, 174–211. Leiden: Brill, 2011.

———. "The Presentation of Sickness in a Community of Non-Muslim Hausa." In *Social Anthropology and Medicine*, edited by Joseph B. Loudon, 104–49. London: Academic Press, 1976.

———. "The Search for Security in Muslim Northern Nigeria." *Africa* 78, no. 1 (2008): 41–63.

———. "Some Economic Aspects of Conversion in Hausaland (Nigeria)." In Levtzion, *Conversion to Islam*, 236–46.

Leonard, Lori. "'Looking for Children': The Search for Fertility among the Sara of Southern Chad." *Medical Anthropology* 21, no. 1 (2002): 79–112.

Lesch, John E. *The First Miracle Drugs: How the Sulfa Drugs Transformed Medicine.* Oxford: Oxford University Press, 2007.

Levtzion, Nehemiah, ed. *Conversion to Islam.* New York: Holmes and Meier, 1979.

Linden, Ian. "Between Two Religions of the Book: The Children of the Israelites (c. 1846– c. 1920)." In *Varieties of Christian Experience in Nigeria*, edited by Elizabeth Isichei, 79–98. New York: Macmillan, 1982.

———. "The Isawa Mallams c.1850–1919: Some Problems in the Religious History of Northern Nigeria." Paper presented at the Ahmadu Bello Social Sciences Seminar, 1974.

Livingston, Julie. *Debility and the Moral Imagination in Botswana.* Bloomington: Indiana University Press, 2005.

Longman, Timothy. *Christianity and Genocide in Rwanda.* New York: Cambridge University Press, 2009.

Lovejoy, Paul E. "Concubinage and the Status of Women Slaves in Early Colonial Northern Nigeria." *Journal of African History* 29, no. 2 (1988): 245–66.

Lovejoy, Paul E., and Jan S. Hogendorn. "Revolutionary Mahdism and Resistance to Colonial Rule in the Sokoto Caliphate, 1905–6." *Journal of African History* 31, no. 2 (1990): 217–44.

———. *Slow Death for Slavery: The Course of Abolition in Northern Nigeria, 1897–1936*. Cambridge: Cambridge University Press, 1993.

Ludwig, Frieder. "Christian-Muslim Relations in Northern Nigeria since the Introduction of Shari'ah in 1999." *Journal of the American Academy of Religion* 76, no. 3 (2008): 602–37.

Luedke, Tracy J., and Harry G. West, eds. *Borders and Healers: Brokering Therapeutic Resources in Southeast Africa*. Bloomington: Indiana University Press, 2006.

Lugard, Frederick. *The Dual Mandate in British Tropical Africa*. 5th ed. London: Cass, 1965.

Lydon, Ghislaine. "A Paper Economy of Faith without Faith in Paper: A Reflection on Islamic Institutional History." *Journal of Economic Behavior and Organization* 71, no. 3 (2009): 647–59.

Lynn, Martin, ed. *British Documents on the End of Empire*. Series A. London: Commonwealth Institute, 2001.

Lyons, Maryinez. *The Colonial Disease: A Social History of Sleeping Sickness in Northern Zaire, 1900–1940*. Cambridge: Cambridge University Press, 1992.

Mafu, Hezekiel. "The Impact of the Bible on Traditional Rain-Making Institutions in Western Zimbabwe." In West and Dube, *The Bible in Africa*, 400–414.

Maier-Katkin, Birgit, and Daniel Maier-Katkin. "At the Heart of Darkness: Crimes against Humanity and the Banality of Evil." *Human Rights Quarterly* 26, no. 3 (August 2004): 584–604.

Mani, Lata. *Contentious Traditions: The Debate on Sati in Colonial India*. Berkeley: University of California Press, 1998.

Mann, Kristin. *Slavery and the Birth of an African City: Lagos, 1760–1900*. Bloomington: Indiana University Press, 2010.

Manton, John. "Leprosy in Eastern Nigeria and the Social History of Colonial Skin." *Leprosy Review* 82 (2011): 124–34.

Marsala, Vincent J. "U.S. Senator Joseph E. Ransdell, Catholic Statesman: A Reappraisal." *Louisiana History* 35, no. 1 (Winter 1994): 35–49.

Masquelier, Adeline. *Prayer Has Spoiled Everything: Possession, Power, and Identity in an Islamic Town of Niger*. Durham, NC: Duke University Press, 2001.

———. *Women and Islamic Revival in a West African Town*. Bloomington: Indiana University Press, 2009.

Masud, Muhammad Khalid. "The Obligation to Migrate: The Doctrine of *Hijra* in Islamic Law." In *Muslim Travellers: Pilgrimage, Migration, and the Religious Imagination*, edited by Dale F. Eickelman and James Piscatori, 29–49. Berkeley: University of California Press, 1990.

McGarvey, Kathleen. *Muslim and Christian Women in Dialogue: The Case of Northern Nigeria*. Bern: Peter Lang, 2009.

Meinhof, Karl. "A Plea for Missionary Work among the Moslems of Central Africa." *Muslim World* 1, no. 2 (1911): 155–63.

Miles, William F. S. "Development, not Division: Local Versus External Perceptions of the Niger-Nigeria Boundary." *Journal of Modern African Studies* 43, no. 2 (2005): 297–320.

———. *Hausaland Divided: Colonialism and Independence in Nigeria and Niger.* Ithaca, NY: Cornell University Press, 1994.
Miller, Ethel P. *Change Here for Kano: Reminiscences of Fifty Years in Nigeria.* Zaria: Gaskiya, 1959.
———. *Hausa Heroines.* Minna: Niger Press, 1923.
———, trans. *Marshal Feng: Nagarin 'dan Yako Mai-Bin Isa Almasihu.* Minna: Niger Press, 1925.
———. "Things as They Are: The Problem in Nigeria." *Muslim World* 2, no. 4 (1912): 436–42.
———. *The Truth about Muhammad: An Appeal to Englishmen in Nigeria.* Minna: Niger Press, n.d.
Miller, Stephen M. "In Support of the 'Imperial Mission'? Volunteering for the South African War, 1899–1902." *Journal of Military History* 69, no. 3 (July 2005): 691–711.
Miller, Walter R. "Islam from the Medical Standpoint: A Symposium." *Muslim World* 3, no. 4 (October 1913): 367–85.
———. *Reflections of a Pioneer.* London: Church Missionary Society, 1936.
Miran, Marie, and El Hadj Akan Charif Vissoh. "(Auto)biographie d'une conversion à l'islam: Regards croisés sur une histoire de changement religieux dans le Bénin contemporain." *Cahiers d'etudes africaines* 3, no. 195 (2009): 655–704.
Molla, Claude F. "Some Aspects of Islam in Africa South of the Sahara." *International Review of Mission* 56, no. 224 (October 1967): 459–68.
Moraes Farias, P. F. de. "A Letter from Ki-Toro Mahamman Gaani, King of Busa (Borgu, Northern Nigeria) about the 'Kisra' Stories of Origin (c. 1910)." *Sudanic Africa* 3 (1992): 109–32.
Morel, Edmund D. *Nigeria: Its People and Its Problems.* London: Smith and Elder, 1911.
Morgan, Sue, ed. *Women, Religion and Feminism in Britain, 1750–1900.* New York: Palgrave Macmillan, 2002.
Mudimbe, V. Y. *The Invention of Africa: Gnosis, Philosophy, and the Order of Knowledge.* Bloomington: Indiana University Press, 1988.
Muffett, D. J. M. *Concerning Brave Captains: Being a History of the British Occupation of Kano and Sokoto and of the Last Stand of the Fulani Forces.* London: Deutsch, 1964.
Muir, E. *Leprosy in Nigeria: A Report on Anti-Leprosy Work in Nigeria with Suggestions for Its Development.* Lagos: Government Printer, 1936.
Musisi, Nakanyike B. "Morality as Identity: The Missionary Moral Agenda in Buganda, 1877–1945." *Journal of Religious History* 23, no. 1 (February 1999): 51–74.
Newbury, Catharine. "Ethnicity and the Politics of History in Rwanda." *Africa Today* 45, no. 1 (January–March 1998): 7–24.
Newbury, Colin W. *British Policy Towards West Africa: Select Documents, 1875–1914.* Oxford: Oxford University Press, 1971.
Newman, Paul. *The Etymology of Hausa* boko. Mega-Chad Research Network, 2013. http://www.megatchad.net/publications/Newman-2013-Etymology-of-Hausa-boko.pdf.
Nunn, Nathan. "The Importance of History for Economic Development." *Annual Review of Economics* 1 (2009): 65–92.
———. "Religious Conversion in Colonial Africa." *American Economic Review: Papers and Proceedings* 100, no. 2 (May 2010): 147–52.

Obadare, Ebenezer. "White-Collar Fundamentalism: Interrogating Youth Religiosity on Nigerian University Campuses." *Journal of Modern African Studies* 45, no. 4 (2007): 517–37.

O'Brien, Donal B. Cruise, and Christian Coulon, eds. *Charisma and Brotherhood in African Islam.* New York: Oxford University Press, 1989.

Ochonu, Moses E. *Colonialism by Proxy: Hausa Imperial Agents and Middle Belt Consciousness in Nigeria.* Bloomington: Indiana University Press, 2014.

Ojo, Matthews A. "The Contextual Significance of the Charismatic Movements in Independent Nigeria." *Africa* 58, no. 2 (1988): 175–92.

Oldham, J. H. "Northern Nigeria." *International Review of Mission* 7 (1917): 43–44.

Olofson, Harold. "*Yawon Dandi*: A Hausa Category of Migration." *Africa* 46, no. 1 (1976): 66–79.

Omoti, A. E. "Complications of Traditional Couching in a Nigerian Local Population." *West African Journal of Medicine* 24, no. 1 (January–March 2005): 7–9.

Otobo, Dafe. "Bureaucratic Elites and Public-Sector Wage Bargaining in Nigeria." *Journal of Modern African Studies* 24, no. 1 (1986): 101–26.

Paden, John N. *Ahmadu Bello, Sardauna of Sokoto: Values and Leadership in Nigeria.* London: Hodder and Stoughton, 1986.

———. *Religion and Political Culture in Kano.* Berkeley: University of California Press, 1973.

Pandya, Shubhada S. "The First International Leprosy Conference, Berlin, 1897: The Politics of Segregation." *Historia, Ciencas, Saude-Manguinhos* 10, supp. 1 (2003): 161–77.

Parascandola, John. "Chaulmoogra oil and the Treatment of Leprosy." *Pharmacy in History* 45, no. 2 (2003): 47–57.

Parrott, W. F. "An Epidemic Called Apollo: An Outbreak of Conjunctivitis in Nigeria." *Practitioner* 206, 232 (1971): 253–55.

Pearson, Karl. *The Life, Letters and Labours of Francis Galton.* London: Cambridge University Press, 1914–1930.

Peel, J. D. Y. "Postsocialism, Postcolonialism, Pentecostalism." In *Conversion after Socialism: Disruptions, Modernisms and Technologies of Faith in the Former Soviet Union,* edited by Mathijs Pelkmans, 183–99. New York: Berghahn Books, 2009.

———. *Religious Encounter and the Making of the Yoruba.* Bloomington: Indiana University Press, 2000.

———. "Two Northerners Contrasted in Their Visions of Nigerian Unity." *Canadian Journal of African Studies* 22, no. 1 (1988): 144–48.

Peterson, Brian J. *Islamization from Below: The Making of Muslim Communities in Rural French Sudan, 1880–1960.* New Haven, CT: Yale University Press, 2011.

Peterson, Derek R. *Ethnic Patriotism and the East African Revival: A History of Dissent, c.1935–1972.* New York: Cambridge University Press, 2012.

Peterson, Derek R., and Giacomo Macola, eds. *Recasting the Past: History Writing and Political Work in Modern Africa.* Athens: Ohio University Press, 2009.

Porter, Andrew. "The Hausa Association: Sir George Goldie, the Bishop of Dover, and the Niger in the 1890s." *Journal of Imperial and Commonwealth History* 7, no. 2 (January 1979): 149–79.

Powell, Eve M. Troutt. *Tell This in My Memory: Stories of Enslavement from Egypt, Sudan and the Ottoman Empire.* Stanford, CA: Stanford University Press, 2012.

Prevost, Elizabeth E. *The Communion of Women: Missions and Gender in Colonial Africa and the British Metropole*. New York: Oxford University Press, 2010.
Quirin, James. "Caste and Class in Historical North-West Ethiopia: The Beta Israel (Falasha) and Kemant, 1300–1900." *Journal of African History* 39, no. 2 (1998): 195–220.
———. "The Process of Caste Formation in Ethiopia: A Study of the Beta Israel (Felasha), 1270–1868." *International Journal of African Historical Studies* 12, no. 2 (1979): 235–58.
Rain, David. *Eaters of the Dry Season: Circular Labor Migration in West African Sahel*. Boulder, CO: Westview Press, 1999.
Reeves, Sherman W. "Advances in Cataract Surgery and Intraocular Lenses." *Minnesota Medicine* (June 2009).
Renne, Elisha P. *The Politics of Polio in Northern Nigeria*. Bloomington: Indiana University Press, 2010.
Reynolds, Jonathan T. "Good and Bad Muslims: Islam and Indirect Rule in Northern Nigeria." *International Journal of African History Studies* 34, no. 3 (2001): 601–18.
———. "The Politics of History: The Legacy of the Sokoto Caliphate in Nigeria." *Journal of Asian and African Studies* 32, nos. 1–2 (1997): 50–65.
Robert, Dana L. *Christian Mission: How Christianity Became a World Religion*. New York: John Wiley, 2009.
———. "'The Crisis of Missions': Premillennial Mission Theory and the Origins of Independent Evangelical Missions." In *Earthen Vessels: American Evangelicals and Foreign Missions, 1880–1980*, edited by Joel A. Carpenter and Wilbert R. Shenk, 29–46. Grand Rapids, MI: Eerdmans, 2012.
Robinson, Charles H. *Hausaland, or Fifteen Hundred Miles through the Central Soudan*. London: Sampson, Low, Marston, 1897.
———. "The Hausa Territories: Hausaland." *Geographical Journal* 8, no. 3 (September 1896): 201–11.
Robinson, David. *Muslim Societies in African History*. New York: Cambridge University Press, 2004.
———. *Paths of Accommodation: Muslim Societies and French Colonial Authorities in Senegal and Mauritania, 1880–1920*. Athens: Ohio University Press, 2000.
Ross, Will. "Nigeria: Kano Reels after Emir Attack." BBC, 7 February 2013. http://www.bbc.co.uk/news/world-africa-21340480.
Rothiot, Jean-Paul. "Une chefferie précoloniale au Niger face aux représentants coloniaux: Naissance et essor d'une dynastie." *Cahiers d'histoire* 85 (2001): 67–83.
Rowbotham, Judith. "'Soldiers of Christ'? Images of Female Missionaries in Late Nineteenth-Century Britain: Issues of Heroism and Martyrdom." *Gender and History* 12, no. 1 (April 2000): 82–106.
Russell, Mrs. C. E. B. "The Leprosy Problem in Nigeria" *Journal of the Royal African Society* 37, no. 146 (January 1938): 66–71.
Salamone, Virginia A., and Frank A. Salamone. *The Lucy Memorial Freed Slaves' Home: The Sudan United Mission and the British Colonial Government in Partnership*. Lanham, MD: University Press of America, 2008.
Salau, Mohammed B. "The Role of Slave Labor in Groundnut Production in Early Colonial Kano." *Journal of African History* 51, no. 2 (2010): 147–65.
Sanneh, Lamin. *Translating the Message: The Missionary Impact on Culture*. Maryknoll, NY: Orbis Books, 1998.

Saul, Mahir. "Islam and West African Anthropology." *Africa Today* 53, no. 1 (2006): 3–33.

Schildkrout, Enid. "Age and Gender in Hausa Society: Socio-Economic Roles of Children in Urban Kano." *Childhood* 9, no. 3 (2002): 342–68.

Schrader, W. E. "Traditional Cataract Treatment and the Healers Perspective: Dialogue with Western Science and Technology in Nigeria, West Africa." *Annals of African Medicine* 3, no. 3 (2004): 153–58.

Schramm, Ralph. *A History of the Nigerian Health Services*. Ibadan: Ibadan University Press, 1971.

Shankar, Shobana. "A Fifty-Year Muslim Conversion to Christianity: Religious Ambiguities and Colonial Boundaries in Northern Nigeria, c. 1910–1963." In Soares, *Muslim/Christian Encounters*, 89–114.

———. "Medical Missionaries and Modernizing Emirs in Colonial Hausaland: Leprosy Control and Native Authority in the 1930s." *Journal of African History* 48, no. 1 (March 2007): 45–68.

———. "The Social Dimensions of Christian Leprosy Work among Muslims: American Missionaries and Young Patients in Colonial Northern Nigeria, 1920–40." In Hardiman, *Healing Bodies*, 281–305.

Sharkey, Heather J. *American Evangelicals in Egypt: Missionary Encounters in an Age of Empire*. Princeton, NJ: Princeton University Press, 2008.

———. "Christians among Muslims: The Church Missionary Society in the Northern Sudan." *Journal of African History* 43, no. 1 (2002): 51–75.

———. "Muslim Apostasy, Christian Conversion, and Religious Freedom in Egypt." In *Proselytization Revisited: Rights Talk, Free Markets and Culture Wars*, edited by Rosalind I. J. Hackett, 139–57. Durham, NC: Acumen, 2008.

Soares, Benjamin F., ed. *Islam and the Prayer Economy: History and Authority in a Malian Town*. Ann Arbor: University of Michigan Press, 2005.

———, ed. *Muslim-Christian Encounters in Africa*. Leiden: Brill, 2006.

———. "The Prayer Economy in a Malian Town." *Cahiers d'etudes africaines* 36, no. 144 (1996): 739–53.

Spartalis, Peter J. *Karl Kumm: Last of the Livingstones; Pioneer Missionary Statesman*. Bonn: Kultur and Wissenschaft, 1994.

Stackhouse, John G., Jr. "The Emergence of a Fellowship: Canadian Evangelicalism in the Twentieth Century." *Church History* 60, no. 2 (June 1991): 247–62.

Stewart, Marjorie Helen. "The Kisra Legend as Oral History." *International Journal of African Historical Studies* 13, no. 1 (1980): 51–70.

Stilwell, Sean. "Constructing Colonial Power: Tradition, Legitimacy and Government in Kano, 1903–1963." *Journal of Imperial and Commonwealth History* 39, no. 2 (2011): 195–225.

Stirrett, A. P. "Threefold Appeal for Special Work in Nigeria." *Missionary Witness* (August 1911): 203–4.

Stock, Robert. "Environmental Sanitation in Nigeria: Colonial and Contemporary." *Review of African Political Economy* 15, no. 42 (1988): 19–31.

Stuart, Emmeline. "The Ministry of Healing." In Van Sommer and Zwemer, *Daylight in the Harem*, 133–48.

Sundkler, Bengt, and Christopher Steed. *A History of the Church in Africa*. Cambridge: Cambridge University Press, 2000.

Tarhule, Aondover, and Ming-Ko Woo. "Towards an Interpretation of Historical Droughts in Northern Nigeria." *Climatic Change* 37, no. 4 (1997): 601–16.

Thomas, Lynn M. *Politics of the Womb: Women, Reproduction, and the State in Kenya*. Berkeley: University of California Press, 2003.
Thompson, Joseph E. *American Policy and African Famine: The Nigeria-Biafra War, 1966–1970*. Westport, CT: Greenwood Press, 1990.
Tibenderana, Peter K. "The Beginnings of Girls' Education in the Native Administration Schools in Northern Nigeria, 1930–1945." *Journal of African History* 26, no. 1 (1985): 93–109.
———. "The Role of the British Administration in the Appointment of the Emirs of Northern Nigeria, 1903–1931: The Case of Sokoto Province." *Journal of African History* 28, no. 2 (July 1987): 231–57.
Tonkin, T. J. "A Missionary Martyr in West Africa." *Wide World Magazine* (April 1900): 670–76.
———. "Muhammedanism in the Western Sudan." *Journal of the Royal African Society* 3, no. 10 (January 1904): 123–41.
Travers, E. A. O. "The Treatment of Leprosy at Kuala Lumpur, Federated Malay States." *Journal of the Royal Society of Medicine* 19 (1926): 1–9.
Tremearne, A. J. N. *Hausa Superstitions and Customs: An Introduction to the Folklore and the Folk*. London: John Bale, Sons and Danielsson, 1913.
Turaki, Yusufu. *Theory and Practice of Christian Missions in Africa: A Century of SIM/ECWA History and Legacy in Nigeria, 1893–1993*. Vol. 1. Nairobi: International Bible Society Africa, 1999.
Ubah, C. N. "Christian Missionary Penetration of the Nigerian Emirates, with Special Reference to the Medical Missions Approach." *Muslim World* 77, no. 1 (1987): 16–27.
Umar, Muhammad S. *Islam and Colonialism: Intellectual Responses of Muslims of Northern Nigeria to British Colonial Rule*. Leiden: Brill, 2006.
Usman, Yusufu Bala. *The Manipulation of Religion in Nigeria, 1977–1987*. Kaduna: Vanguard, 1987.
Van der Veer, Peter. *Religious Nationalism: Hindus and Muslims in India*. Berkeley: University of California Press, 1994.
Vansina, Jan. "The Politics of History and the Crisis in the Great Lakes." *Africa Today* 45, no. 1 (January–March 1998): 37–44.
Van Sommer, Annie, and Samuel M. Zwemer, eds. *Daylight in the Harem: A New Era for Moslem Women*. Edinburgh: Oliphant, Anderson, and Ferrier, 1911.
Vaughan, Megan. *Curing Their Ills: Colonial Power and African Illness*. Stanford, CA: Stanford University Press, 1991.
Vongsathorn, Kathleen. "Gnawing Pains, Festering Ulcers and Nightmare Suffering: Selling Leprosy as a Humanitarian Cause in the British Empire, c. 1890–1960." *Journal of Imperial and Commonwealth History* 40, no. 5 (2012): 863–78.
Wall, Martha. "Life or Death." *Sudan Witness* 16, no. 6 (November–December 1940): 2–3.
———. *Splinters from an African Log*. Chicago: Moody Press, 1960.
Walls, Andrew F. "Africa as the Theatre of Christian Engagement with Islam in the Nineteenth Century." *Journal of Religion in Africa* 29, no. 2 (1999): 155–74.
———. "The Heavy Artillery of the Missionary Army: The Domestic Importance of the Nineteenth-Century Medical Missionary." In *The Church and Healing: Studies in Church History*, edited by W. J. Sheils, 287–97. Oxford: Oxford University Press, 1982.

Wariboko, Waibinte E. "I Really Cannot Make Africa My Home: West Indian Missionaries as 'Outsiders' in the Church Missionary Society Civilizing Mission to Southern Nigeria, 1898–1925." *Journal of African History* 45, no. 2 (2004): 221–36.

Watts, Michael. "Hazards and Crisis: A Political Economy of Drought and Famine in Northern Nigeria." *Antipode* 15, no. 1 (1983): 24–34.

Weiss, Holger. "German Images of Islam in West Africa." *Sudanic Africa* 11 (2000): 53–93.

West, Gerald O., and Musa W. Dube, eds. *The Bible in Africa: Transactions, Trajectories and Trends*. Leiden: Brill, 2000.

White, Luise. *The Comforts of Home: Prostitution in Colonial Nairobi*. Chicago: University of Chicago Press, 1990.

———. *Speaking with Vampires: Rumor and History in Colonial Africa*. Berkeley: University of California Press, 2000.

———. "Vampire Priests of Central Africa: African Debates about Labor and Religion in Colonial Northern Zambia." *Comparative Studies in Society and History* 35, no. 4 (1993): 746–72.

White, Stanhope. *'Dan Bana: The Memoirs of a Nigerian Official*. London: Cassell, 1966.

Wilson, John F. "Blindness in Colonial Africa." *African Affairs* 52, no. 207 (1953): 141–49.

Windel, Aaron. "British Colonial Education in Africa: Policy and Practice in the Era of Trusteeship." *History Compass* 7, no. 1 (2009): 1–21.

Woodberry, Robert D. "The Missionary Roots of Liberal Democracy." *American Political Science Review* 106, no. 2 (May 2012): 244–74.

Wooding, Anne, and Dan Wooding. *Blind Faith*. Garden Grove, CA: ASSIST Books, 1996.

Worboys, Michael. "Colonial and Imperial Medicine." In *Medicine Transformed: Health, Disease and Society in Europe, 1800–1930*, edited by Deborah Brunton, 211–38. Oxford: Manchester University Press, 2004.

———. "The Colonial World as Mission and Mandate: Leprosy and Empire, 1900–1940." *Osiris*, 2nd ser., 15 (2000): 207–18.

Works, John A. *Pilgrims in a Strange Land: Hausa Communities in Chad*. New York: Columbia University Press, 1976.

Index

Abarshi, Ahmadu John, 130
Abbas, Emir of Kano, 26–31
Achebe, Chinua, xiv
Action Group, 123
Adamawa Province
    African Christians in, 125, 135
    Christian missions in, 78, 121
    Muslim conversion campaigns in, 129, 132
    slaves from, 12, 15
Adichie, Chimamanda, xiv
African Missionary Service (AMS), 100, 118
Agades, Ayuba, 134–135
Aguiyi-Ironsi, Johnson, 133
Ahmadiyya, 33
Akawu (*see* Garba, John), 38–42
al-Fatiha, xxiii
alcohol consumption and sale, 16, 17, 33, 47, 81, 89, 98, 132, 143
Alhamdu, 103, 123
Almasihu (*see also* Masihiyawa), 89
alms (*zakat*) (*see also* charity)
    for leprosy sufferers, 75–76, 80
    for soldiers, 101–102
    for the blind, 97, 114–115
    Native Administration use of, 106, 112
    seekers xx, 32
Alvarez, Thomas, 28
Amanawa (*see* Sokoto, Leprosarium), 130
American Mission to Lepers, 81, 83, 102, 164 n29, 165 n57
Anglo-French border (*see also* French Niger), 11, 19–21, 113
anti-imperial resistance, xxiv, 10–11, 94–95, 101, 118
anti-missionary sentiment, 26, 139
apostasy, xxiii, 23, 35, 59, 119, 141, 158 n41

Arabs, 8, 26–27, 32, 140, 156 n5
Arabic language or script, xiii, xix, 15–16, 33, 79, 91, 122, 145 n8
Ari Biu, 35–37, 40–41, 45
aristocracy (*see also sarakuna*), xv, 11, 20
Ariye, Pastor Moses, 131
Arnett, E. J., 21, 57
Atiku, George Rufus, 40
Audu (Miller), 7–9, 16–17, 45
Awolowo, Chief Obafemi, 123
Azikiwe, Nnamdi, 117–118

babbar riga (gown), 22, 123, 131, 133
Babbar Ruga (*see* Katsina, Leprosarium)
backsliding, xxv, 22, 128
Bako, Garba, 107–108, 110
Bakori, 79, 108
'Balewa, Tafawa, 116–117, 131, 132, 136, 138
baptism, 8–9, 17, 34, 58, 118–119, 120
baraka (*see* religious authority)
Barber, Karin, xxiv
'Barewa College (*see* Katsina College), 139
Bargery, C. P., 34
Battersby, Thomas Harford, 5
Bauchi
    City, 101
    Emirate, 15–16, 117
    Leprosarium, 79, 117, 136
    Province, 9, 16, 44, 97, 107, 121, 141
Bawa, Ibrahim, 67
Bayero, Abdullahi (Emir of Kano), 35, 37, 47
Bayero, Ado (Emir of Kano), 132
Beitzel, Charles, 97
Belgian colonialism, xvi, 25
Bell, Hesketh, 28

199

Bello, Ahmadu (Sardauna)
　assassination of, 132–133
　conversion campaigns of, xx, xxvi, 129–134, 137, 143
　perceptions of, 133–134, 137, 139
　relations with Christian missions and African Christians, 116–118, 130–132, 136–138, 176 n72
　view of violence in Kano, 123
Bello, Ishaku, 102–104
British Empire Leprosy Relief Association (BELRA), 73, 78, 80–81
Beminster, Fred, 35–36
Benani (Yangola), 18–19
Benedict XVI, 53
Benin, xvi
Biafran War (see Civil War), xiv
Biamuradi, 22, 51–52
Bible (see also Injil)
　copies of, 22, 33, 35, 59, 83, 91, 102, 122
　Hausa translation of, 14, 34, 67, 153 n65
　innovations in, 5, 14
　reading of, xix, 72, 88, 99, 104
　school (see also Tofa), 123
　stories from, 73, 87
　talismanic use of, xxi, 40, 46
Bida, 9
Bima Hill, 137
Bingham, Rowland, 7
Birnin Kano (see Kano Old City)
Birnin Kebbi, 21, 63
Boas, Franz, 81
boko (see also literacy), xiv, xviii, 19, 21, 35–36, 40, 52, 55, 79, 85, 93, 145 n8
Boko Haram, xiv
Bompai, 29, 47, 53, 67
bookshop (Christian), 33–36, 38–41, 44, 59, 130
'bori, 19, 114
Borlase, Howard, 88–89
Borno Province, 36, 38–40, 121
born again, xix-xx, xxvi, 83, 118–119, 138–139
Bourdillon, Bernard, 95–96, 106, 112
Boy Scouts, 42, 104
braille, 97–98, 100, 115
Brigades, Boys' and Girls', 108–110
British colonial government
　abolition of slavery, xvii, 11–13, 28, 140
　African workers in, 30, 39, 45
　demobilization, 101–102, 106
　disagreement with Native Administration, 37, 48, 59
　division of responsibilities with Native Administration (see also indirect rule), 61–64, 95
　grants in aid (see also Colonial Welfare and Development Act), 96
　medical welfare for Africans, 72–73, 75–76, 77–78, 111, 121
　loyalty to, 32, 57
　plans for decolonization, 111–112, 118, 126–127
　relations with Christian missions, xiv, xv, xviii, 23–24, 28–30, 32–35, 37, 49, 61–62, 78–79, 90, 111–112, 127
　treatment of Christian converts, 21, 59, 92, 120–121
British Cotton Growing Association, 16
British Foreign Bible Society (BFBS), 91
British National Leprosy Fund, 75
Brooke, Graham Wilmot, 5, 150 n5
Buell, Raymond Leslie, 34
Buganda (later Uganda), 55, 108
Burdon, Major Alder, 14
burqa, 140

Cairo, 7, 52, 58
Cameron, Donald, 43–44, 78–79
Cameroon, 117–118, 129, 135
Campbell, Dugald, 35, 58
Canada (see also North America), 53–54, 131
Carney, Mabel, 81
Carrow, John, 35, 104
Carville leprosarium, 75, 102
Catholic mission (see also individual mission institutions), xvi, 27–28, 42, 49, 74, 104, 122, 156 n10
Central Soudan Mission, 7
Central Sudan region, xvii, 7, 9
Chad (see also French Equatorial Africa), 101
Chadians (see also Sara), 103–104, 112, 115, 118, 123, 135, 141
Challawa, 44, 53
charity, 36, 41, 111–112, 142, 178 n17
chaulmoogra, 76
children
　concerns about immorality of, 107, 110–111, 137

evangelism to, 55, 89, 92, 99, 101
hawkers, 39, 101
Christian mission care of, 17, 40, 51, 86, 104, 106–107, 110, 111
   orphans (waifs), 41–42, 51 photo 3.1, 52, 64, 103–104, 107, 119, 171 n81
   religious identity of, xxii-xxiii, 42, 89–90, 120
   separation of, 86, 90, 142
Christian Association of Nigeria (CAN), 140–141
Christian Council of Nigeria, 127
Christian fundamentalists
   disagreement amongst Christians, 5, 14, 81, 165 n59
   views of secular scholars, 6, 179 n25
   relations with Muslims, xxv, 47
Christian missions (*see also* missions by individual name), xiii
   Africans' employment with, xix, 15–16, 41, 51, 74, 85, 123, 130, 148 n31
   and Islam, xvi-xvii, 3–5, 7, 12, 57, 91, 128
   education (*see* schools, Christian mission)
   experimental farming, 28, 78
   gender dynamics in, 49, 52–53, 86, 88
   medical work, xxi, xxvii, 52, 54, 71, 73–74, 76, 78, 100, 142, 164 n25
   Muslim perceptions of, 26, 29, 34, 37, 55, 81–83, 99, 130, 139
   relations with British authorities, 12–14, 23, 28–30, 32–35, 49–50, 57, 77–79, 90, 96, 111–112, 121, 125–126
   relations with African Christians and churches, 21, 74, 100, 127, 132
   relations with Muslim authorities, 27–28, 34–35, 90, 92, 97, 116–118
   social difference in, xvi, 4, 9, 18, 44–46, 84–85, 137–138, 140
Christian Missions in Many Lands 121–122
Church Missionary Society (CMS), xvii, 5, 7, 12–13, 16, 23, 28–29, 33, 43, 47, 71, 122, 124
Church of the Brethren, 44, 78, 81, 121
Civil war (*see also* Biafran War), 117, 130, 134, 139
civilizing influence
   Christian, xxii, 50
   Muslim, xxvi, 4, 6, 57, 131, 162 n52
Clark, Emily, 51–52

clash of civilizations, 142
Clayton, Tubby, 80
clerks (native), 21, 39–40, 44, 62, 89
clientage (*see also* wealth in people), xix-xxi, 15, 37, 45, 71, 104, 107, 113
Clifford, Hugh, 32–34, 41
clothing and identity (*see also* Babbar riga), xxii, 131
Colonial Welfare and Development Act, (1940) 90, 95
colportage, xxi, 21, 91, 102
commoners (*see also* talakawa), 33, 59
Congo (Zaire), 3, 5, 25, 81, 135
constitutional negotiations, xxiii, 116–118, 123, 128
conversion
   challenges of Christian, xxiii, xxv, 8–9, 44, 67–68, 92, 110, 119, 120, 140–141
   changing modes of, xx-xxii, 67, 88, 136–137, 143
   governmental protection for freedom of, 128–129
   mass, xxvi, 129, 131–133
   narratives of, xxvi, 56
   prevention of, (*see also* recantation), 59, 92, 141
   to Christianity, xvii, 31, 35–37, 83, 135, 143
   to Islam, xx, 35–36, 40, 46, 59, 83, 139, 143
Cook, Norman, 108
Cotton, Rev. James, 33–35, 38, 41 photo 2.2, 42, 124
coup d'état, 132–133, 139
crèches, 92, 121
crypto-Christians, xxvi-xxvii, 29, 40, 45, 142
cultural authenticity, xiv, xxi, xxiv, 96, 135–136

Dala, 97–98, 114–115
Dalziel, J.M., 75
Damagaram 38
'Dan Agundi gate, 28–29, 40, 102, 142
'Dan Darma, 83
'Dan Daura, Haruna, xxii-xxiii, 124, 128, 134
'Dan Daura, Istifanus, xxii, 40, 46
'Dan Fodio, Usman (*see* Shehu), 12, 20, 117, 123
Danielsson, Daniel, 74
dar-al-Harb, xvii

dar-al-Islam, xvii, xx
Dass, xxii, 97, 121, 138
de Foucauld, Charles, 53
demographics
- of conversion campaigns, 129
- of Hausaland, 6
- of religions in Northern Nigeria (*see also* Willink Commission), 128
- insecurity of Christian population in Northern Nigeria, xx

dependence on foreign assistance, 112, 123, 126, 142
development work, xvi, 64, 131–132, 142
Dikko, Muhammadu (Emir of Katsina), 105
diseases
- blindness, 76, 97
- cancer, 72
- cataracts of the eyes, 76, 97, 113
- cerebrospinal meningitis, 33, 76, 84, 85, 102, 105, 121, 142
- conjunctivitis, 100, 170 n36
- infertility, xx, xxii, 106
- influenza, 56
- leprosy, 71, 73–75, 81, 96, 102
- madness, 16, 154 n70
- maternal, 49, 52, 72
- pneumonia, 96, 102
- polio, 142
- rabies, 87
- relapsing fever, 72–73, 76
- river blindness, 97
- sleeping sickness, 23, 52, 76, 101, 108
- spirit-caused (*see also* 'bori), 16, 87
- syphilis, 72–73, 96, 102
- trachoma, 97
- tuberculosis, 72–73, 96, 102, 119, 134
- yaws, 74, 96

dispute resolution (*see also* Interfaith Mediation Center), xxiii-xxiv, 120–121
dissenters
- Christian, xxiv, 9, 48, 49, 59, 138
- government containment of, 23, 48, 59–61, 95, 128
- Muslim, xviii, 9, 12, 23–24, 138

divorce, xix, 19, 31, 120, 140
Dogon Yaro, Adamu, 123
Donham, Donald, 5
Dosso, 10–11, 15, 17, 19–24
drought, 82–83, 105, 137
Dutse, 102, 119, 124

Dyce-Sharp, N. A., 72–73
education (*see also* schools), 122, 131
- Christian mission, xv, 36, 43, 46, 52, 64, 78, 91–92, 122
- Islamic, 134
- Montessori method, 62
- value of, 43–45, 110–111, 131
- Western, xiv, 59, 61, 64, 66, 72, 81, 95, 117, 131

Egypt (*see also* Cairo), 7, 8, 29, 30, 53, 54, 58, 71, 91
Eklisiyar Krista a Sudan (EKAS), 135, 138
English language, xxiii, 33, 39, 42, 46, 54, 55, 60, 91, 113, 114,
Eritrea, xvi
eschatology (*see also* Mahdism), xv, xxvi, 4, 52, 55, 89, 137
Ethiopia, xvi, 12, 81, 97, 146–147 n17
Ethnicity
- enclaves based on, 26
- minorities, xv, xxii, 128, 139
- multiethnic communities, xxi, xxii, 141, 176 n73
- origins, xix, 17–19, 24, 99, 104, 137–138, 141
- predominantly Muslim, 4, 7, 103, 134, 141
- tensions, xvi, 11, 19–20, 72, 124, 134, 138, 178 n15

Evangelical Churches of West Africa (ECWA) (*see also* Christian missions, relations with African Christians and churches), 118, 122–123, 125, 129, 134
evangelism (*see also* preaching)
- as an occupation, xix, 18, 24, 101, 104
- independent of white missionaries, 15, 22, 127
- conducted by Muslims, xxi, 7, 9, 33, 92, 128–129, 143
- itinerant, xix, 15, 22, 24, 52, 54, 85, 91, 118, 136, 138
- medical, xv, xx, 76, 89–90
- prohibition on, 37–38
- women's, 22, 48, 51–52, 160 n16

Fagge, 26, 33, 42, 44, 60, 79, 124, 126, 133
Fago, 119
famine, 105–107, 137
Father Damien, 74
Fati, 16, 52, 67

Fatu, 39–40
feasts of repentance, 132
feminism, 65
Feng, Marshal, 55
Fraser, Alec, 62–63
French Equatorial Africa (*see also* Chad), 77, 101
French Niger (*see* Anglo-French border), xvi, 19, 110, 113
French Soudan, 72
French West Africa, xviii, xxviii
Fulani, xv, xvii, 4, 11, 15, 19–20, 26, 107, 113–114, 130
Funtua, 79

Gagare, Bete, 97–100, 103, 115
Garba, John (*see also* Akawu), xiii–xiv, xx, xxiv, 38, 41–46, 124, 138, 140, 158 n49
Garkida, 44, 78–79, 81, 82, 85, 86, 121
Garko, 79
Gaskiya ta fi kwabo, 95
Gbagyi, 22, 128, 132
German colonialism, xvi, 32
German, Harold and Eugenie, 106–107
Ghana (*see also* Gold Coast), xvi, 137
Gibbon, Edward, 58
Gimi, 23, 56
Gindiri, 97
Girouard, Percy, 49
Glerum, Mike, 125
Gold Coast (*see also* Ghana), 14, 28, 40, 62, 73, 92, 95
Goldie, Sir George, 5–6
Gorsuch Commission, 126
Gould, Michael, 133
Gowans, Walter, 6
Gowers, W. F., 29
Gowon, Yakubu, 133, 134, 139
Guenter, Henry and Rita, 134
Guinness, H. Grattan, 3, 5, 12
Gummi, Abubakar, 139
Gumsuri, Sule, 38–39
Gusau, 43, 105, 130, 136
Guyer, N. Pauline, 86
Gwandu, 59, 72, 91

Ha'be, 38
Had'ejia emirate, 59
Hadith, 35
hajj (*see also* pilgrimage), 8, 9, 21

Hansen, Armauer, 74
Haruna, Dauda, 126
Harris, Edwin, 81–84
Harris, Hermann, 7–8
Hausa Association, 5, 8
Hausa
　ethnic group (*see also* ethnicity, Maguzawa), xiii, xvii, xx, 4, 6, 38, 103, 117, 146 n12
　language, xiv, 5, 9, 33, 104
　traders, xvii, 6, 28
Hausa Heroines, 55–57, 65
Hay, John, 21
Helser, Albert, 81, 85–86, 96–97, 104
Hershelman, Chuck, 131
Higazi, Adam, 144
hijra, 137
history-production
　Christian revisionism in, xiii–xiv, xxiv–xxvi, 97–98, 138, 179 n25, 145–146 n9
　concerning the jihad, xv, xxii, 19–20
　construction of difference in, xiv, xvi, 140, 143–144
　Islamist, xiv–xv
　oral, xiii, xxv–xxvi, 129
　politics of forgetting, xiv, 136, 144
　problem of religious fluidity in, xiii, 140–141
　scholarly, xv, 6, 57, 68
　separatist, xvi–xvii
Holy Trinity School, 42–44
Horton, Robin, xx–xxi
Howard, Carlton, 80
human rights, 91, 127, 129
Hursh, Douglas Marion, 98–100, 113–114
Hussey, E.J., 61, 81

Ibiam, Francis, 116–117
Idda, 19–20, 121
Igbirra, 18
Igbo, 116–117, 123–124, 132–133
Imam, Abubakar, 95
independent (freelance) missionaries, 5
　conflicts with missions, 52–53, 59
　relations with government, 35, 57, 60, 71
independence (Nigerian), xxiii–xxiv, 116–117, 124–125, 128, 132
India, xxvii, 25, 33, 58, 71, 73, 75, 113

indigeneity of Christians, xv, 96, 118, 125, 137, 146 n12
Indigenization Decree (1972), 134, 137
indigenous African religious practices, 4, 22–23, 132, 149 n44
indirect rule *(see also* British colonial government), 30, 66–67, 128, 151 n18
imprisonment, 11, 16, 21, 35
Injil, xiii, xxiii, 91
Interfaith Mediation Center, 142
International Missionary Council, 52, 62
Inusa Samuila, xxiv, 10–11, 14–16, 19–24, 52–53, 128–129, 132, 137, 152 n36
Isa (Jesus), xxi, xxiii, 9, 15, 20, 21, 55, 57, 83
Isawa, 15–16, 22–24, 91, 105, 137
Islam
 Euro-American attitudes toward, xix, xxvi, 3–4, 7–9, 17–18, 33, 50, 57–58, 80, 128
 Gender relations in, xix, 13, 17, 48, 50, 58, 61, 65
 Geography of, in Northern Nigeria, xvii-xviii, xx, 26–27
Itu, 77–78, 80

Jebba, 11, 14
Jega, 87–88, 133
Jihad, xv, xviii, xxii, 20, 38, 123, 138
Joe, Ladi, 67, 133–134
Johnston, Harold, 127
Jones, Bishop Melville, 59
Jos, xxiv, 76, 110, 116, 135
Jos Plateau, 27, 97, 136
Jotcham, William, 81, 84

Kabba Province, 121, 125
Kaduna, xxv, 130, 142
Kagadama, 112
Kagwa, Apollo, 55
Kano
 Old City of Kano *(see* Birnin Kano), 6, 15, 26, 29–30, 34–36, 40, 78, 97–98, 100
 Emirate, xvii
 Leprosarium *(see also* Ya da Kunya), xviii, 83–84, 87–88, 95, 98, 112, 120, 124
 Province, 79
 Township, xxii, 30, 79, 96, 100, 114, 131
Kano City Hospital, 79, 85, 119, 124

Kano Eye Hospital (SIM), 96, 98–99 photo 5.1, 100, 103, 113, 121, 124, 126, 129
Kano Motor Club, 47, 53, 67
Kano School of Arabic Studies, 45
Kanuri, 38, 103
Karu, 129
Katsina
 City, 127, 138
 Emirate, 8, 16, 86, 105
 Leprosarium (*See also* Babbar Ruga), xviii, 79, 81, 84–87, 91, 105–107
 Province, 61, 79, 105, 121
Katsina College *(see also* 'Barewa College), 68
Katsina Women's Training Center, 133
Kazaure, 91, 103–105
Kelsey, H. A., 105–106
Kibby, Leona, 97
Kobkitanda, 10–11
'Ko'ki, Muhammadu, 26, 31, 34
Krusius, Paul, 16
Kuala Lumpur General Hospital, 77
Kumm, Karl, 12, 17
Kuta, 129, 132, 175–176 n67
Kwoi, 133

Lagos, xviii, 14, 25, 43–44, 62, 72, 101, 123
Laka, 15, 19
Lambert, Will, 80, 82–83
Lambie, Thomas, 81
Land and Native Rights Act (1910), 29
Lang, E.F., 15
Last, D. Murray, xvi, xvii, 141, 142, 143
Layi, Umaru, 112
lazaret, 76, 80
League of Nations, 121
Lebanese, 39, 123
Leith-Ross, Sylvia, 62–63, 65
Lepers Proclamation (1910), 75–76
leprosariums, xviii, xxvi, 71, 73–74, 79, 81, 85, 86, 88, 91–92, 104, 110, 121, 134, 137
Levtzion, Nehemia, xxi
Lindsell, H.O., 61
literacy, xiv, xviii, xxiv, xxvi, 21, 31, 34, 36, 39–40, 46, 59, 85–87, 93, 122, 131
Livingstone College, London, 80
Livingstone, David, 104, 126
Lokoja, 5, 12, 51

London School of Economics, 45
Lord's Supper, 58, 118–119
Lot, David, 126
Lugard, Frederick, xiv, xvii, 12–14, 23, 49, 66, 95

Maguzawa, 110
   Christian evangelism among, 105, 137
   conversion of, 119, 132
   relations with Muslims, 16, 89, 119, 131
Mahdi, 7, 10, 157 n25
Mahdism, xxiv, 10, 66
Mahdists, 11, 33, 137
Maiduguri, 40, 135
Malumfashi, 86, 89, 105–106, 108, 111, 119
Mariri, 55, 58, 99
marriage
   among missionaries, 49–50
   arranged by missionaries, 16–19, 50, 88
   indigenous Christian practices of, 120, 138, 148 n33
   Muslim practices of, xix, 13, 31, 63–64
   sadaka, 56–57
Masihiyawa (*see also* Almasihu), xiii, 141
Maska, 108
masu bi, xiii, xix, 161 n31
Matazu, 91, 105
materialism, 27, 33, 48, 50, 68, 85
Mawri, 22
Maxwell, J. Lowry, 17, 48, 49–50
McClay, John Scott, 98, 99 photo 5.1
Mecca, 8, 15, 17, 131, 137
medicines, xix-xx, 72, 106, 164 n29
   Alepol, 77
   asibiti (hospital), 86, 94–95, 113
   botanical oils (*see also* chaulmoogra), 74, 76, 94
   Chinese traditional medicine, 76–77
   dapsone, 74, 121
   Indian traditional medicine, 76–77, 113, 172 n104
   indigenous medicines (*maganin gargajiya*), 16, 91, 94, 113
   penicillin, 74, 91, 97
   quinine, 91
   Salvarsan, 73
   sulfa, 74, 96, 102
   trials, 75, 76, 102, 142
migrants (*see also* soldiers, demobilized)
   identities of, xix, 148–149 n41
   new urban communities of, 21, 107, 141
   refugees, xxiv, 5, 11–13, 17, 38, 135, 137
   workers, xviii, xix, 14, 16, 72
Middle Belt movement, 125, 129, 138–139, 149 n42
Middle East, xiii, 53, 128, 133
Miller, Ethel Paddy, xxv, 17, 19, 34, 35, 47–49, 51–60, 65–66, 78, 143
Miller, Dr. Walter, xxv, 7–8, 13–14, 16–17, 23, 34–35, 42, 44, 56, 59, 76, 80, 138
Minna, 33, 76, 81
Minorities (*see also* ethnicity), 125, 127–128, 139
modernization, xiv, 65–66, 72, 117
Molla, Claude, 129
Morel, Edmund Dene, 25–27, 30–31, 128
Morris, Cecil, 81
Moyer, Faye, 64
Muhammad, Murtala, 139
Muhammadu (Katsina), 38–41
Muir, Ernest, 73, 80
Muri Province, 27, 32

Nagogo, Usman (Emir of Kano), 35
Nassarawa Province, 13
National Church of Nigeria and the Cameroons, 118
National Council of Nigeria and the Cameroons (NCNC), 117
nationalism, xxii, 92, 95, 101, 115, 118, 135, 138, 178 n9
Native Administration
   competition with Christian missions, 89, 92, 107, 130
   cooperation with Christian missions, 27, 68, 74, 78–80, 104, 111–112, 122
   Christian employees of, 40, 42, 120
   educational and medical work, 35, 60, 63, 76, 92, 107, 131
   independence-era politics, 123
   policies concerning Christians, 34–37, 59, 104
   popular resentment toward, 105–106, 112
New Life for All, 134, 136
Nicodemus, xxvi, 83
Niger Province, 51, 64, 129
Nigerian Television Authority, xxii
North Africa, xvii, 7, 8, 58
North America (*see also* Canada; United States), xvii, 3–4, 96

Northern Elements Progressive Union (NEPU), 128, 146 n9
Northern People's Congress (NPC), 117, 123, 128–129, 138, 145–146 n9
Nuffield Scholarship, 45
Nupe, xvii, 7, 15, 33
Nuruddin, Muhammad Ashafa, 142

Obasanjo, Olusegun, xxiii
Ochonu, Moses, xxii
Oil boom, 139
Oldham, Joseph, 53, 62–63
Omaru, John Tafida, 120
ordination, 22, 97, 116, 123, 169 n33
Oswold, Cris, 133
Ottoman empire (see also Turkey), 32
outpatient medical treatment, 44, 73, 86, 100, 112

pagans (see also Maguzawa)
    Christian convert-evangelists, 118, 132
    inferiority of, xxvi, 4, 17–18, 131
    lack of political protection for, 7, 90, 128–132
    mission work among, 17, 78, 81, 88, 105, 110, 121
    Muslim-Christian competition to evangelize among, xx-xxi, 36, 92–93, 129, 131–132, 139
    origins among converts, 140–141
    relations with Muslims, 4, 12, 15–16, 18, 36, 73
    resistance to Islamization, xxii, 22, 105, 138
Palmer, H. R., 16, 152 n29
Pankshin, 139
Pategi, 9, 14–15
Payne, Titus, 87–88, 132
Peel, J. D. Y., 138, 176 n72
Pentecostalism, 137
Perham, Margery, 65–67
persecution of Christians, 58, 83, 127
Peterson, Derek, xxvi
Pfizer, 142
Phelps-Stokes Commission, 81
Philippines, 75
pilgrimage (see also hajj), 17
pilgrims, xvii, 6–8, 12, 15, 45, 137, 178 n9
Pilgrim's Progress, 104
Playfair, G.W., 91

police, 14, 21, 30, 60, 110, 124, 128, 130, 133
polygyny, xix, 49–50, 140
porters, 7, 11, 14, 15–16, 21
Potiskum, 101
prayer
    communal, 9, 141
    economy, xxi, 159 n70
    groups, 91, 101
    healing, 114, 164 n25
    Islamic, 9, 82, 140, 143
propaganda
    Christian, 5, 35, 37, 59, 78, 138
    Muslim, xvii, 32
    political, 32, 139
Propaganda-Treatment Survey, 73
Prophet Muhammad, 15, 35, 48, 52, 57–58, 138
Preaching (see also evangelism)
    Africans' itinerant, 16, 20–21, 26, 134
    market, 34, 40, 80, 99, 108, 132, 143
    missionary, 3, 15, 55, 94, 122
    public, 4, 30, 34, 37, 52, 59, 67, 80, 89, 99, 137
public health, 71, 73–74, 92, 100, 142
purdah (see also women, seclusion of), 60

qadi (alkali), 30, 104, 113, 126, 139, 143
Qadiriyya, 33, 129
Qur'an, xv, xxiii, 15, 22, 58, 129, 140, 146 n11, 149 n47
paternalism
    of British toward Muslim rulers, 61, 137
    of Muslim rulers toward Northern Nigerian Christians, xxi, 68, 134, 137
    shared missionary and Muslim, 142

racial equality, 55, 94–95
racial science, 3–4, 6, 66
railway, xviii, 7, 14, 24, 25, 27–28
Ramadan, 40, 89
Ransdell, Jospeh, 75
recantation, xxi, xxiii, xxv, 40, 45, 56, 59, 119–121, 131, 140–141
reformism, xv, xxvi, 12, 48, 58, 67, 105, 139
relativism, 5, 6, 57
religious authority, xix, xx, 15–16, 22, 46, 87, 93, 98, 136
religious competition, xvi, xxii, xxiv, 12, 57, 61, 89, 90–91, 115, 137
religious freedom, 37–38, 59, 116, 121, 128

religious tolerance, 4, 53, 62, 79, 128, 162 n51
revivalism, 21, 33, 99, 136, 138, 140
Rhine, Charles, 135
ri'ko, 41
Robinson, Charles, 5–7
Rogers, Leonard, 73
Royal Niger Company, 3, 5
Rwandan genocide, xvi

Sabon Gari
　courts in, 126, 128
　development of, xviii, 27–29, 33, 141
　migration to and from, 42, 45, 84, 98,
　　100–101, 141
　negative perceptions of, 98, 140
　violence in, 117, 123–126
Saint Andrew's College, 44
Saint Bartholomew Hospital (CMS), 43,
　71, 121
Saint Louis School (Kano), 122, 141
Saint Thomas School, 104
Saint-Germain-en-Laye Treaty (1919),
　121
Sanderson, Cyril, 34
Sani, Joseph Mohammed, xxiv, 42, 45,
　46
sanitation, 29, 32–33, 62, 63, 67, 73, 75
Sara (see also Chadians), 101, 103–104,
　134–135
sarakuna (see also aristocracy) xxii, 59, 75,
　94, 98, 129, 130
Sarkin Kutare, 94, 96, 97
Sarkin Makafi, 97, 115
Satiru, 11–14, 21, 24
Saul, Harold, 82, 88
schools
　blind (SIM), 97–100, 103
　Christian mission, 42, 52, 104, 107, 112,
　　122, 127
　Church Missionary Society Zaria/
　　Wusasa, 23, 42–45, 61, 120
　girls (see also Saint Louis School),
　　44–46, 60–65, 92, 133
　government, 28, 31, 34–36, 38, 40, 60,
　　79, 107, 131, 141–142
　Islamiyya schools, 140
　Kabo Girls' School (SIM), 104, 111,
　　119–120
　leprosarium, 78
　Qur'anic, 11, 15, 42, 140

religious knowledge classes, 141–142,
　179 n18
Roni Boys' School (SIM), 91, 103–105,
　108, 111, 112
secret, xxii, xxvii, 39, 40, 41 photo 2.2,
　44, 124, 131
Sciortino, J. C., 13
secret believers, xxv-xxvi, 83, 89, 92, 131,
　166 n73
secularism, 26–27, 58, 65
segregation
　racial, 26–27, 32–33
　religious, xviii, xx, 23, 38
　residential, xviii, xxvi, 74, 101
　leprosy, 73–76, 80, 90, 94, 108, 112
Seko, Mobutu Sese, 135
Selassie, Haile, 5, 81
Selborne, Maud, 56–57, 63
Shaibu (blind cleric), 10–11
Shar'ia
　non-Muslims and, xxiv, 35, 91
　post-2000 implementation of, xv, xxi-
　　xxiii, 143
　support for, xv, 30–31, 125
　women and, 13, 17
Shehu (see 'Dan Fodio, Usman), 20, 38
Slavery
　concubinage, 13, 50
　emirs' practices of, 28, 31
　freed slaves, 5, 11–14, 27, 38, 41, 51, 149
　　n49
　freed slave home, xviii, 12–13, 17–19, 28,
　　48, 63–64
　slave-raiding, xvii, 6–7, 10–11, 18–19, 103
　slave descent, 15, 17, 176 n72
social gospel, xv, 26, 52, 79, 111–112, 122
Society for the Victory of Islam, 131
soldiers 132
　British West African Frontier Force, 14,
　　19, 30, 38–39
　demobilized (see also British colonial
　　government, demobilization), xx,
　　101–102,
　　106, 118
　ethnic identity of, 139
　French tirailleurs, 10, 72, 101
　Nigerian army, 132
　slave, 13
　World War II, xxvii, 95, 100–102,
　　105–107

Index ～ 207

Sokoto
    Caliphate, xv, xvii, 6, 20, 117, 123, 125, 138
    Leprosarium (see also Amanawa), xviii, 81, 83, 86, 104, 108, 134
    Province, 10, 14, 53, 59, 63, 72, 75, 79, 87, 105, 112, 121, 130, 133
    Town, 10–11, 19, 21, 88
Soudan Pioneer Mission, 3
South Africa, xxvii, 48, 56, 160 n23
Southern Nigeria
    amalgamation with Northern Nigeria, 21, 24, 25, 32, 43
    anti-colonial agitation in, 60, 92, 95, 101
    Christians hailing from, xxviii, 42, 45, 78, 89, 92, 104, 122, 134, 142
    migration, to 14
    regional tensions, 3, 98, 117–118, 123–124, 133, 138, 140
Stirrett, Andrew, 30, 59, 64, 76
Stuart, Emmeline, 52
Sudan (Anglo-Egyptian), xiv, xvi, 6, 45, 91
Sudan Interior Mission (SIM), xvii, 5, 9, 46, 64, 79, 81–82, 88, 111, 116, 129, 138
Sudan United Mission (SUM), xvii–xviii, 12–13, 17, 97, 135
Sumaila, 80–84
Sultan of Sokoto, 59, 75, 91, 130, 137
Syrians 39, 55

talakawa (see also commoners), xxii, 63
Tasa, 108–109
Temple, C.L., 29–30
Ter Meer, Albert, 119
Truth about Mohammed, 35, 47, 55, 57–58
Thompson, W. A., 17, 23
Thomson, Graeme, 62, 77–79
Tijaniyya, 33, 129
Toc H, 80
Tofa Bible training school, 122, 125
Tombalbaye, Ngarta, 135
Tonkin, Dr. T.J., 6, 8
tracts (pamphlets) (see also select pamphlets by title), xviii, xix, xxiii, 17, 19, 21–22, 33–35, 55–56, 59, 102, 122, 127, 129
Tripoli, Libya, 8, 29
Tsakani, Rev. Musa, 97
Tuareg, xviii, 26
Tudun Wada, 100–101, 103–104, 119
Turkey (see also Ottoman empire), 21, 65

ulema (clerics), xxi, 30, 59, 89, 91, 94
Ungogo, 35, 126
UNICEF, 134, 142
United Nations, 121, 127
United States (see also North America), 3, 5, 55, 58, 74–75, 81, 98, 112, 139
Usman, Yusufu Bala, 139

Vander Schie, John, 86–87, 89
vigilantism, 123, 128, 133, 144
violence/riots, xiv-xv, xxii, 141, 145 n7
    against Africans working for the British administration, 30
    against Christians, 16, 127
    against missionaries, 82
    against Native Administration, 98
    between Hausa and Igbo, 117, 123–124, 133–134
    Muslim-Christian, 140
Virchow, Rudolf, 74

Wahhabism, xvii, 12
Wakefield, Frances Daisy, 52–53, 65
Wall, Martha, 87–88
Wallace, William, 13
wealth in people (see also clientage), xxi-xxii, 18
West African Medical Service, 72
Willink Commission (see also minorities), 128–129
Whale, Fred, 107–108, 110
Whitmore, Jessie, 111
Wilson, John Foster, 114–115
Women xxv, xxvii, 13
    Christian identity of, 19, 23, 133–134, 140–143, 159 n69
    freed slave, xix, 13, 17, 31–32, 50–51
    interaction between Christian and Muslim, 87, 141–142
    leprosy patients, 86–88, 94, 112
    missionaries, 28, 37, 48–49, 51, 54, 64, 87, 97
    Muslim, 57, 62–63, 140, 178 n13
    reformers, 45, 47, 53, 62–63
    seclusion of (see also purdah), xix, 39, 50, 59
    teachers, 63–65, 67, 133–134
Women Count, 55, 58
Wooding, Anne, 97–98, 115
Wordless Book, 55

workers' strikes, 96, 123, 126
World War I, xxii, 21, 32, 38, 40, 54, 72, 80, 124
World War II, 95–96, 98, 121
Wusasa, 43–45, 61, 71, 108, 120–121, 133–134, 138–139
Wushishi, xvii, 9, 17–19, 22, 51 photo 3.1, 64, 85, 130
Wuye, James, 142

Ya da Kunya (see also Kano, Leprosarium), 83, 84, 87, 112, 124

Ya'ki da Jahilci, 122
Yepwi, 22, 128–129, 134
yondo, 134–135
Yoruba, xvii, 33, 42, 62–63, 123, 125, 138

Zabarmawa, 10–11, 14, 17, 19–20, 72–73
Zaria
   City, xxv, xxvii, 8, 13–15, 17, 42, 124–125
   Emirate, xvii, 16, 23, 120
   Province, 105, 121
   Sabon Gari, xviii
Zungeru, 12–13, 40

www.ingramcontent.com/pod-product-compliance
Lightning Source LLC
Chambersburg PA
CBHW020647300426
44112CB00007B/277